A History of Social Psychology

The term 'social psychology' was first established in the 1860s but the issues surrounding the subject have evolved over a much longer period. This book follows the history of the discipline over two and a half centuries, demonstrating the links between early and current thought. The first attempts at empirical approaches were made in France during the Enlightenment whilst some modern ideas were also being anticipated in Scotland. The search for laws of mind and society began in nineteenth-century Europe and, by the end of the century, it changed direction. Darwinian theory made a powerful impact on the emerging discipline and the centre of gravity began to move to America where it reached maturity during the inter-war period. *A History of Social Psychology* is viewed against a background of radical social and political changes and includes sketches of the major figures involved in its rise.

GUSTAV JAHODA is Emeritus Professor of Psychology at the University of Strathclyde. He has published more than 200 journal articles and is the author of *The Psychology of Superstition* (1969), *Psychology and Anthropology* (1982) and, most recently, *Images of Savages* (1999).

A History of Social Psychology
From the Eighteenth-Century Enlightenment
to the Second World War

GUSTAV JAHODA

CAMBRIDGE
UNIVERSITY PRESS

CAMBRIDGE UNIVERSITY PRESS
Cambridge, New York, Melbourne, Madrid, Cape Town, Singapore, São Paulo

Cambridge University Press
The Edinburgh Building, Cambridge CB2 8RU, UK

Published in the United States of America by Cambridge University Press, New York

www.cambridge.org
Information on this title: www.cambridge.org/9780521687867

First published 2007

Printed in the United Kingdom at the University Press, Cambridge

A catalogue record for this book is available from the British Library

ISBN 978-0-521-86828-0 hardback
ISBN 978-0-521-68786-7 paperback

For Andrea, Eve, and Ruth

Contents

Illustrations

Acknowledgements

Over the years many friends and colleagues, some alas no longer with us, have had some part in shaping my thinking. I should like to take this opportunity of paying tribute to them. They include John Berry, Ernest Boesch, Kofi Busia, Michael Cole, Pierre Dasen, Jan Deregowski, Lutz Eckenberger, Rob Farr, Nico Frijda, Cigdem Kagitcibasi, Bernd Krewer, Ioan Lewis, Walt Lonner, Serge Moscovici, Ype Poortinga, Marshall Segall, Robert Serpell, Durganand Sinha, Henri Tajfel, Harry Triandis, Jaan Valsiner, Ibolya Varine-Szilagyi, and Geneviève Vinsonneau.

Special thanks are due to Ivana Markova, herself steeped in the historical background of social psychology, who provided advice and inspiration in the course of numerous discussions.

I am also indebted to the Nuffield Foundation, devoid of 'ageism', and in particular to Louie Burghes, for generous support.

Last but not least, Brian Calder and Bill Woodside managed, in their very different ways, to keep me going.

Introduction

> Social psychology is an ancient discipline ... Our intellectual ancestors, for all their fumbling, were asking precisely the same questions as we are asking today ... It is true that our intellectual forefathers lacked tools of precision for empirical research and that they were sometimes naïve in their theories; yet they bequeathed to us an important store of shrewd insights that have stood the test of time.
>
> (Allport 1954a, vol. 1, p. 5)

There are many books on the history of psychology, but few among them devote much space to social psychology. As a rule they do not go further back than 1908, the year when two texts with the title 'social psychology' were published. The term 'social psychology' was coined just after the middle of the nineteenth century, and did not come into more general use until its end. How then, it might be asked, can there be a history of social psychology before it had been recognised as a distinct discipline? The answer is that it is not the label that matters, but the kinds of problems addressed. Histories of biology do not confine themselves to the period after the subject received its name in the early nineteenth century. As Gordon Allport rightly stated, many of the topics with which social psychology is concerned have been discussed from classical antiquity onwards. This was acknowledged by a recent author who wrote that 'Many regard Aristotle as the first social psychologist' (Taylor 1998, p. 59). Then he moved smartly on to the twentieth century, but a great deal happened in between!

There are those who might ask 'why history?' and recall Henry Ford's notorious dismissal when he said 'History is more or less bunk.' As against that, a distinguished modern historian has written: 'if you think of the past as a landscape, then history is the way we represent it, and it's that act of representation that lifts us above the familiar to let us experience vicariously what we can't experience directly: a wider view' (Gaddis 2002, p. 5). In the light of such a perspective one can gain a better understanding of how the subject has evolved, and this in turn provides a platform from which to regard our current state of knowledge more critically. The story of the struggles of our predecessors is also in itself a fascinating one, and it will become apparent that some of the ideas presented in textbooks as fresh and original have in fact been *anticipated* long ago. This is not to claim that there is always a direct line of descent from past to present ideas, but sometimes continuity can be demonstrated. For instance, the notion that our self-image is largely determined by our social milieu can be traced back some two-and-a-half centuries.

What then, it may further be asked, is the subject matter that defines what is now called social psychology? In other words, what were the criteria employed for inclusion and exclusion in this narrative? There is no easy answer, since even today there is a lack of consensus about what social psychology is or ought to be, notwithstanding the slick textbook definitions along the lines of 'the scientific study of social behaviour'. For the present purpose the following broad formula has been adopted to delimit the area: social psychological topics concern the relationships between individuals and between individuals and their society or culture, considered both synchronically and diachronically. Admittedly this is a debatable choice, but that would also be true of possible alternatives. It could further be objected that the above formula might apply equally to sociology. While that is quite correct, it should be pointed out that the separation between sociology and social psychology came late and was a gradual process – there remains a good deal of overlap even today.

Given that discussions of what could be regarded as such social-psychological issues date back millennia, the question as to when one should start is bound to be somewhat arbitrary, but the eighteenth-century Enlightenment marked a new beginning. The weakening of religious authority, coupled with the Newtonian revolution in science, made it possible to view humans as part of the natural as well as the social world. From then onwards numerous attempts were made to provide systematic if not truly scientific accounts of social relations among people. Many brilliant individuals applied themselves to this endeavour, and the aim here is to present an – inevitably superficial – survey of their ideas. These were bound to be influenced by contemporary socio-cultural and political atmospheres and events, which will sometimes be sketched in. For instance, German thought during the nineteenth century has to be seen in the context of the quest for national unity; or again, the terror during the French Revolution and the trauma of the Paris Commune after the Franco-Prussian war gave rise to 'crowd psychology'.

Many of the early theoretical schemes were 'armchair speculations' of a kind dismissed by tough-minded empiricists. But the armchair is not to be despised, since a great deal of our knowledge originally stems from it – even empiricists need some time in the armchair before starting their investigations! In any case, the mind of the person in the armchair is not a *tabula rasa*, being furnished with a great deal of information conveyed directly or indirectly from the outer world. An example would be a field manual for the study of 'savages' produced by Degérando, who had never himself visited distant shores. Yet the principles laid down in his work (described in chapter 1), based purely on his extensive reading, were still found to be largely valid in the twentieth century. Or again, the armchair pronouncements of Scottish philosophers must have been the product of shrewd observations; they led at times to remarkable *anticipations* of modern ideas, as for example of some of the hypotheses of experimental social psychology. I have stressed that they were usually *anticipations* so as not to imply continuities of development, though these could also be found. It should be added that from the mid-eighteenth century onwards one also encounters applications of probability theory and the use of statistics. The historical development of ideas that will be traced is varied and intricate, so that only some very broad trends can be discerned, and a brief preliminary overview may be helpful.

In eighteenth-century Europe a faith in continuous human progress prevailed, and in France there was a search for empirical method designed for better understanding of human nature and the improvement of society. In Scotland interpersonal relationships and national stereotypes were analysed.

The first part of the nineteenth century saw a move in Germany, France, and Britain towards grand theories seeking to define the relationships between mind and society. In the second half of the century Darwinian theory began to exert an increasing influence on psychology in general and also on discussions of social and societal issues. Another factor during that period was the process of democratisation in Europe, which stimulated an interest in the 'masses' and collective behaviour. Towards the end of the nineteenth century social psychology started to acquire an identity of its own under that name, and its centre of gravity began to shift towards the United States.

By the early twentieth century that change was well under way, and group psychology that had originated in Germany started to take root in America. Explanations of social behaviour in terms of 'instincts' – a Darwinian heritage – came to be abandoned with the rise of behaviourism. Yet in the midst of much activity a consensus about the objectives and scope of social psychology was slow to emerge. The division between sociological and psychological social psychology hardened, and here the focus will mainly be on the latter. During the 1920s and 1930s the major fields of teaching and research consisted of the study of attitudes and an experimental social psychology focused firmly on individuals. Two handbooks published in the mid-thirties provide a picture of the landscape of social psychology at that time. Some classical studies are described, undertaken over two decades to the onset of the Second World War, the terminus of this account.

The general story is framed mainly in terms of biographies of outstanding figures, with brief sketches of their backgrounds and lives. Some of these were humdrum, others adventurous or even tragic. Prior to the twentieth century the professional role of social psychologist did not exist, and ideas about human sociality were generated by a widely varying set of thinkers, by no means confined to philosophy: they included people from the fields of anthropology, astronomy, biology, economics, history, mathematics, medicine, and philology.

The ordering of the topics is broadly but not rigidly chronological, subdivided by countries. Many of the original sources are in French or German, and when translated versions existed and were accessible I used them. In other cases, where references are to French or German originals, the translations are my own.

Finally, it should be stressed that this modest volume does not pretend to be an authoritative history – such a history is still awaited. Rather it is intended to give those concerned with social psychology a broad picture of how the subject is rooted in the past.

PART I

The eighteenth century:
Enlightenment precursors

1 France: a short-lived dawn of empirical social science

Nature and nature's law lay hid in night;
God said 'let Newton be', and all was light.

(Alexander Pope)

It may seem odd to start a chapter on the French *Lumières* with a quotation from Alexander Pope, but Newton's prestige was high in France, and even there these lines were quite well known. Isaac Newton and his friend the philosopher John Locke strongly influenced French thought during the second half of the eighteenth century. It was a period when age-old dogmas and beliefs about the world and the place of humans within it began to be questioned, and radically new ideas emerged. Among them a key one in the present context was a question suggested by Newton's success in demonstrating the lawfulness of the physical universe: could there not be analogous causal laws governing mind and society? Such a wish to take physics as a model for psychology in general and social psychology in particular recurred during the following two centuries.

Already in the seventeenth century William Petty in England and Ludwig Seckendorf in Germany had elaborated a system of demographic statistics dealing with births and deaths, showing that human life is subject to order and regularity, and can be studied quantitatively. One of the first attempts to formulate general laws of social processes was made by the philosopher Charles de Montesquieu (1689–1755). In an introductory passage to his *De l'esprit des lois* (1748) he stated that: 'every particular law is linked with another law, or depends on another more general one'. Montesquieu had visited England and been introduced to the Royal Society, though Newton himself was then no longer alive; he also met the translator of Locke. It is perhaps worth mentioning that already at that time the works of prominent writers on either side of the Channel were nearly always promptly translated. As will be shown below, Locke inspired a new kind of psychology that long held sway in France. It opposed the rationalist nativism of René Descartes, a dualist who regarded the body as essentially a mechanical device. Descartes acknowledged that information about the physical world is transmitted through the senses, but believed that basic ideas – such as those concerned with God, or logical concepts – are innate. Locke, by contrast, was an empiricist who stressed the need for observation rather than mere speculation. Knowledge, for him, is based on experience and gradually built up from birth onwards.

Another admirer of Locke was François Marie Voltaire (1694–1778), whose life in several ways illustrates the intolerant and arbitrary nature of the French monarchy. An aristocrat treated the great man with contempt, and Voltaire responded with his caustic wit. This resulted in his being beaten up by the servants. When Voltaire challenged his opponent, he was incarcerated in the Bastille and only let out on condition that he would leave for England at once. There he was welcomed and introduced to, among others, Alexander Pope, who had written the lines cited above. Voltaire also studied the work of Newton, and later published a book on *The elements of the philosophy of Newton*. Madame du Chatelet, his mistress for many years, was a mathematician who astonished French society by translating Newton's *Principia*! Voltaire was a complex character, anti-clerical but not anti-religious, who believed in a vague deism of a kind then common. He denounced the shams and political follies of his time, but he was no revolutionary and did not fundamentally question the established order. He was a believer in progress, but not in equality; higher education, he observed, is not for cobblers or kitchen-maids. However, Voltaire had a passion for truth and justice, and a hatred of oppression. At considerable personal risk he intervened repeatedly to save people from miscarriages of justice. For instance, he defended an abbé accused of homosexuality, for which the penalty was being burnt alive, a Huguenot accused of having murdered his son, and a manic depressive who had committed suicide. Voltaire glorified the revolution in science, the product of 'reason', which he regarded as the most important attribute of humanity.

Such rationalism, typical of the Enlightenment, was also embodied in the famous Encyclopaedia published between 1751 and 1765, a massive work of seventeen volumes of text. Under the editorship of Denis Diderot, it was ostensibly a compilation of knowledge in all its branches; but in so far as the censor could be hoodwinked, it was also a tool for propagating views opposed to tradition and existing institutions. This is not to say that the Encyclopaedists were preaching revolution; their aim was reform, but they did contribute to a climate of opinion in which radical change was coming to be seen as inevitable.

Some of the figures whose ideas will be discussed were directly involved in the events leading to the Revolution, or were active during and after it, and one of the most outstanding among them became its victim. While historians are still debating the causes of the Revolution, there is consensus that progressive economic deterioration, coupled with catastrophic failure of harvests leading to widespread protests and disorders, were salient factors. In due course (chapter 6) it will be shown that the excesses of the revolutionary period had an effect on theories of crowd behaviour elaborated a century later. This account of ideas prevalent during the *Lumières* begins with a psychological theory that held sway for the second half of the eighteenth century.

Condillac: the statue that comes alive

A priest and a firm believer in the Catholic faith, content with the political state others found so objectionable, Etienne Bonnot, Abbé de Condillac (1715–80), was far from typical of Enlightenment luminaries. And yet his account of human psychology, which he regarded as a branch of metaphysics, remained unrivalled for half a century. Born in Grenoble into a family of the minor nobility, he was delicate as a child and by the age of twelve had not yet learned to read. He was so withdrawn that his family thought for a while that he was retarded. The local priest saw to his elementary education, and little is known about the transition to his intellectual flowering. At any rate, one of his brothers took him to Paris, where he enrolled at the Sorbonne to study theology. Subsequently he read widely, including translations of Newton and Locke, whose empiricism greatly appealed to him. He met and became friendly with Rousseau and with Diderot, editor of the Encyclopaedia mentioned above. A few years later he began to publish his own works, which soon spread his fame. He frequented the salons where ideas were being discussed, but owing to his retiring personality made few contributions himself. While being exposed to the turbulence of reformist sentiments, he kept his own counsel. After delays caused by illness, his *Treatise on sensations* appeared in 1754.

The twin pillars of Locke's theory had been sensation and reflection, the latter accounting for the higher mental processes such as comparing, judging, and willing. However, Locke abandoned his genetic approach at that point, treating these as basic 'faculties' without seeking to trace them to their source. Condillac decided to concentrate on pure experience and, by means of a descriptive analysis, reduce everything to 'sensation' as the root of all cognition, feeling, and action. While he recognised the physiological aspects of mental phenomena, Condillac resolutely set them aside; he began not with the senses, but with sensation, the inner life. The resulting system had the virtues of logical simplicity and elegance, and as such was widely acclaimed.

In expounding his system Condillac made use of a thought-experiment, imagining a statue endowed only with a sense of smell, engendering the simplest possible sensations. The statue is of course a model of a person prior to any experience, and as such is not to be viewed as passive. If we present the statue with a rose to smell, its capacity for feeling is entirely taken up with the scent of the rose, and this Condillac called *attention*. The statue may enjoy or suffer but cannot as yet envisage any other state of being; nor has it any sense of its own identity.

Let us now offer a second flower, and the statue's whole *attention* is given over to the second scent. If we now go on to repeated alternating presentations, something new emerges: the statue gains awareness of more than one state of being because of the *memory* of the other state, leading to a *comparison* of the two existences. At this mode of consciousness the stage of ideas is reached, and other operations can be performed, including for instance *imagination* and *abstraction*. A notion of self arises, this being the sum total of sensations experienced and recalled. All cognitive processes, according to Condillac, essentially consist of different modes of *attention*. A similar analysis is devoted to the progression from the simple dichotomy of pleasure and pain to the whole gamut of emotions. The radical conclusion is that since attention and desire can ultimately be reduced to *sensations*, it follows that *sensation* is the fundamental element underlying all mental processes – hence the label of 'sensationism'.

Condillac's attempt to show how, beginning with the simple sensation of smell, the association of what we would call various stimuli and then ideas leads to such functions as imagination and memory was of course a *tour de force*, a kind of analytical model devoid of any empirical basis. But it should be stressed that the condensed presentation offered here does scant justice to the subtlety and complexity of his scheme. In particular, the association of ideas was for him not something free-floating, but a process ultimately governed by human needs or wants:

> The connection of ideas can arise from no other cause than from the attention given to them, when they presented themselves conjunctly to our minds. Hence as things attract our attention only by the relation they bear to our constitution, to our passions, to our state, or, to sum up all in one word, to our wants; it follows that the same attention embraces at once the idea of wants, and of such things as are relative to those wants, and connects them together.   (Condillac 1746/1971, p. 46)

The fundamental driving force of *wants* constitutes a constant thread in Condillac's arguments, and is applied by him to the social sphere. Take for instance his discussion of differences between peoples: he believed, in common with many eighteenth-century writers, that climate determines temperament, which in turn influences the type of government, and both jointly create the character of a people in terms of their 'passions' and wants – 'passions' being much the same as what we would call emotions. Furthermore, the language of a people is said to reflect their character by expressing their dominant interests and values. The general thesis may be summarised in modern terminology by saying that ecology determines culture, which in turn shapes mentality.

The spread of 'sensationist' psychology

The general aim of Condillac, whose sphere of activity was much wider than the topics touched upon here, was to construct a philosophy that was as exact as mathematics, though he was no great mathematician himself. Yet his aspiration to create a rational system of human nature was typical of his time. Among those who adopted Condillac's psychology was Claude-Adrien Helvétius (1715–71), whose crass materialism in his book *De l'esprit* (1758) scandalised many others besides Condillac. He held that humans have no divine soul but only senses and a passive, though receptive mind that can be completely shaped through education. It must be said, however, that he used the term 'education' in a very broad sense, meaning:

> Everything that serves for our instruction, and thus I say that no one receives the same education, because everyone has, if I dare say, as teachers the form of government under which he lives, his friends, his mistresses, the people surrounding him, his reading, and lastly chance, i.e. an infinity of events whose causal change our ignorance prevents us from perceiving.   (Helvétius 1758/1973, p. 208)

This long list indicates that Helvétius was really referring to what we would call 'the social environment'. He denied the existence not merely of group or race but also of innate *individual* differences, claiming that, given the right circumstances, anybody could achieve anything. In this he was a forerunner of J. B. Watson, founder of twentieth-century behaviourism, who guaranteed that he could make a doctor, lawyer, artist or other specialist out of any healthy infant. Helvétius also followed Condillac in believing that 'passion' is what drives us. Some passions tend to distort reason and thus lead to error, yet without passion reason becomes ineffective. One of the chapters in his work is headed 'One becomes stupid as soon as one ceases to be impassioned.'

Although the lucidity and coherence of Condillac's doctrine ensured its dominance for much of the eighteenth century, its metaphysical and speculative character was at variance with the temper of the latter part of that century. Thus it came to be modified by two of Condillac's disciples, Destutt de Tracy (1754–1836) and Pierre Cabanis (1757–1808). Tracy invented the term 'ideology' to denote the 'science of ideas', which he claimed was part of zoology: 'One has an incomplete knowledge of an animal, if one does not know its intellectual faculties. Ideology is part of zoology, and it is with regard to man that it is particularly important and deserves to be dealt with in depth' (de Tracy, cited in Copans and Jamin 1978, p. 490). This sounds almost as though he had anticipated modern evolutionary psychology; but in fact his claim was rather spurious, since he failed to depart very much from Condillac and viewed the object of study as the analysis of ideas into their constituent sensations. None the less he was deeply involved in contemporary debates; his circle came to be known as *idéologues* – so dubbed disparagingly by Napoleon.

More interesting is the contribution of Cabanis, the son of a lawyer who had also helped the reforms of the economist Anne Robert Turgot in reclaiming barren land. The son was initially a disappointment to his successful father because he neglected his studies and seemed shiftless. Hence the father sent him to Paris, where he had to fend for himself. There he began reading widely, including the classics, French philosophers like Descartes, but also Locke and Adam Smith, and extended his knowledge over several years. Then he suddenly decided to study medicine, qualified as a physician and later became a professor of medicine. The major focus of his work was the relation between body and mind. Abandoning the traditional image of a body subordinated to its soul, he substituted a model in which the physical and the 'moral' (read psychological) aspects of humans are dynamic and interdependent systems – a view remarkably close to our own. He is rightly regarded as one of the pioneers of physiological psychology. His early writings were concerned with the then topical question as to whether the people who had been guillotined felt any pain after decapitation. His conclusion was that they did not, since what he called 'the central self' had been destroyed so that any apparent signs of life in the body separated from the head was due to the activities of neural ganglia independent of the brain.

Cabanis delivered a series of lectures on the natural history of man at the prestigious Institut National, which were subsequently published under the title *Rapports du physique et du moral de l'homme* (1802). In this the chief remaining link with Condillac was his emphasis on receptivity to sensations from the external world; he showed that this existed even in the foetus. Accordingly, he stressed the importance of environmental influences for human development, both individual and collective. In the latter context, following Rousseau, he regarded 'true' education as the proper development of the natural powers, a process involving primarily the relations of individuals in society.

His discussion of social relations is based in part on Condillac's concepts of 'needs' or 'wants', but even more on the writings of the Scottish philosophers, among whom he mentioned particularly Hutcheson and Adam Smith (both discussed in chapter 2). This meant that he invoked 'sympathy', which he regarded as an instinct in all social species. Cabanis proposed that signs, be they gestures, facial expression, voice, ways of looking, and so on, constitute a kind of universal language enabling us to gauge the feelings of our fellow-humans. As the capacity for such communication increases, 'we exist no less in the others than in ourselves' (Cabanis 1802/1985, p. 97). He stressed the fundamental importance of sympathy as the foundation of all sociability, adding that it is linked to imitation described as 'a faculty that characterizes human nature and is the principal means of education for individuals as well as for societies' (1802/1985, p. 551).

Cabanis attempted to establish links between Condillac's psychology and his own physiological researches. For instance, he suggested that sense impressions reach the brain through the nerves and are there transformed into ideas, which are then communicated to one's fellows through gestures or verbal language. This kind of speculation about the transformation of the organic into the 'moral' came to be regarded as unsatisfactory by many French scientists and scholars by the end of the eighteenth century, when an alternative approach began to emerge.

In sum, Condillac inspired a number of disciples, and his theory of motivation was adopted even by some of those who strongly disagreed with his conservative outlook, such as Condorcet. Like so many prominent figures of the period, the two men knew each other socially. This is clear from the fact that shortly before his death Condillac complained to his niece that he had been given some bad chocolate to drink at Condorcet's house, and had felt the effects ever since!

Condorcet on social science and social decision-making

Marie Jean, Marquis de Condorcet (1743–94), an only child, came from an impoverished aristocratic family in the provinces. His father, a cavalry captain, was killed shortly after his birth and his holy-minded mother dressed him like a girl and kept him isolated at home until the age of nine. Then his uncle, a bishop, arranged a Jesuit tutor for him and then sent him to a Jesuit school in Reims. Writing about his experiences there later, Condorcet described his intense dislike of the rigid discipline enforced by beatings and hellfire threats. The curriculum was narrow, largely confined to Latin and religion. He also mentioned priests abusing boys, and was greatly relieved when he went on to the University of Paris, where he blossomed. He was particularly keen on mathematics and decided to make it his career, against the opposition of his family who had hoped that he would follow his father into the army.

In Paris Condorcet met the great mathematician Jean d'Alembert, who became his mentor, and Alembert's companion, Julie de l'Espinasse, who sought to polish his rough edges – 'Don't bite your fingernails!' With the influential support of Alembert he was elected to the Academy of Sciences in 1769, later becoming its permanent secretary. In 1770 he met Voltaire, whose anti-clericalism he shared and who aroused his interest in politics. Both opposed an antiquated and oppressive legal system responsible for many cruel injustices. For instance, in 1766 a young man was accused of failing to remove his hat at the passage of a religious procession, of blaspheming, and of hitting a crucifix. He was tortured and burned alive. This, with other instances of judicial brutality, was one of the reasons why Condorcet advocated the abolition of capital punishment – another is mentioned below.

1   *Marie Jean Antoine Nicolas de Caritat, Marquis de Condorcet (1743–94)*

Condorcet had a close relationship with Turgot, economist and adminis-
trator, who was, for a period, appointed by the king as controller-general of
finances. In that capacity he sought to reform a system in which the nobility,
the richest section of the population, was exempt from taxes that fell heavily
on the poor. Condorcet collaborated with Turgot until the latter was dismissed, having threatened the privileges of the aristocracy. Apart from his
involvement in politics, Turgot was also an important exponent of the theory
of progress, stressing the cumulative character of socio-cultural change:

> The arbitrary signs of speech and writing, by giving men the means
> wherewith to make sure of the possession of their ideas and to commu-
> nicate them to others, have formed from individual stores of knowledge
> a common treasure-house, that one generation transmits to another, an
> inheritance which is always being enlarged by the discoveries of each
> age.   (Turgot 1750/1973, p. 41)

This is precisely what Tomasello et al. (1993, p. 495) called 'the ratchet
effect' in human culture. Turgot's ideas evidently took root in Condorcet,
as shown by the last work he left to posterity, the *Sketch of a history of the
progress of the human mind*, on which more anon.

After Turgot's fall Condorcet became for a while disillusioned with
practical politics and turned back to mathematics, and in particular to
probability theory. As he himself explained, it had begun in the seventeenth

century with questions posed about how the stakes ought to be divided up among players of games of chance, questions that were answered by Pascal and Fermat. Only gradually did it become apparent that these methods could be used more widely, and Condorcet applied them to the kinds of social issues which for him were matters of passionate concern. He was convinced that they constituted tools which relate either to social interests or to the analysis of the operations of the human mind in society, and he called this 'social mathematics'. Examples of his applications will be offered later, but in the meantime the remainder of his life-history will be sketched.

At the time of the America Revolution he became friendly with several notable American figures. These included Benjamin Franklin, American ambassador in Paris, whom he also valued as a scientist; Thomas Jefferson, Franklin's successor and later American President, who was considerably influenced by Condorcet's ideas; and the radical Tom Paine, born in England to a modest Quaker family and whose political writings became highly influential.

In 1786 Condorcet married Sophie de Grouchy, the young niece of a reforming magistrate who saved the lives of three peasants who had been unjustly accused. His wife shared Condorcet's ideals, and they were a devoted couple. Altogether it was a good year for him: he had achieved wide recognition as a scientist and thinker and enjoyed numerous distinctions. It was not to last. An enthusiastic political radical, he supported the Revolution, advocating the setting up of a republic, and in 1792 was made president of the Legislative Assembly. But as a more moderate *Girondin* he aroused the hostility of Robespierre, was accused and condemned, and declared an outlaw. He had to flee, and after finding refuge for several months in the house of a friend he was recognised and lodged in jail, where he was found dead the next morning.

Like most of his contemporaries, Condorcet originally referred to 'moral science' and explained that 'We understand by this term all those sciences which have as the object of their researches either the human mind in itself, or the relations of men one to another.' He did not believe that the 'moral sciences' were in principle inferior to the physical ones, since both are concerned with factual knowledge and adopt similar methods. However, he conceded that there is an important difference, since the 'moral sciences' express their findings in everyday language and so lay people feel that they can make judgements without having previously acquired the necessary knowledge. It was a comment that has not lost its sting.

Returning to the relationship between the 'moral' and physical sciences, there is an interesting passage whose intent has been disputed:

> All would be equal between [moral and physical sciences] for a being foreign to our species, who would study human society as we study that of the beavers and the bees. But here the observer himself forms part of the society that he observes, and the truth can only have biased or prejudiced judges.   (Cited in Baker 1975, p. 192)

The conservative thinker Joseph de Maistre treated this as simply a silly statement, since beavers and bees have no thirst for knowledge. Others took it that Condorcet displayed an awareness of reflexivity, which prevents any objective study of human behaviour. But it should be noted that he referred to 'the truth', and therefore cannot have been of a quasi-postmodernist persuasion. Condorcet wished to say neither that the moral sciences are less certain than the physical ones, nor that the former are subjective while the latter are objective. Rather he implied – and directly stated elsewhere – that the findings of physical science tend to be more readily accepted by society at large, because they remain unaffected by the preconceptions and biases which constitute an obstacle to the acceptance of the 'truths' provided by the findings of moral science. Subsequently Condorcet was one of the first to use the term 'social science'.

Underlying these statements was the conviction that one has to distinguish between rational 'enlightened' people and the majority whose ideas are distorted by prejudice and superstition. This is not to say that he despised the majority and disputed their right to have opinions on social matters, but, as far as the attainment of 'truth' is concerned, he viewed them as less qualified. On these grounds he for a time also disapproved of one-person-one-vote democracy, because he regarded it as incapable of arriving at decisions valid in terms of 'truth'. This led him to advocate the use of probability theory, whereby decisions taken collectively by the enlightened minority could be rendered more rational. For instance he demonstrated that simple majority voting in order to select one of several candidates could result in a candidate preferred only by a minority being elected. This is still a topical issue, as shown by the numerous calls for 'proportional representation'. He also discussed risky decisions, judicial as well as political, and suggested methods for assessing the probability that a decision reached is 'true'. The 'truth' criterion has been abandoned as unattainable, and voting confined to an enlightened elite is now unacceptable. But this does not detract from the fact that Condorcet formulated a theory about how groups of people arrive at decisions, thereby anticipating a problem area taken up in social psychology some two centuries later.

In his later writings Condorcet came to advocate a much wider 'social mathematics' that would help to guide everyone in their economic and political decisions, and thereby extend rationality in everyday life. Thus he noted that people usually form beliefs and opinions on the basis of general impressions rather than factual evidence, and discussed in detail how to avoid pitfalls. Here is one of his examples, showing how far in advance of his time he was. On the basis of direct observation, he noted, it seems highly probable that men are more talented than women. However, if one compares not men and women in general, but only a sample of men who have received an advanced education with the small subset of women who have also benefited in this way, then the probability of a real difference becomes almost zero.

Condorcet expected that prejudices of that kind would be eliminated by a transformation of society on scientific principles, ushering in an age in which rationality prevailed. It was an ideal that governed his own beliefs and attitudes. Thus he opposed the death penalty on the grounds of the high probability of some people being condemned to death though innocent – an argument that regained its force during the twentieth century. Accordingly, when president of the Revolutionary Assembly he proposed that the king should receive the severest penalty short of death. This did not endear him to his opponents, and probably was a factor in bringing about his sad fate.

One would have thought that his experiences during the increasingly bloody Revolution would have undermined his faith in rationality; yet his last work remains optimistic in tone, even though its completion coincided with the start of his prosecution. It has also been suggested that the philosopher, in despair over the ruin of his hopes, sought refuge in a rosy view of the future. Whatever the answer, his completion under such circumstances of the *Sketch of the history of the progress of the human mind*, published posthumously in 1795, compels admiration.

That famous work begins with a summary of Condillac's 'sensationist' psychology, which informs the rest of the work. Condorcet followed the structure of Turgot's account of historical stages of humankind, but he differed in wanting to establish more directly the high probability, if not inevitability, of future advances. He argued that the natural sciences rest on the conviction that necessary and constant laws regulate all phenomena in the universe. Why should that be less true, he asked, of the intellectual and moral development of humans who, he implied, are also part of nature? The argument is of course questionable, since Condorcet himself believed that society could be deliberately changed by human action. None the less it is worth asking to what kinds of 'laws' he had been referring, and his contention was that the collective progress of the human mind

> is subject to the same general laws that are observed in the individual
> development of our faculties, since it is the result of that development,
> considered at the same time among a great number of individuals united
> in societies.   (Condorcet 1794/1966, p. 76)

From this analogy between individual and historical development it is clear that Condorcet was not concerned with history as such, using it merely as a source of evidence for his assertions about progress. Furthermore, the 'laws' envisaged are evidently psychological ones, based on 'sensationism'. Saint-Simon and Comte – about whom more in due course – later misinterpreted this as a blueprint for historical sociology as they envisaged it;

but it was nothing of the kind. For Condorcet's conception was essentially trans-historical, a lawful unfolding of the potentialities of the human mind, with steadily increasing rationality and reduction of errors. He himself was passionately dedicated to further this process and to create for this purpose mathematically based principles capable of application in practical life.

The Society of the Observers of Man

In the summer of 1798 three hunters in the district of Aveyron came across a naked wild and mute boy seemingly aged about eleven or twelve. They took him to a neighbouring village, but after about a week he escaped. A year later he suddenly appeared again and allowed himself to be captured without offering resistance. He was taken to a hospice, where the professor of natural history at the local college visited him and produced a report. This story of 'the wild boy of Aveyron' is of course well known, and it was certainly not the first case of its kind. What is less well known is the significance of this particular case. In order to appreciate this, a detour is necessary.

It occurred at a time in France when, as already mentioned, the foundations were being laid by philosophers and physiologists of a new 'science of human nature' which would elicit the 'laws' governing it. For much of the eighteenth century all this had remained purely theoretical, but towards the end of the century such theoretical speculations were felt by some to be inadequate and lacking empirical support. As noted above, the groundwork for an empirical approach as regards *collective* phenomena such as birth and death rates had already been laid before the Enlightenment. However, there were at that time no suitable methods for dealing with issues of the kind we would now call social-psychological. Such methods were first developed during the latter stages of the Enlightenment.

The theoretical discussions in this sphere during most of the eighteenth century were concerned with two chief questions, namely what the universal features of humans are, and what accounts for national differences. The term 'national' in that context included 'primitive' nations as they were then called, the concept of 'race' having barely emerged at that time. National differences in that sense were usually attributed to climate, a view that prevailed in simplistic form for much of the nineteenth century. Montesquieu even speculated about the processes whereby climate exerted its effects. He proposed that heat and cold differentially affect nerve and muscle 'fibres', people in cold countries having stronger 'fibres' and eating rougher kinds of food.

The problem for those anxious to move away from such dubious conjectures, and towards collecting evidence, was that of method. Experimentation – in the modern strict sense – that had already begun in physiology was not, with some odd exceptions, seen as a possibility. The main solution adopted was systematic observation. One other avenue was the use of what is now called 'a natural experiment', taking advantage of naturally occurring circumstances – a method now employed in cross-cultural psychology. As will be shown in more detail below, one example would be the case of the 'wild boy' mentioned above.

Jauffret and the beginnings of the *Société*

The initiative to bring together people interested in the empirical study of humans in society was taken by Louis-François Jauffret (1770–1850) who in 1799 founded the *Société des Observateurs de l'Homme*. Adopting the motto 'Know thyself', it attracted some sixty members, including a veritable galaxy of illustrious names in France, drawn from a diversity of fields, including naturalists, linguists, philosophers, medical men, historians, and explorers. It was probably the first interdisciplinary effort on such an ambitious scale, dedicated to the 'physical, moral and intellectual aspects of the science of man'. Jauffret, a man of lively curiosity and rigorous scientific spirit, was one of the first to address the problems of method in the human sciences. These are set out in his introduction to the *Mémoires* of the *Société*. Unfortunately the major part of them has been lost, but what has been preserved is sufficient to convey a clear sense of its purpose and activities. Here Jauffret's introduction and some accounts of the kinds of empirical studies he envisaged will be presented.

The introduction constitutes an outline of his guiding philosophy. He started by noting that the very name *Observateurs de l'Homme* indicates the method whereby a more profound understanding of humans is to be acquired. The emphasis was to be on the multiplication of factual observations, leaving aside 'vain theories'. The research will involve

> Casting an attentive glance at the physiognomy of the various inhabitants of the earth, it will study the causes that distinguish one people from another, and which alter in various countries the form and primitive colour of the human species.   (In Copans and Jamin 1978, p. 73)

Jauffret proposed an exploration of the relationship between animal and human nature, continuity being already taken for granted. Equally, ethnic and regional differences between humans ought to be studied. He expressed some cautious reservations on the validity of 'physiognomy', the diagnosis of character from faces, a fashionable doctrine at the time. The interdependence between the physical and moral aspects of humans is stressed, with comments suggesting an interpretation that comes close to what we understand by psychosomatic medicine.

Other topics mentioned include the study of the history of various peoples, their customs and migrations – all on a comparative basis. This also covers languages and gestures, especially the signs and gestures of 'savages' believed to be related to those of deaf-mutes. This no doubt reflects the influence of Abbé Sicard, a pioneer of the education of deaf-mutes, who had directed a famous institution in Paris. The establishment of an anthropological museum was also suggested.

Observation should also be the chief method for the study of the properties of the 'soul' or mind, and in this connection a proposal was put forward for observing the genesis of these properties from the cradle onwards. When Jauffret sought to justify this plan, he did so in florid prose:

> Why should one not find the same charm in following with an attentive eye the development of the first light of the spirit, in keeping a detailed record of the progress of intelligence in a child, in seeing the birth of the faculties one after the other, as in closely watching the habits and industry of an insect, or observing the blooming of some exotic plant?   (In Copans and Jamin 1978, p. 80)

Jauffret could not have been aware that such a study had already been pioneered half a century earlier by a German philosopher, Dietrich Tiedemann, who had published his observations on the mental development of an infant. Jauffret also mooted – not for the first time – an extravagant experiment whereby children would be brought up in social isolation and their development observed. It is to be expected, he noted, that a host of problems concerning the origin of language and of ideas could be resolved thereby.

The peroration strikes a political note, condemning the evils of the *ancien régime* that outraged human dignity, and ending as follows:

> May this Society, in whose success one might say Europe is interested today, fulfil in due course the glorious destinies that seem to await it, and merit that one should say of it one day that its foundation served both the advancement of science and the happiness of mankind.

> (In Copans and Jamin, p. 85)

Even this brief summary should convey something of the effervescence of ideas generated by the *Société*, the feeling of liberation with which they were embraced, and the idealistic purposes they were meant to serve.

The case of the 'wild boy'

Against this background we can continue the story of this boy, briefly mentioned above. We are now in a position to understand why the news of the discovery of Victor, as he came to be called, aroused considerable excitement when it reached Paris. This was because the appearance of the 'wild boy' seemed to present an excellent opportunity for studying the process of transition from what was believed to have constituted *raw* human nature to becoming an ordinary *socialised* person. Hence it was decided to set up a quasi-experiment in which a talented young medical man, Jean-Marie Itard (1757–1838), was charged with the task of educating and civilising Victor, carefully observing and recording the stages of his progress.

Itard's programme of education was based on Condillac's sensationism, combined with some of the physiological ideas of Cabanis. The main objectives were to teach him language, to integrate him into the life of society, and to increase his receptiveness by exposing him to suitable stimuli and arousing his affect. In a sense Victor was the embodiment of Condillac's statue, which has to be awakened and filled with affect and ideas. Itard's methods may be illustrated by his efforts to 'waken' Victor's sensitivity. Since he appeared quite indifferent to cold, Itard made him lie for hours in a hot bath and dressed him very warmly; and he did in fact become more sensitive to cold. He also used games, such as hiding objects Victor needed, in order to improve attention and memory.

Itard's labours were – at least initially – crowned with some success, and he felt able to draw wide-ranging theoretical conclusions. He suggested that in a pure state of nature, man is inferior to a great many animals. The moral superiority of humans, usually believed to be natural, is in fact only the result of civilisation, which leads humans to acquire new needs and new sensations. The imitative faculty necessary for learning, especially languages, weakens rapidly with the duration of isolation; and isolation also blunts nervous sensibility. Lastly, from the most isolated savage to the most refined urbanite, there is a constant relationship between ideas and wants; so any local circumstances increasing or decreasing wants thereby necessarily widen or narrow the range of knowledge. This emphasis on 'wants' is of course also derived from Condillac. What was new about Itard's conclusion was not so much that there can be no true humanity without culture, but his claim that this was a deduction from his observations – a claim that gave rise to considerable debate.

It was pointed out, for instance, that nothing was known about Victor's origins, so that assertions about his experience or lack of it were bound to be speculative; and to describe him as a 'natural man' was therefore questionable. Furthermore, in a discussion somewhat reminiscent of modern debates about environmental deprivation, it was argued that the natural environment provides a rich source of stimulation, and as such might have been expected to give rise to some learning.

While such shrewd critiques were entirely theoretical, an even more telling blow to Itard's conclusions was delivered by the famous alienist Philippe Pinel (1725–1826), commissioned by the *Société* to investigate Victor. In a closely reasoned memoir Pinel showed that the 'wild boy' displayed many of the characteristics well known to him from the behaviour of the profoundly mentally handicapped. For instance, Pinel described how Victor had witnessed for many months doors being opened with a key, and realised that this had to be done. Yet he was unable to learn in all that time how to turn a key, so that he had to lead someone to the door to let him out. Pinel concluded that Victor, far from being a prototypical 'natural man', was a mental defective whose parents had probably abandoned him as ineducable, and who thereafter spent time roaming in the wild before being found.

This was an experiment that failed, yet it was still instructive. Among other empirical studies reported, one concerns a young Chinese, Tchong-A-Sam, who after some adventures – including capture by privateers – reached France. Although he was by no means the first Chinese to do so, the *Société* felt that the skills required for adequate study had previously been lacking, and that his presence provided an opportunity for learning something about Chinese language and culture. The first step was to make sure that he was really Chinese; and Georges Cuvier (1769–1832), distinguished comparative anatomist, believed he could confirm this from skull measurements. The *Société* did not manage to discover a great deal about Chinese language and writing, but did find common ground in modes of calculation. What they described as the most interesting exercise involved an abacus, used by their subject with extraordinary skill. The work was cut short by the government's decision to send Tchong-A-Sam back to the Orient.

On methods of fieldwork with savages

The study of Victor, promising as it appeared at the time, eventually turned out to be a failure. Similarly, the hope that Tchong-A-Sam would provide valuable insights into Chinese personality and culture proved a disappointment. It foreshadowed a period in anthropological research a century later when it was mistakenly believed that a single 'omniscient informant' should make it possible to determine the major traits of a whole culture. However, the *Société* did not abandon its aim of studying 'savages', and an opportunity presented itself when an expedition to Australia was being planned. The leader was to be Nicolas Baudin (1754–1803), a distinguished explorer and himself a member of the *Société*, which was invited to take part in the preparations. While the ostensible purpose was strictly scientific, Napoleon, in approving it, was perhaps not unmindful of its potential intelligence value. The expedition, in addition to collecting data on the flora and fauna, geology, and so on, was also intended to include studies of the physical, moral, and intellectual characteristics of the inhabitants of southern Australasia. It was decided that a kind of 'field manual' should be prepared for the scientists responsible for studying these savages, and the task was entrusted to Degérando.

It is rather surprising that he was chosen to give advice on how to study savages, since he himself had never travelled to any exotic lands. In the event, the choice of Joseph-Marie Degérando (1772–1842) turned out to be a fortunate one. Although from a royalist background, he served with the Republican army for a time and then became a scholar of repute. He won a prize from the prestigious *Institut* for an essay on signs inspired by Locke and Condillac. Its sub-title referred to 'the art of thinking' and dealt with the influence of what we would call 'symbols' on the formation of ideas, an early indication of his psychological interests. After this success he was called to Paris, joining the ranks of the *idéologues* and becoming a member of the *Société*. Subsequently he had a distinguished administrative career, becoming readily adapted to the increasingly reactionary political climate of the Empire and the *Restauration*.

The memoir he wrote for Baudin, which ensured his lasting fame, was entitled *Consideration of the methods to follow in the observation of savage peoples* (1800/1969). It is a remarkable document, which often has an astonishingly modern ring. Some of its recommendations would not be out of place in a text on methods in social psychology or anthropology.

Degérando began by stating that the science of man is also a natural science, a science of observation. In accordance with the then prevalent notion of the progressive development of humanity, he suggested that the 'philosophical traveller' who journeys to the end of the earth is, by the same token, travelling backwards in time; in other words, we can see ourselves as we once were in the past – an evolutionary idea that persisted in similar form during the nineteenth century. The behaviour of civilised people is determined by complex multiple causes, that are hard to tease out. Savage life, by contrast, is simpler and, basic human nature being constant, its development is governed by natural laws which we can discover by means of the 'comparative method'. This mistaken belief in the simple life of primitive peoples persisted until the twentieth century. On the other hand Degérando was under no illusion that researches are simple, and proceeded to list the faults of previous explorers and travellers that ought to be avoided. Some of these will be summarised:

1   Many travellers tend to judge a whole nation by a few people, or their character by observing a few of their actions; they are apt to rely on the testimony of those people they have happened to encounter – in our terms, inadequate sampling.
2   The inquiry is usually conducted unsystematically, focusing randomly on individuals without first establishing a good relationship or considering the broader social context.
3   There is a common tendency for observers to judge things by their own alien standards – now known as 'ethnocentrism'.
4   It is important to consider the effects of the observer's presence upon those being observed, a phenomenon now called 'reflexivity'.

5   One needs to be sure of effective communication: those ques-
         tioned may not have understood properly because of failure to
         make oneself sufficiently clear; or perhaps they were not inclined
         to tell the truth – or the whole truth. They may misinterpret what
         is being asked, or we may misinterpret what they are saying.

Degérando also suggested that the widely accepted notion, which long
persisted, that to know one savage is to know all of them is fallacious.
There is certainly much diversity among them, and therefore any
studies must take account of such factors as age, sex, lifestyle, the
organisation of their society, and the particular circumstances prevailing
at the time.

These principles remain highly relevant for present-day social-psychological studies. Unfortunately it cannot be said that they were properly
applied in the course of the Baudin expedition. The representative of the
'science of man', François Péron (1775–1810) was recruited only at the last
moment. He had studied medicine, and an unhappy love affair led him to
abandon his studies and apply for membership of the expedition. When he
was in the field, Péron was guilty of the very faults against which
Degérando had warned, as will be shown by an example.

After landing in Tasmania with three sailors, Péron found himself and
his companions surrounded by a large group of armed natives. Both sides
dropped their weapons as a sign of peaceful intentions, and after some
mutual gazing at this first encounter the Tasmanians began to scrutinise
the strangers, whose white skin astonished them. They evidently also
wanted to find out what was under their clothes, which the Europeans
were reluctant to display. Owing to the Tasmanians' insistence, and the
difficulty of refusing them in view of their superior numbers, Péron asked
the youngest sailor to satisfy their curiosity. What followed is quoted from
Péron's report:

> Michel suddenly displayed such a striking proof of his virility that all of
> [the Tasmanians] exclaimed loudly in surprise interspersed with loud
> bursts of laughter. Such a state of force and vigour ... surprised them
> greatly, and they gave the impression of applauding that state, like
> people for whom it is out of the ordinary.

From this episode Péron drew the conclusion that the Tasmanians were
lacking in sexual vigour!

The expedition itself, which had set out in 1800 in two ships, was dogged
by ill-fortune from the start. Owing to friction between Baudin and several
of the scientists, artists, and technicians, ten of the twenty-four staff
disembarked on reaching what is now Mauritius. Among the remainder,
illness took such a toll that only six returned in 1804, Baudin himself
having died before the end of the voyage.

At the time when the remnants of the expedition reached France, the *Société* also found itself in terminal decline. The Empire had been declared by Napoleon, and the more radical section of the membership objected to Jauffret's request to Napoleon for permission to add 'imperial' to the name. The attempt at currying favour failed, since Napoleon had become hostile to the radical spirit that inspired the *Société*. Thus ended a brief flowering of the idea of an empirical social science, which was only gradually renewed during the nineteenth century.

2 Britain: interpersonal relations and cultural differences

Britain in the eighteenth century was a hive of enterprise: building canals and factories, and pioneering the 'age of steam'. In England much of this was achieved by members of the 'Lunar Society' (so named because they met every month), who came together to exchange ideas on almost every topic under the sun. It was founded by Erasmus Darwin (1731–1802), grandfather of Charles, a big man in every sense of the word whose wide-ranging interests included aspects of what we would call psychology.

Another member was Joseph Priestley (1733–1804), about whom I shall say a little more in order to illustrate the manifold talents of most of these men. Priestley came from a modest background, his father having been a cottage weaver. He was sent to the local grammar school, where a teacher introduced him to the writings of Locke and Newton. He went on to train for the ministry in a nonconformist Academy, where he came across David Hartley's *Observations on man* (1749), a psychological treatise. As a minister his study of the Bible led him to regard the doctrine of the Trinity as untenable, which did not endear him to his congregation, and he retained only a belief in a vague 'Providence'.

Subsequently he became a teacher, and when he met Benjamin Franklin in London he revived his early interests in experimental science and is now best known as a chemist – he discovered no fewer than ten gases, including oxygen. Apart from that, he wrote a good deal on social and political topics, and was sympathetic to the French Revolution, which got him into trouble. He also retained his interest in human nature, and in 1775 published a new edition of Hartley's *Observations*. Since Hartley's theories were concerned purely with individual psychology, a brief indication of his twin approaches will be sufficient. One was a modification of Locke's theory of association, taken up later by James Mill. The other was the theory of 'vibration', inspired by a remark of Newton's in his *Optics* where he had suggested that a 'sensation' makes an impression on the physical body and creates a disturbance of the nerves. Hartley developed this further, proposing that a sense impression creates 'vibrations' which travel along the nerves to the brain, and from the brain to the muscles. Thus anticipation of physiological psychology appealed to Priestley, and even this brief and superficial sketch should be enough to show what a remarkable man he was.

While some of the members of the Lunar Society were Scots, they tended to be like James Watt, whose work was in science and technology. But outstanding contributions to the understanding of the social nature of humans were made in Scotland, as part of a remarkable intellectual spurt that occurred there in philosophical and scientific fields. Its impact on the rest of Europe and America was powerful and long lasting (cf. Herman 2003). Geographically the movement was mainly centred on the triangle of Aberdeen, Edinburgh, and Glasgow, consisting of networks of people who knew each other and were engaged in vigorous exchanges of ideas. Like the French writers discussed in the preceding chapter, they were nearly all 'Newtonians'.

Among numerous distinguished figures, only those whose writings appear most germane to what much later became social-psychological problems are singled out here. They mostly sailed under the flag of 'moral philosophy', a term that had a wide range of meaning at the time – it will be recalled that 'moral' was often more or less synonymous with 'social'. It is clear that 'moral behaviour' essentially meant for them how people behave towards one another, and therefore shades imperceptibly into what is now known as 'interpersonal behaviour'. They commonly dealt with cognate areas such as history, economics, or law. At the end of this chapter one of the greatest German philosophers is briefly smuggled in, because he dealt with related issues and also provides a transition. It should be stressed that what is presented here is inevitably a very small part of a massive body of work, and many potentially relevant themes have had to be omitted.

There is one area, however, that should receive at least some mention, and that concerns the theme of language. During the eighteenth century there were numerous discussions about the origins and functions of language, and its relation to society. It was that relation which posed fundamental problems, on which diametrically opposite positions were taken. In a book on *The origin and progress of language* the rather eccentric James Burnett (1714–99), known as Lord Monboddo after he had become a judge, put forward the view that language is an acquired ability, as is speech. Both are the product of human industry and effort, so that improvements of language can be taken as a measure of intellectual advance. Language could not have been invented without society, which therefore must have preceded it. Moreover, on the basis of reports about orang-utans, which at that time had never been seen alive in Europe, he inferred from their physical similarity to humans, and from the alleged fact that they lived in societies, that they might in due course acquire language. This would require abandoning their indolence and manifesting a wish to learn. There are modern primatologists who, possibly unawares, share to some extent Monboddo's belief.

A very different position was taken by his contemporary, Thomas Reid (1710–96), professor of philosophy first at Aberdeen and then at Glasgow, in a work entitled *Essays on the intellectual powers of man* (1785). For him, the notion of inventing a language without previously having any was untenable. Reid drew a distinction between 'natural' and 'artificial' languages. He postulated an innate 'natural' language consisting of modulated cries and gestures and bodily signs which are universally understood. Such paralinguistic communication, as we would call it, is an essential prerequisite for an artificial language to be created. While that was a more reasonable position than Monboddo's, it fails of course to solve the problem of origins that is still being extensively debated. In any case, the role of language in social relations is a topic that has come to the fore in modern social psychology.

Enough has been said to convey some feel for the intense intellectual ferment that characterised the Enlightenment in general and its Scottish version in particular. In what follows it will be shown in more detail how Scottish 'moralists' tackled questions that are still of concern to social psychologists after more than two centuries.

Hutcheson's moral calculus

One of the figures who sought to provide a new basis for morality was Francis Hutcheson (1694–1746), a clergyman who later became professor of moral philosophy at Glasgow University. His views were not well received among the more orthodox clergy, but he influenced both David Hume and Adam Smith, and his ideas will therefore be briefly outlined. Hutcheson began with a simple psychological assumption, namely that humans have an innate moral sense. Loving one's fellow-creatures and caring for them gives us pleasure, while harming them causes us pain. He was of course not so naïve as to imagine that such *benevolence* (his key term) was universal, but thought that in behaving badly we go against our original nature. He had imbibed the ethos of Newtonianism, and in *An inquiry into the origin of our ideas of beauty and virtue* (1725) he wrote that the treatise was also intended to 'introduce a mathematical calculation in subjects of morality'. He produced a quasi-algebraic set of formulae designed to compute the morality of any action. For instance, the *Moral Importance* (M) of any agent is a function of his *Benevolence* (B) multiplied by his *Abilities* (A), which is then expressed as $M = B \times A$; a series of such spurious equations was then combined to arrive at general conclusions about relationships.

It would be wrong to end with this aberration that constituted only a very minor part of his writings, and is noted only to show that he partook of the Enlightenment ethos. In this connection it might also be mentioned that Hutcheson broke with the tradition of teaching only in Latin, and often lectured in English. He was a champion of liberty in the spirit of

Locke, an opponent of slavery, and an advocate of equal rights for women. Moreover, he was probably the first to regard even animals as having a right to happiness, so that no pain or misery should be inflicted on them. He also supported freedom of religion and initially encouraged Hume, who in turn regarded Hutcheson as the first *modern* philosopher. However, when Hume declared that he saw no good reason why one should believe in God, it was too much; and so Hutcheson was one of those who prevented Hume from gaining an academic post.

Hume on 'sympathy' in social relations

David Hume (1711–76) ranks as one of the world's great philosophers, whose ideas challenged many then prevalent doctrines. He was born in the Scottish Borders and descended from a long line of lawyers on both sides of his strictly Presbyterian family. His father died in 1713, leaving a widow with three children. Hume was expected to follow in his forebears' footsteps and was sent to Edinburgh University at the age of twelve; it was then common to be admitted during the early teens, but fourteen was more usual. He does not seem to have been unduly impressed by his teachers, for he is reported as having commented that 'there is nothing to be learned from a professor, which is not to be met with in books'. Hume found the study of law uninspiring, failing to graduate, but became fascinated with philosophy. Forced to earn his living, he became for a while a counting-house clerk in Bristol and in 1734 left for France, where he spent three years. While there, he began writing his *Treatise on human nature* (1739), which has as its sub-title *An attempt to introduce the experimental method of reasoning into moral subjects*. However, the term 'experiment' should not be understood in today's strict sense, as indicated by his subsequent elaboration: 'We must ... glean up our experiments in this science from a cautious observation of human life, and take them as they appear in the common course of the world, by men's behaviour in company, in affairs, and in their pleasures.'

Hume had high hopes for his *Treatise* and was disappointed that it was initially ignored, becoming famous only much later in a revised version. After that he published his *Essays moral and political* (1741), which were an immediate success. In spite of his brilliance Hume failed to obtain a chair at either Edinburgh or later Glasgow, his views being unpalatable at universities then still dominated by theology. In 1745 he became tutor to a young aristocrat who was mentally ill and impossible to teach. Then he was invited by General St Clair to join him on an expedition, and he subsequently became secretary to embassies in Vienna and Turin.

As his writings became more widely known his reputation grew, and when he was back in France from 1763 to 1765 he was fêted in all the major *salons* frequented by the intellectual luminaries of the period, including Helvétius, d'Holbach, Turgot, Diderot, and Alembert. At the end of his life he did not abandon his sceptical outlook, typified by his remark that any book on divinity that does not contain any abstract or 'experimental' reasoning should be burnt. He joked to his close friend Adam Smith about his imminent demise. He imagined that he might ask Charon, boatman of the Styx, to wait and let him see the downfall of all superstitions. However, Charon would have none of it and was said to reply 'Get into the boat this instant, you lazy loitering rogue!' Thus even at the end Hume remained true to his convictions.

While Hutcheson had postulated an innate 'benevolence', Hume's general thesis was that people are subject to 'passions' which, when left uncontrolled, would make civil society impossible; and since reason is 'the slave of the passions', appeals to reason would be useless. Hence the existence of social institutions, customs, and rules that act as external constraints, redirecting the passions towards behaviour compatible with the functioning of society – e.g. sex into marriage, aggression into military institutions protecting society from enemies.

There is, however, according to Hume another psychological feature which plays a crucial role in social interaction, namely *sympathy*, whose 'nature and force' he described as follows:

> The minds of all men are similar in their feelings and operations; nor can any one be actuated by any affection of which all the others are not in some degree susceptible. As in strings equally wound up, the motion of one communicates itself to the rest, so all the affections readily pass from one person to another, and beget corresponding movements in every human creature. When I see the *effects* of passion in the voice and gesture of any person, my mind immediately passes from these effects to their causes, and forms such a lively idea of the passion as is presently converted into the passion itself. In like manner, when I perceive the causes of any emotion, my mind is conveyed to the effects, and is actuated with a like emotion.   (Hume 1739/1911, vol. 2, p. 272; emphasis in original)

This vivid description does not really tell us what processes are involved. The metaphor of the strings implies some kind of contagion. The subsequent elaboration suggests that consideration of the *causes* of an emotion plays a critical role. But this would entail the necessity of prior reflection and thereby contradict the *immediacy* of the experience of sympathy, on which Hume also insisted. This is a vexed problem, and it will be shown that Adam Smith took a somewhat different line.

Hume also discussed the relevance of sympathy to the relationship between self and others:

> A man will be mortified if you tell him he has a stinking breath; though it is evidently no annoyance to himself. Our fancy easily changes this situation; and either surveying ourselves as we appear to others, or

considering others as they feel themselves, we enter, by that means, into sentiments which in no way belong to us, and in which nothing but sympathy is able to interest us. And this sympathy we sometimes carry so far, as even to be displeased with a quality commodious [convenient] to us, merely because it displeases others, and makes us disagreeable in their eyes.   (Hume 1739/1911, vol. 2, p. 284)

So the man with the stinking breath starts to worry about it as soon as he becomes aware that other people dislike it. Sympathy leads him to put himself in the position of others, and thereby he comes to view himself in a different light. This means that sympathy is a force towards social conformity.

In sum, Hume regarded sympathy as one of the most salient character-istics of humans, which makes us respond to the feelings of others and forms the basis of our attachment to society. He discussed the variations in the intensity of its operation, pointing out that its effectiveness is a function of the closeness of our relations in both physical and social terms: we feel more sympathy with friends than with strangers, with our country-men than with foreigners. This statement was subsequently to be echoed by Charles Darwin when discussing the adaptive function of sympathy. Hume's writings on sympathy inspired his friend Adam Smith, who further elaborated them.

Adam Smith and his quasi-social-psychology

Best known for the groundbreaking economic thesis expounded in *The wealth of nations* (1776), Adam Smith also made a significant contribution towards the understanding of social behaviour in *The theory of moral sentiments* (1759). The birthplace of Adam Smith (1723–90) was the small port of Kirkcaldy. His father, who died shortly before his birth, was a local customs official while his mother came from a land-owning family. He was sent to the small (two-room) local grammar school, where he learned Latin, Roman history, rhetoric, grammar, and arithmetic. At the age of fourteen he went from there to Glasgow University, where his favourite subjects were mathematics and natural philosophy. But the teacher who most impressed and inspired him was Hutcheson.

In 1740 Smith was awarded an exhibition to Balliol College, Oxford, where he spent six years. He was not happy there. The college was 'anti-Scotch', and the university as a whole intellectually conservative and rather idle as compared with Glasgow. Hence his often-cited remark that 'In the University of Oxford, the greater part of the public professors have, for these many years, given up altogether even the pretence of teaching.' So Smith spent most of his time reading philosophy and litera-ture in several languages. After Oxford he returned to Kirkcaldy, where he

2   *Adam Smith (1723–90)*

lived with his mother and maiden cousin. Smith was without a job for some time, until invited to give a course of public lectures on rhetoric in Edinburgh. There he made a number of distinguished friends, including Adam Ferguson, William Robertson, and, above all, David Hume, who was twelve years his senior. Unlike Hume, who was partial to the ladies, Smith's social life had little to do with women. In 1751 he was called to

Glasgow, first as professor of logic, and shortly afterwards moving to the chair of moral philosophy vacated by Hutcheson. In 1763 he resigned his chair to become tutor to the young Duke of Buccleuch and travelled with him on the continent, spending time in Paris. On his return he resumed his post in Glasgow and wrote the work which established his greatest fame.

Adam Smith was a liberal and open-minded man, who deplored national prejudices and, unlike many of his contemporaries, was strongly opposed to slavery. He wrote that 'There is not a negro from the coast of Africa who does not . . . possess a degree of magnanimity which the soul of his sordid master is too often scarce capable of conceiving.'

The quasi-psychological character of *The theory of moral sentiments* is readily apparent from its sub-title: *An essay towards an analysis of the principles by which men naturally judge concerning the conduct and character, first of their neighbours, and afterwards of themselves.* However, the actual thesis presented by Smith is much wider, notably in its examination of the consequences of such judgements in terms of *reciprocal* relations between people. Smith believed that *sympathy* is centrally involved in all kinds of social behaviour, and one of his students commented that for Smith sympathy was for the social world what gravity is for the natural world. He started with the fact that we are interested in and have sympathy with the fortunes of others, and regarded the need for mutual sympathy as a fundamental human characteristic. Smith defined sympathy essentially as 'our fellow-feeling with any passion whatso-ever', but the simplicity suggested by this definition is misleading, for we have no direct access to other people's feelings, and can only imagine what we ourselves would be feeling in their situation. But that is also not straightfor-ward, since we cannot assume that everybody reacts in the same way:

> Sympathy, therefore, does not arise so much from the view of the passions, *as from the situation which excites it.* We sometimes feel for another, a passion of which he himself seems to be altogether incapable; because, when we put ourselves in his case, that passion arises in our breast from the imagination, though it does not in his from the reality. We blush for the impudence and rudeness of another, though he himself appears to have no sense of impropriety of his own behaviour; because we cannot help feeling with what confusion we ourselves should be covered had we behaved in so absurd a manner.   (Smith 1790/1984, p. 12; emphasis added)

Generally we gain satisfaction from the sharing of feelings, which is closest in one's immediate kin, and 'What is called affection, is in reality nothing but habitual sympathy.' But sympathy also functions to cement other relationships, from friends to wider social circles, and society as a whole is the sum-total of these networks. Much of the work discusses the various forms taken by sympathy and its role in social life. While Smith took sympathy to be an innate human characteristic, nineteenth-century evolu-tionists, and notably Darwin, proposed that it served an adaptive function not merely among humans but also among animals. Early in the twentieth century the newly emerging social psychology still regarded sympathy as an explanation of social behaviour. But with the advent of a behaviouristic social psychology it became discredited as a concept unsupported by empirical evidence. However, in the twenty-first century the neural mechanism underlying it has begun to be identified, and so it has come to be once again viewed as highly significant for understanding social behaviour.

Let us return from this brief excursion to consider another of Smith's ideas that has stood the test of time. He showed that the kind of person we become is largely shaped by our interactions with other people. In describing this process Smith made use of the twin metaphors of the *mirror* and the *internal spectator*:

> Were it possible that a human creature could grow up to manhood in some solitary place, without any communication with his own species, he could no more think of his own character, of the propriety or demerit of his own sentiments and conduct, of the beauty or deformity of his own mind, than of the beauty or deformity of his own face. All these are objects which he cannot easily see ... and with regard to which he is provided with no mirror which can present them to his view. Bring him into society, and he is immediately provided with the mirror which he wanted before.   (Smith 1790/1984, p. 110)

The idea that we see ourselves reflected in the behaviour of others towards us (hence the *mirror* or the *looking-glass*) was not a new one, and could be found in Hume. What was a new and powerful notion was that of the *impartial spectator*, who is set up *internally* in the course of development. This part of the mind is in a sense detached from myself as well as from those who may be affected by my conduct. The *impartial spectator*, regarded as being aware of both social norms and my motivation, acts as a kind of judge between myself and those with whom I live. I consult the *impartial spectator* and try to act in such a way as to gain approval.

The *impartial spectator*, who strides repeatedly through Smith's pages, constitutes the internal counterpart of the acting agent whose conduct is being judged, and a good deal of the argument of the book turns on the play of their interactions. There are indications that Smith saw the *impartial spectator* as being a function of primary group membership, since the influence of the immediate social environment was stressed: 'The natural disposition to accommodate and assimilate, as much as we can, our own sentiments, principles, and feelings, to those which we see fixed and rooted in the persons with whom we are obliged to live.' The metaphor of the mirror was adopted a century later by Cooley, who referred to the 'looking-glass self', and the social psychologist George Herbert Mead re-christened the *impartial spectator* 'the generalized other', i.e. the internalised collective norms, rules, and values. G. H. Mead in particular sought to show how these values are internalised in the course of development, unlike Smith, who had hardly anything to say about child development or education; thus

Smith was apt to write as though people came into the world as adults. On the other hand Smith fully acknowledged cultural differences:

> The different situations of different ages and countries are apt ... to give different characters to the generality of those who live in them, and their sentiments concerning the particular degree of each quality, that is either blameable or praise-worthy, vary, according to that degree which is usual in their own country, and in their own times. That degree of politeness, which would be highly esteemed [in our country], perhaps would be thought effeminate adulation in Russia, would be regarded as rudeness and barbarism at the court of France.   (Smith 1790/1984, p. 204)

While agreeing that sentiments of attachment are proportionate to the closeness of kinship, he dismissed the then prevalent belief in the power of 'blood' that was widely supposed mysteriously to attract even those unaware of their relationship.

Throughout the work one finds perceptive and sensitive comments on emotional responses to the attitudes and actions of other people in the social field. One of the few psychologists who noted this was Fritz Heider, who in his book on *The psychology of interpersonal relations* (1958) explained his dual approach: 'We shall make use of the unformulated or half-formulated knowledge of interpersonal relations as it is expressed in our everyday language and experience – this source will be referred to as common-sense or naïve psychology; we shall also draw upon the knowledge and insights of scientific investigations.' Such investigations of course did not exist in Adam Smith's time, but his insights into 'common-sense psychology' were acute. Accordingly, Heider had frequent occasion to cite him.

Heider was the originator of what has become known as 'balance theory', which sought to systematise various patterns of interpersonal relationships. It is of course not possible to expound this theory here in detail, but some of the basic principles need to be summarised. The classical case concerns three entities, p, o, and x, where p is the individual perceiver, o is another person, and x is an impersonal object or issue. Each of the three relations between each pair of entities can take the form of positive or negative 'sentiments' (e.g. likes or dislikes). There are eight possible relationships between these entities, some of which are 'balanced' or harmonious, and others 'unbalanced'. For instance, if both people support the same political party, the triad is 'balanced'. The relationships need not be all positive for there to be 'balance', as implicit in the saying 'my enemy's enemy is my friend'. It is assumed that the object is an important one for the two people concerned, about which they feel strongly.

Now in his discussions of the intricacies of affective and cognitive aspects of interpersonal relations, Smith sketched a hypothetical situation which contains the germ of Heider's 'balance theory' in the emotional sphere:

> Though you despise that picture, or that poem, or even that system of philosophy, which I admire, there is little danger of our quarrelling upon that account. Neither of us can reasonably be much interested about them. They ought all of them to be matters of great indifference to us both; so that, though our opinions may be opposite, our affections may still be very nearly the same. But it is quite otherwise with regard to those objects by which either you or I are particularly affected. Though your judgements in matters of speculation, though your sentiments in matters of taste, are quite opposite to mine, I can easily overlook this opposition; and if I have any degree of temper, I may still find some entertainment in your conversation, even upon those very subjects. But if you have either no fellow-feeling for the misfortunes I have met with, or none that bears any proportion to the grief which distracts me; or if you have either no indignation at the injuries I have suffered, or none that bears any proportion to the resentment which transports me, we can no longer converse upon these subjects. We become intolerable to one another. I can neither support your company, nor you mine. You are confounded at my violence and passion, and I am enraged at your cold insensibility and want of feeling.   (Smith 1790/1984, p. 21)

Curiously, this passage was not among those cited by Heider. It is not the only instance of Smith anticipating elements of a social-psychological theory, and another example would be Festinger's 'theory of social comparisons', outlined below.

Festinger's (1954) first hypothesis was that a human being has 'a drive to evaluate his opinions and abilities', arguing that both are connected since they jointly affect behaviour. Smith was not concerned with abilities in this context, so references to that will be omitted. At any rate, Festinger elaborated a series of hypotheses, among which the second was the fundamental one, most relevant in the present context. It ran as follows: 'To the extent that objective, non-social means are not available, people evaluate their opinions … by comparison … with the opinions … of others.' One could rephrase this by saying that, in situations of uncertainty, other people become a major source of information. Here is the analogous version provided by Smith:

> The agreement or disagreement both of the sentiments and judgements of other people with our own, is, in all cases, it must be observed, of more or less importance to us, exactly in proportion as we ourselves are more or less uncertain about the propriety of our own sentiments, about the accuracy of our own judgements.   (Smith 1790/1984, p. 122)

While Smith referred to moral 'sentiments' and 'judgements', the principle is exactly the same. Moreover he suggested that the greater the uncertainty, the more likely we are to rely on other people.

The fact that there is some congruence between the writings of Smith and the theories of some modern social psychologists can hardly be coincidental. It indicates that he was a careful and shrewd observer of people's social behaviour, and that social-psychological theories also tend to have their roots in 'common-sense' observations. However, it would be quite wrong to assume that Smith saw himself engaged in some kind of 'social science', for, unlike some of his French contemporaries, his attitude to any kind of science was sceptical. When he wrote a history of astronomy (probably begun at Oxford) he declared that his purpose was to consider various cosmological systems not in terms of their closeness to reality, but rather in terms of their capacity 'to soothe the imagination, and to render the theatre of nature more coherent'. He shared the widespread Enlightenment aim of throwing light on the nature of human nature, which for him constituted a sort of exercise of the imagination, and his approaches included the study of language and communication as well as his work on what is now called economics.

It should now be clear why his *Theory of moral sentiments* has been labelled above *quasi*-psychological. Its central focus was on the 'passions' (in our terms 'emotions') experienced either directly or sympathetically. Like Hume, he regarded reason as subordinate to passion. There is one noteworthy absence from Smith's account of the passions, namely that of sex. One might surmise that the explanation lay in his personal life, and as one commentator wrote wittily, if rather unkindly: 'Smith couldn't be doing with sex because it was sand in his great sympathetic machine: the last thing lovers need is an Impartial Spectator.'

Millar on culture and behaviour

One could not accuse John Millar (1735–1801) of a lack of interest in sex. He published a kind of cultural history of the development of humanity, in which it figured prominently. Millar was the eldest of four children of a Church of Scotland minister. His mother was a cousin of William Cullen, a professor of medicine who was one of the first to clarify the functions of the nervous system; and Cullen took an interest in the education of his nephew. Millar enrolled at the University of Glasgow, where he became a friend of James Watt, prominent engineer and inventor. He was expected to follow his father into the ministry, but studied law instead. When Adam Smith came to Glasgow University, Millar attended his courses in logic and moral philosophy. He was a favourite student of Smith's and later they became close friends. Millar married in 1759 and had thirteen children, two of whom died in infancy.

Two years after his marriage he obtained the regius chair of civil law at Glasgow University. His predecessor in the chair was not popular, having an average of three or four students per year and sometimes none. After a few years Millar had ten times that number, owing to his very different style. Instead of effectively dictating lectures in Latin, he gave them in English, and he was an inspiring teacher who frequently held informal discussions with his students. His theoretical orientation owed much to both Hume and Smith, and in his approach to jurisprudence he made use of the metaphor of the 'impartial spectator'.

Millar was much concerned with politics, taking a Whig line in favour of parliamentary reform that would lead to 'a much more general diffusion of political power'. He supported American independence and was active in the anti-slavery movement. He also welcomed the early stages of the French Revolution, before it had become a messy bloodbath. One of his sons adopted an even more radical stance, and was forced to emigrate to America. The same was true of some of his former students, one of whom was transported to Australia as a result of his radical agitation.

Millar published a constitutional history that was the first of its kind, but it is his earlier work, the famous *Observations concerning the distinction of ranks in society* (1771), that is relevant in the present context. In the preface he explained his aim: 'When ... we consider how much the character of individuals is influenced by their education, their professions, and their particular circumstances, we are enabled, in some measure, to account for the behaviour of different nations.' He shared with many other Enlightenment figures the view that 'Man is everywhere the same, and we must necessarily conclude, that the untutored Indian and the civilized European have acted upon the same principle.' This is in sharp contrast to the belief in 'racial' determinism widespread during the nineteenth century. Millar's work could be said to have been, in our terminology, a study of the influence of culture on behaviour. Moreover, he stressed the importance of doing this on the basis of actual data: 'Thus by real experiments, not abstracted [*sic*] metaphysical theories, human nature is unfolded.' At the time, as already mentioned, the meaning of the word 'experimental' corresponded to our 'empirical'. As was usual in the eighteenth century, the empirical data consisted of reports by travellers and explorers, and historical accounts. The material he used varied widely in time and space, ranging from classical Greece via Columbus to contemporary voyages of exploration to exotic places.

During the Enlightenment, as already mentioned, it was held that humankind went from 'savagery' to civilisation, passing through four main stages named according to the dominant mode of gaining subsistence, namely hunting and fishing, pastoralism, agriculture, and commerce; in essence these broad stages are still accepted to the present. Within the overall topic of 'rank' – more or less equivalent to our 'status' – Millar concentrated on particular categories of people, showing how their position changed during the upward move through the stages. The categories included the condition of women, the authority of the father over his children, and that of the chief over his people. Here only the first chapter, the changing condition of women, will be discussed.

It begins with the general statement that 'Of all our passions, it should seem that those which unite the sexes are most easily affected by the peculiar circumstances in which we are placed, and most liable to be influenced by the power of habit and education.' In order to understand the import of a passage that follows, it should be explained that the image of the 'savage' at the lowest stage he presented, well-nigh universal at the time, was of people with few if any institutions and entirely dominated by a struggle for mere subsistence. Thus he wrote about the 'savage' that 'his great object is to be able to satisfy his hunger ... He has no time for cultivating a correspondence with the other sex, or in attending to those enjoyments which result from it; and his desires ... are allowed to remain in that moderate state which renders them barely sufficient to answer the purposes of nature in the continuation of the species.' In other words, 'savages' are under-sexed. At the same time, sex for them is a straightforward matter: 'It cannot be supposed, therefore, that the passions of sex will rise to any considerable height in the breast of the savage. He must have little regard for pleasures which he can purchase at so easy a rate.'

Pastoral peoples are no longer under grim survival pressures, and so 'the mere animal pleasure is often accompanied with the more delicate correspondences of inclination and sentiment'. Hence, it is suggested, the status of women in such societies is somewhat better. Jumping now to civilisation, their status is further improved: 'Whatever has a tendency to create more attention to the pleasures of sex, or to raise the estimation of the different arts and occupations which are suited to the female character, must also have an influence in procuring respect to the fair sex.' The advent of courtship in which the woman had to be wooed, and the rise of romantic love, conferred on women a more elevated status.

In a similar manner Millar traced the changing status of other categories of people. For instance servants were at one time barely distinguishable from slaves, and only gradually gained individual rights. While the general thesis is a reasonable one, the material he was able to use was often unreliable. For example, the notion that 'savages' had unregulated access to women was little more than a European fantasy. On the other hand, when Millar said that in the Congo and other parts of Africa women were usually not permitted to eat together with the men, that was correct; in fact it still remains the custom in parts of Africa less affected by western practices.

At the end of his book Millar discussed the 1778 Scottish judgement against slavery, an institution held to be unjust. In previous judgements the rights of the masters over their property had been upheld, and Millar heartily approved of the change, which was a matter of pride for him.

Generally, Millar has to be credited with a systematic attempt to analyse the manner in which changing socio-cultural conditions influenced social behaviour. In doing so he was forced to rely on secondary sources, as were all those who embarked on comparable enterprises. But as has been shown, at the end of the century in France the *Observateurs* advocated the need for direct observation. Knowing Hume well, Millar was almost certainly influenced by a famous essay of Hume's that will now be considered.

Hume on national stereotypes and characters

First of all it should be said that the term 'stereotypes' was not coined until the twentieth century, but the label fits. Discussions of the characters of nations go back a long way. Niccolò Machiavelli (1469–1572) had suggested that nations preserve their particular positive and negative characteristics over long periods. Not everybody agreed, and Seckendorf (1626–92) was a sceptic who pointed to the dangers of what we would call inadequate sampling:

> The origin, nature and sentiments, virtues and vices, of the inhabitants of a country, are made quite a lot of by old and new writers, although they are made without basis on uncertain assumptions, and they are too easily generalized from the example of a few people to whole nations and peoples.   (Cited in Slotkin 1965, p. 128)

Hume shared Seckendorf's reservations, and in his essay *Of national characters* (1741) considered two main questions. To what extent are generalisations about national character valid? And in so far as there are real national differences in characters, what are their causes? He used the expression 'national character' for both 'national stereotypes' and features taken to be real and typical. This is clear from his first paragraph:

> The vulgar are apt to carry all *national characters* to extremes; and having once established it as a principle, that any people are knavish, or cowardly, or ignorant, they will admit of no exception, but comprehend every individual under the same censure.   (Hume 1741/1894, pp. 116–17; emphasis in original)

He stressed that though such lack of discrimination is unreasonable, there *are* national differences, but these are differences in *frequencies* of traits. Essentially the same point was made later by Gordon Allport in his classic work on *The nature of prejudice* (1954b). One of Hume's examples refers to the 'common people' in Switzerland, said to be on average more honest than those in Ireland. It is noteworthy that he specified social status, and elsewhere he commented that occupations also shape character in similar fashion across nations. Other examples are rather quaint, as when he suggested that one would expect more knowledge in an Englishman than in a Dane, though Tycho Brahe was a Dane.

Hume then went on to consider the causes of national differences, distinguishing between 'moral' and 'physical' ones, the latter referring mainly to climate. Unlike some other writers, he did not think that climate was a major factor, except for some very general tendencies such as a greater liking for strong liquors in northern peoples, and more intense love of women in southern ones. This again was an old story: Jean Bodin (1530–96) had been among those who drew contrasts between peoples living north and south. Bodin had further suggested physical causes for the difference: in the cold, liquor warms the blood, while a hot climate inflames the blood 'and exalts the passion between the sexes'.

Beliefs in the inferiority of those living further north or south were combined with the conviction that one's own location was the optimal one. This applied for instance to Muslims at the end of the first millennium, who lived in the lands stretching from Spain across North Africa to the Middle East. Muslim scholars were agreed that peoples further north and south were, respectively, white and black barbarians. The northern climes, which included Hume's Scotland, were said to produce people with frigid temperaments and raw humours who were ignorant, stupid, and apathetic. As will be shown in chapter 7, even Wundt in his earlier years still shared this kind of preconception.

While accepting the supposed effects of climatic extremes, Hume placed less weight on the influence of climate than did several of his contemporaries. One problem regarding the notion of 'climate' is that the term was often used in a sense that corresponds more or less to our 'ecology'. In any case, Hume put more emphasis on what he called 'moral' causes and explained what he meant by that:

> By *moral* causes, I mean all the circumstances, which are fitted to work on the mind as motives or reasons, and which render a peculiar set of manners habitual to us. Of this kind are, the nature of the government, the revolutions of public affairs, the plenty or penury in which the people live, the situation of the nation with regard to its neighbours, and such like circumstances.   (Hume 1741/1894, p. 117; emphasis in original)

As already indicated, the term 'moral' then had a much broader meaning than it has now. As employed by Hume in this context, it corresponds roughly to our 'social', and he elaborated what might well be called a social-psychological interpretation:

> The human mind is of a very imitative nature; nor is it possible for any set of men to converse often together, without acquiring a similitude of manners, and communicating to each other their vices as well as virtues. The propensity to company and society is strong in all rational creatures; and the same disposition, which gives us this propensity, makes us enter deeply into each other's sentiments, and causes like passions and inclinations to run, as it were, by contagion, through the whole club or knot of companions.   (Hume 1741/1894, p. 119)

The point to note here is the stress on 'imitation' and 'contagion' as a source of social and emotional communalities. This was a widespread notion, expressed by Erasmus Darwin – Charles's grandfather, it will be recalled – in the form of a poem, part of which is reproduced below. The first lines seem rather odd and require explanation. Erasmus Darwin held the rather quaint belief that humans make greater use of imitation than animals, because we have a greater facility for discovering the outlines of an object by touch, and can afterwards transfer these to the sense of sight.

> Trace on hard forms the circumscribing line;
> Which then the language of the rolling eyes
> Hence when the inquiring hands with contact fine
> From distant scenes of earth and heaven supplies;
> Those clear ideas of the touch and sight
> Rouse the quick sense to anguish and delight;
> Whence the fine power of IMITATION springs,
> And apes the outlines of external things;
> With ceaseless action to the world imparts
> All moral virtues, languages and arts
> First the charmed Mind mechanic power collects,
> Means for some end, and causes of effects;
> Then learns from other Minds their joys and fears,
> Contagious smiles and sympathetic tears.
>
> (Erasmus Darwin 1803/1824, p. 39)

In other words, it is *imitation* which not only is responsible for progress, but also governs social relationships of all kinds. It will also be noted that imitation is linked here with sympathy, and both were and still are seen as important factors in social life.

Coming back to Hume's essay, it ends on a rather curious note, comparing the passions for liquor and for love. The former is bad, but even the latter carries risks, for 'when love goes beyond a certain pitch, it renders men jealous, and cuts off the free intercourse between the sexes, on which the politeness [i.e. refinement] of a nation will commonly much depend'. The point of the argument is that southern nations, who drink less and are more inclined to love, do not thereby necessarily have an advantage. In claiming that people in temperate zones are most fitted to progress, Hume revealed himself as a child of his time.

Kant's *Anthropology*

The inclusion at this point of an eminent German philosopher, who was definitely not part of the Scottish Enlightenment, requires some justification. It could be said that Kant was linked to Hume in as much as it was Hume's *Enquiries into human understanding* (1748) that was supposed to have awakened Kant from his 'dogmatic slumbers'; and it prompted Kant into a determined but finally inconclusive attempt to counter Hume's scepticism about causation. But the real reason is that the *Anthropology* fits into the present theme and provides a transition to the subsequent one.

Immanuel Kant (1724–1804) was born in Königsberg, in Prussia, the son of a saddler. He stayed there throughout his life, becoming professor of logic and metaphysics at the university in 1770. He was an intellectual giant, but his everyday life was regular and uneventful – it was said that one could set one's watch by his daily walk. His early publications were in the natural sciences, and he made significant theoretical contributions to astronomy. In the Newtonian spirit, he equated science with measurement and mathematics, and hence concluded psychology was not, and could not become, a science. In common with many of his contemporaries, he called the study of man as part of nature 'anthropology', and saw psychology as an empirical and pragmatic discipline.

Kant's account of psychology is therefore to be found in his *Anthropology from a pragmatic point of view* (1797/1974). The book is organised according to the tripartite scheme of knowing, feeling, and willing set out in his *Critique of judgement* (1790), which set a pattern for the future. In the *Anthropology* metaphysical discussions of self and soul are eschewed, and the focus of the last part in particular is on human characteristics and behaviour. It has rarely been pointed out that some of this has a distinctly social-psychological flavour. He had a lot to say about how people manipulate each other, and similar down-to-earth topics. Thus Kant discussed the 'inclination for power' in the following terms:

> This inclination comes closest to technically practical reason, that is, to the maxim of prudence. For getting other men's inclinations into our power, so that we can direct and determine them according to our own purposes, is almost the same as *possessing* other men as mere tools of our will. No wonder that the striving for this kind of *power* to influence other men becomes a passion.
> This power to influence others contains three kinds of might, so to speak: *honor*, *dominion*, and *money*. If we have these we can get at every man and use him for our purposes – if one of them fails to influence him, the others will.   (Kant 1797/1974, p. 138; emphasis in original)

In a later part there is a great deal about 'characters' of individuals, but what is of interest in the present context is Kant's account of the characters of *categories* of people, such as the sexes, on which he makes some amusing comments, e.g. 'We call feminine ways weaknesses, and joke about them. Fools jeer at them, but reasonable men know very well that they are precisely the rudders women use to steer men and use them for their own purposes.' Perhaps it was this shrewd insight that prevented Kant from ever marrying!

Another section deals with the character of nations, and the probable origins of such characters are discussed. He regarded them as innate and/or the result of combined effects of climate, history, government, etc.

As a sample of how characters are presented, here is part of a sketch about Englishmen:

> The English character renounces all amiability toward others, even among the English people, whereas amiability is the most prominent social quality of the French. The Englishman claims only respect and, for the rest, each wants only to live as he pleases. – For his compatriots the Englishman establishes great benevolent institutions, unheard of among other peoples. But if a foreigner whom fate has driven ashore on his soil falls into dire need, he can die on a dunghill because he is not an Englishmen – that is, not a man.   (Kant 1797/1974, p. 177)

It will be evident from these examples that, compared with his disquisitions on metaphysical issues, the tone of these sections is light; unlike Hume, he apparently was content to deal in stereotypes. It is not certain how seriously this was meant, since much of the *Anthropology* was based on popular lectures delivered over a period of some thirty years. Understandably, Kant was unwilling to have them published until he had retired. He treated psychology lightly, almost jocularly, and the contrast with his philosophical writings is striking. His thesis that psychology could never become a genuine science was disputed by Herbart, his successor in the chair at Königsberg. It was also Herbart who elaborated an early form of social psychology.

PART II

The nineteenth century: the gestation of social psychology in Europe

3   Germany: Herbart's and his followers' societal psychology

Kant's view that psychology could never become a real science because, as he contended, it is not susceptible to mathematical treatment was challenged by Herbart's elaboration of a mathematical approach. However, it was not so much his mathematics as his other writings on psychology, and especially on pedagogy, that gained him international fame. For more than a century nearly everyone concerned with psychology or education in German-speaking countries – and sometimes beyond – *had* to engage with Herbart and his students, one of the most prominent of them having been Fechner. It was Herbart's theories that inspired Lazarus and Steinthal when they formulated their *Völkerpsychologie* long before that of Wundt. Later two Austrian scholars carried Herbart's ideas further, and it is not clear whether the earlier one, Lindner, or the Italian, Cattaneo, was the first to give social psychology its name. Lastly an unorthodox student of Herbart will be discussed, whose ideas were opposed to the then prevailing 'racist' ethos and well in advance of his time.

Herbart's contributions to mathematical and educational psychology are generally recognised in histories of psychology. What one rarely finds in English-language publications is any reference to Herbart as a pioneer of social psychology. Yet in Germany it has long been taken for granted that he was the originator of that discipline, although the term 'social psychology' did not yet exist in his time. For instance Moede (1920, p. 25), one of the earliest of experimental social psychologists, wrote: 'None other than Herbart was ... the pioneer of exact social psychology.' Similarly, Lauken (1998) attributes to Herbart the first great project of a social psychology, which came to be further developed by his followers. None of the followers considered here pursued his mathematical project, but they took over the fundamental analogy proposed by Herbart between individual and collective psychological functioning. Since for Herbart the collective was the society or the state – neither he nor his followers distinguished these clearly – the term 'societal psychology' is used in the title of this chapter.

Herbart: from individual to societal psychology

A quiet academic life

Johann Friedrich Herbart (1776–1841) was born in Oldenburg and went to school there. At the age of sixteen he was selected to give the customary leaving address and he chose as his topic 'Some observations on the most general causes responsible for the growth and decline of morality in countries' – a harbinger of his remarkable talents. His father was a distant figure who would have liked him to become a businessman, while his domineering mother had all kinds of unspecified ambitions for him. His home situation seems to have been less than congenial, and so he was glad to leave in 1797 to become tutor to a Swiss family in Berne. It was this experience of teaching children, to which he often referred later, that initially kindled his interest in pedagogy.

He then went to university in Jena, and there told one of his fellow-students that he never felt a sensual inclination towards the other sex. Moreover, he expressed the view that whoever devotes himself to science should not consider marriage before the age of forty, but should marry then so as to able to guide one's children to maturity. He later married a woman from an English family, the marriage remaining childless. But she helped him to set up a school for boys in his house and they adopted a mentally handicapped child.

On leaving university he became a *Gymnasium* (grammar school) teacher in Bremen. There Herbart was introduced by a friend to three women in the latter's family circle, giving them some instruction in mathematics and Greek, and discussing child development and learning. Apparently Herbart enjoyed this, displaying no trace of male superiority – something most unusual at the time. As that friend later commented, he treated them as though they were men. Herbart discussed with these ladies the methods of Pestalozzi, and in 1802, at the age of twenty-six, he published an essay on Pestalozzi's latest work and dedicated it to them. This seems to have been a sign of his burgeoning interest in child development and education, which became a major strand of his work. In 1805 Herbart became extra-ordinary (i.e. less than full) professor of philosophy at the University of Göttingen. In comparison with the relatively democratic spirit at the University of Jena, Göttingen was rigidly hierarchical. Professors addressed students strictly according to their social status, from *Hochgeboren* (literally 'high-born') for scions of the aristocracy, down to *Wohlgeboren* (well-born) for mere bourgeois. In 1806 Napoleon defeated Prussia, to the dismay of Herbart who was intensely patriotic; and in the same year he began to lecture on psychology.

In 1809 Herbart was 'called' as Kant's successor to Königsberg, then the refuge of the Prussian king while Berlin was occupied by the French.

3   *Johann Friedrich Herbart (1776–1841)*

During that time he met Wilhelm von Humboldt (1767–1835), a great scholar who had retained the spirit of the Enlightenment. A pervasive theme in Humboldt's work was the relationship between the languages, thoughts, and mentalities of peoples. Thereby he anticipated the concern in social psychology with national differences and with the social functions of language. They frequently met for discussions, and this probably accounts for the introduction of language as a social factor in Herbart's later writings. In 1833 Herbart returned to a chair at Göttingen, where he remained for the rest of his life.

Herbart lived in the period between the idealism of the Declaration of the Rights of Man and the conservative reaction. Like many bourgeois intellectuals, he was repelled by the Terror in France and declared his belief in freedom of thought. He was a moderate liberal who deplored oppression, but favoured a 'legitimate monarchy' well short of anything approaching democracy. An incident at the University of Göttingen typifies his stance. A new and relatively more liberal regime had been established in the state of Hanover, and the historian Dahlmann had participated in the negotiations leading to the new constitution. On ascending the throne the new king Ernst August summarily dissolved the assembly, declaring the new constitution revoked. Dahlmann sought the help of fellow-members of the faculty of philosophy, where Herbart was dean. Six distinguished colleagues, including the brothers Grimm, supported him and made up the 'Göttingen seven' as they came to be called, who issued a joint protest. Herbart, on the other hand, decided to go along with a deputation of Senate who presented an address of loyalty to the king, who not only dismissed all seven but sent three into exile. For all his brilliance, Herbart was clearly unwilling to rock the political boat. It will become apparent in due course that this political position was reflected in his theoretical writings on social aspects of psychology. Before discussing this, it is necessary to say something about his *individual* psychology, since he sought to show that essentially the same general principles could be applied to social life.

Herbart's individual psychology

It should be said at the outset that it is quite difficult for most of us to understand his psychological system. There are two main reasons for this, one being that Herbart developed a sophisticated mathematical psychology, albeit one devoid of any empirical anchoring. While it is not necessary to understand the details of the mathematics – and I myself do not – at least the broad principles underlying his approach have to be grasped. Secondly, both the language and the concepts used tend to be unfamiliar. Hence, far from seeking to convey the full subtlety and complexity of Herbart's scheme of individual psychology, a mere simplified outline will be sketched. Unlike Kant, he believed that there *can* be a psychological science along the lines of Newtonian physics: 'The lawfulness of the human mind [*Geist*] is exactly the same as that of the starry sky.' His model for psychology was therefore physics.

For Herbart, the underlying unity of all mental activity was the soul. One might suppose that by beginning with the soul he would have landed himself in trouble. Yet he managed to avoid that by declaring that the soul is itself unknown and unknowable, except through its indirect manifestations; and science is only concerned with the latter, so that the mystery of the soul is irrelevant. The key concept for Herbart was the forbidding-sounding term *Vorstellung*, which is often glossed as *Idea*. This is not accurate, since for him a *Vorstellung* could be a thought, an idea, or an imagined object; furthermore, Herbart also applied it to emotional states. It will therefore be safest to retain the German term. Herbart's aim was to show how simple *Vorstellungen* (plural) like 'sweet', 'small', 'red', or 'heavy' could give rise in combination to complex modes of thought. There is a certain resemblance in this respect to Condillac's *sensationism*.

In accordance with his physical model, Herbart conceptualised the movements of *Vorstellungen* as *mechanics*, so that their motions are capable of being represented by sets of equations. Such movements were of several different types, the simplest being that *Vorstellungen* can rise above the threshold of consciousness or sink below it over periods of time. Additionally, different *Vorstellungen* tend to interact in various ways. Thus they may combine and thereby become strengthened, or they may be in opposition and as a result some would become impeded for a time, or they may be pushed altogether below the threshold of consciousness. Corresponding to the *mechanics* there is also *statics*, which refers to a state of temporary equilibrium when different *Vorstellungen* either inhibit each other or are combined.

In sum, *Vorstellungen* were seen by Herbart as active forces, the dominant ones constituting an 'apperceptive mass' open to congruent *Vorstellungen* but presenting obstacles to others. Such quasi-mechanical systems were regarded by Herbart as self-contained within any given individual, which had two significant consequences. Since direct access to the processes was not feasible, it meant for him as it had for Kant that experiment in the strict sense was not possible in psychology. The method advocated was mainly that of self-observation, which he regarded as an empirical approach.

From individual to social

When one looks at Herbart's individual psychology knowing already the later turn towards the social, it seems plausible to argue that the germs of the later formulation were already present. For Herbart, who, it will be recalled, claimed to model his psychology on physics, *Vorstellungen* were *forces* interacting with one another; and it would be easy to go one step further and think of them as quasi-individuals. Imagine an organisation, say a firm in the market. Such an organisation contains a power hierarchy: people within it form coalitions and enter into conflicts with others, sometimes managing to get someone sacked – though under some circumstances they may be rehired. New entrants into the firm at various levels will affect the system of social relationships. One could easily pursue this further, but enough has been said to demonstrate the obvious parallels. One might therefore speculate that Herbart unwittingly modelled his individual psychology not really, as he had declared, on physics but on social relationships. It is therefore not surprising that even early on, far from ignoring the social aspects of human life, Herbart repeatedly stressed their importance: 'Psychology will remain one-sided', he wrote, 'as long as it considers man standing alone.' Or again: 'The human being is nothing outside society.' What, then, is the connection between individual minds and society? Herbart proposed an analogy: the functioning of society is essentially that of individual minds writ large. The way in which Herbart saw such parallels can be seen in the following passage:

> In every society as a whole individual persons behave almost in the same manner as the *Vorstellungen* in the mind of an individual, provided the social bonds are close enough to fully mediate the mutual influences. Conflicting interests take the place of oppositions among the *Vorstellungen*; the inclinations and needs for social contacts yield that which is known from the preceding [i.e. from individual psychology] as combinations and fusions. The immediate consequences of the psychological mechanism, which manifests itself here on a large scale, are as follows: the many are pushed down by a minority leading to a loss of their social significance; in the minority itself only a few gain real ascendance; every society in a state of natural equilibrium takes on a form sharpened at the top [i.e. a social pyramid]. The laws of movement of the psychological mechanism here, as in the case of individuals, do not allow a completely steady state.   (Herbart 1834/1891, vol. 4, p. 425)

In this connection he also considered the power relations within a society. Reminding the reader of the concept of threshold of *Vorstellungen* in individual psychology, Herbart declared that its equivalent in society is the *threshold of social influence*. The way in which this influence operates is seen as basically similar to the play of *Vorstellungen* in the individual mind. A few powerful persons, or those who command a number of supporters, can in a conflict neutralise any number of weaker, isolated individuals. One is reminded of modern social-psychological studies of the influence of consistent minorities (e.g. Moscovici 1985).

More persuasive than this and other analogies is Herbart's argument that an important reason for the similarity between mind and society is *language*, which cements social bonds. It is through words and speech, he noted, that thoughts and feelings are transmitted between minds. Like the *Vorstellungen* which constitute the contents of individual minds, the mother tongue comes originally from the social environment. He did not explicitly consider the relationship between language and thought, a topic extensively explored by Humboldt. It should be added that Herbart insisted that his analysis was a purely theoretical one, describing social processes irrespective of the values entailed, since it is not the business of psychology to moralise. The view that psychology is a value-free science was also widely prevalent for a period in twentieth-century social psychology, but has now been almost completely abandoned.

When considering the relationship between individuals and society, Herbart adopted a stance that was to be more fully developed later by Dilthey (see chapter 7). He considered that it would be a mistake to consider individuals in isolation, since their make-up is largely socially determined, and society itself in turn is a product of history. As he eloquently phrased it:

> no human being stands alone, and there is no known age that was self-contained; in each present there lives the past, and what the individual calls his personality is itself in the strongest sense of the

> word a web of thoughts and feelings; by far the greatest part of these
> merely repeats what the society in which he lives holds and administers
> as shared mental property. (Herbart 1821/1890, vol. 5, p. 16)

In addition to drawing attention to the historical factors that have shaped
individuals and societies, Herbart also noted the importance of what we
would term cultural factors:

> we really only know humans in *advanced* society. The savage is not much
> more familiar to us than the animal. We hear of him and we read about
> him; but we involuntarily search for our own image in him, as in a
> mirror. There is no worse way to observe ... Incidentally, if we were
> also strong enough to avoid this mistake [we might ask]: how many of us
> concerned with psychology have been to New Zealand? How many of us
> have occasion to observe the savages in their home setting? (Herbart
> 1825/1892, vol. 6, p. 16; emphasis in original)

Thus he made it clear that the psychology of his time was confined to an
unrepresentative sample of humanity, a comment that has not altogether
lost its sting at the present day.

Even this brief sketch of his teachings should make it clear why Herbart,
in spite of many flaws evident in hindsight, is justifiably regarded in his
native country as the originator of a social psychology. He made quite
explicit what previously had sometimes been only vaguely implied when
he wrote that 'The forces active in society are undoubtedly, in their origin,
psychological forces'; and he attempted a systematic exposition of the
manner in which these forces operate. In sum, Herbart was a pioneer
whose ideas were taken up and extended in Germany and Austria. Among
the earliest followers in Herbart's footsteps who developed his theoretical
ideas were Lazarus and Steinthal.

The first version of *Völkerpsychologie* (Psychology of peoples)

The first version was elaborated about half a century before
Wundt's more famous one, and constitutes a good illustration of how
intellectual constructions are related to a specific socio-political and
intellectual background. In the Germany of the period there was a rise
of patriotic fervour following the Napoleonic wars. But it had no immediate political effects, since the rulers of the various small kingdoms and
principalities were reluctant to abandon their privileges. The bourgeois
revolution of 1848, which aimed at German national unity based on
democratic institutions, was crushed. None the less, national unity and
national identity remained salient themes, not merely in politics but also
in various spheres of intellectual activity. In spite of the fragmented

political organisation there was the feeling that Germans constituted a *Volk*, a people. This notion of the *Volk* with its quasi-mystical overtones had been extensively treated by Johann Gottfried Herder (1744–1803), for whom a *Volk* was characterised by a shared language and historical tradition which shape the mentality of its members. For Herder it had not mattered whether or not such a *Volk* coincided with a nation-state, but later this came to be regarded as a necessity. Herder's romantic concepts of the *Volksgeist* (spirit of the people), coupled with Herbartian social psychology, provide the background against which the creation of the first version of *Völkerpsychologie* by Lazarus and Steinthal has to be viewed.

Moritz Lazarus (1824–1903) was born in a small town with a mixed German and Polish population, and even as a child he is supposed to have pondered national differences. At grammar school (*Gymnasium*) his German teacher was a Herbartian, and Lazarus also later recalled that one of his essays at school was on German national pride. At university in Berlin, where he first met Steinthal, Lazarus studied physiology, other natural sciences, and philosophy. He was still fascinated by national differences, notably in the characters of peoples, and looked for ways of approaching this issue. Hajim Steinthal (1823–99) read philosophy, philology, and theology, specialising in Chinese languages, and had been planning to visit China. However, he was persuaded to abandon this and join Lazarus in his project. For Steinthal, language was central to psychology, the study of different languages being, in his view, the key to understanding the 'souls' of the people who are their speakers. These views were derived from Humboldt, whom he fervently admired and whose work he sought to continue.

In the first article that had the term *Völkerpsychologie* in its title, Lazarus (1851, p. 112) wrote: 'We have named a field of study that as such does not yet exist.' He defined its task as that of determining the psychological nature of the *Volksgeist* (the spirit of a people), its processes, and the laws governing it. Together with Steinthal he later founded the *Zeitschrift* (journal) for *Völkerpsychologie* and *Sprachwissenschaft* (philology), and in a joint lead article (Lazarus and Steinthal 1860) they developed these ideas further. They explained that the term '*Volksgeist*' was being widely used by historians, philosophers, jurists, and so on, but remained exceedingly vague. Clarification was needed; and the most appropriate discipline for that purpose was psychology. It had always dealt with the individual *Geist* (spirit/mind); and a logical extension would be *Völkerpsychologie*, the study of collective mental phenomena manifested by the *Volksgeist*. As Lazarus was subsequently to write, echoing Herbart: 'in the collective mind . . . the individual minds behave in just the same way as the particular *Vorstellungen*, or mental elements in general, behave within the individual mind'.

The question to be tackled at the outset in their 1860 article was that of the very existence of the *Volksgeist*, since there were those who did not believe in it. Now admittedly, they argued, the *Volksgeist* cannot be regarded as a substantive entity in the same way as the individual *Geist*, yet the whole is greater than its parts. Society has a logical, temporal, and psychological priority over the individual, powerfully influencing individual development and producing a certain mentality characteristic of a particular people. The *Volksgeist* promotes unity and harmony of collective psychological functioning, and may be defined as 'the inner activity common to all individuals'. Naturally, it was added, it cannot be literally *all* individuals, and one has to exclude children, idiots, and exceptional persons of genius, so it can only apply to *average* individuals. This was of course a fallacy, since the *average* individual is an abstraction. At any rate, it was claimed, the *Volksgeist* is governed by the same basic psychological processes as the individual mind, only they are more complex and extended – essentially Herbart's position.

Listing a number of supposed parallels of various kinds, they saw the *Volksgeist* as basically the individual *Geist* writ large. For instance, the collective sentiment of nationality in a people corresponds to the sense of personality in the individual. Or again, just as the psychological well-being of an individual depends on the health of the body, so the state of the *Volksgeist* depends on the health of the 'body politic'. The restriction of consciousness at any one moment to a small fraction of total mental content corresponds to the preoccupation of the *Volksgeist* at any one time with a particular set of events such as the Crusades or the Reformation; a moment for the individual is perhaps a decade for the *Volk* – it is simply a question of scale.

The unity of the *Volksgeist* is reflected in a feeling of being at one with the community. In part this is the outcome of a sense of shared background and fate; but the primary factor is a common language, the creation *par excellence* of the 'national genius'. Language is the instrument mediating social relations; it unites all individuals and unifies their psychic contents. Hence in order to reconstruct the national characteristics and the *Weltanschauung* of peoples of the past, the preferred method must be that of the philologist.

The *Volksgeist* or 'objective spirit', as they sometimes called it in Hegel's terminology, exists in two different modes: one is intra-psychic, consisting of thoughts, sentiments, and dispositions; the other constitutes its material embodiment in books, works of art, monuments, industrial products, etc. Between these two the 'objective spirit' also manifests itself in all types of institutions, be they educational, administrative, commercial, or whatever. Thus the *Volksgeist* is part of the individual – not, of course, as a biological organism, but as a historical being living in society. Moreover the *Volksgeist*, being all-pervasive, also surrounds the individual in material or organisational form. Thus their concept of the *Volksgeist* was perhaps not unlike what we mean by 'culture'.

The *Volksgeist* is said to be the objective spirit of a *Volk*, but what constitutes a *Volk*? Although language is a prime source of unity of a people, it cannot be used as a criterion since the outer boundaries of a language are often as hard to pin down as those of a *Volk*. In fact there cannot be any objective criterion: 'the concept of a *Volk* rests on the subjective views of the members about themselves, their shared identity and feeling of belonging together'. After much subsequent debate on the issue, such a view has come to be generally accepted, usually without awareness that Lazarus and Steinthal had shrewdly anticipated it.

The first version of *Völkerpsychologie* as a whole had a twofold aim, general and specific. The former was historical: 'Just as the biography of the individual person rests on the laws of individual psychology, so does history – the biography of humanity – receive its rational foundation from *Völkerpsychologie*.' It is completely abstract and general, unconcerned with the variations of peoples in space and time; one might say that it treats humanity at large as a *Volk*. It addresses the question of how the processes of elementary individual consciousness come to be combined into the complex of forces that jointly constitute the *Volksgeist*. In sum, it studies the laws of the growth of the *Volksgeist* in general.

The second part, named 'psychological ethnology', descends from abstract humanity in general to the concrete level and is concerned with the variety of actually existing *Volksgeister* (plural) and their development. It is mainly descriptive, dealing with life processes of particular peoples studied by means of observation, which makes possible the ordering and comparison of phenomena. In terms of research strategy, psychological ethnology has to precede *Volk*-historical psychology, for the laws of the latter must be derived inductively from the material assembled by the former. This material is virtually all-embracing: language, writing, myth, religion, custom, law, political constitution, arts, sciences, trade, and all the institutions of public life – everything is grist to the mill.

It will be evident from the above sketch that a major flaw in Lazarus and Steinthal's approach, rooted in the modes of thought of the period, was excessive ambition. They were unable to specify any method whereby they might have achieved the grandiose aim of discovering what they conceived as 'the laws of the development of humanity'. They were also vacillating between a view of humans as the products of historical developments and that of humans as natural organisms and, as such, within the purview of natural science. It was a dilemma shared by those who later tried to pursue similar paths, such as two Austrian scholars, Lindner and Schäffle, who also took up the Herbartian heritage and sought to develop it further. Before going on to that, there will be a brief interlude.

How social psychology got its name

It will not have escaped the attention of the reader that although the topics that preoccupied the authors so far discussed were germane to social psychology, none of them used that expression; and they could not have done so, for it did not exist prior to the 1860s. Lindner, whose ideas will shortly be surveyed, did use it, but he was not the first to do so. That honour almost certainly belongs to the Italian philosopher, journalist, and politician Cattaneo – unless somebody discovers an earlier instance. Carlo Cattaneo (1801–69) was born in Milan and studied at the University of Pavia. After graduating, he obtained a post as a secondary school teacher in Milan. From the early 1830s he began a career as a journalist, and in 1839 founded his own journal, *Il Politecnico*, as a vehicle for his views on a wide range of topics in the arts, sciences, and technology, as well as politics in a broad sense. In 1848, when Milan revolted against Austrian rule, he became for a brief spell a revolutionary leader and had to flee to Switzerland. After the Austrians had been defeated with French help, Cattaneo returned to Milan to resume publication of *Il Politecnico*. His contributions to the journal, and his writings generally, testify to his remarkably wide range of knowledge, untrammelled by disciplinary boundaries. Although a considerable scholar, he is mainly remembered for his contribution to the struggle for the unification of Italy. His democratic ideals inspired the post-*Risorgimento* (unification movement) Italian intellectuals of a progressive cast of mind. Today a new university in Castellanza is named after him.

The title of the crucial article published in 1864 contains the expression *psicologia sociale*. The thesis he developed has virtually nothing in common with lines of thought then prevalent in German-speaking countries. His philosophical inspiration came from Giambattista Vico (1668–1744), an outstanding early exponent of social thought, and Hegel. He praised Vico for dealing with nations, i.e. collectivities rather than individuals, and Hegel for updating Vico by introducing the modern idea of progress through the patterns of thesis–antithesis–synthesis. While Hegel had been concerned with large-scale social movements, Cattaneo transposed Hegel's theme to interactions among individuals. He suggested that in all spheres of human endeavours, be it science, philosophy, technology, or politics, the clash of conflicting ideas results in the generation of new ones:

> Antithesis of associated minds is, in my view, that act by which one or more individuals, in the effort to deny an idea, come to perceive a new idea; or, to be precise, that act by which one or more individuals, when perceiving a new idea, come, even unconsciously, to deny another idea. In the first case that which distinguishes the new idea is that it is born of the conflict of several minds; and that it would not have been born amongst unanimous minds or in a solitary mind.   (Cattaneo 1864, p. 265)

His general point was that change and transformations are ubiquitous, always entailing opposition and conflict. Far from being uniformly undesirable, they often constitute engines of progress. He therefore suggested a need for the study of such processes, a study he named 'the psychology of associated minds'.

Cattaneo's proposals are interesting and challenging, though he does not seem to have pursued them further. The idea has not been directly taken up in modern social psychology, unless one thinks of 'brain-storming' or problem-solving in groups where the emphasis has been on the positive contributions of the members. This is perhaps due to the tendency to concentrate on intra-psychic conflicts, as in Festinger's 'cognitive dissonance'. However, Piaget did discuss the significance of interpersonal disagreements for cognitive development.

Returning to the issue of the term 'social psychology', it is not known how it initially came to spread. It is most likely that Lindner helped to put it on the map, since Cattaneo's article had been published in a relatively obscure Italian periodical. For the same reason it is also likely that Lindner coined the term independently.

Lindner's ideas for a future science

Gustav Adolph Lindner (1828–87) was born in Bohemia and studied philosophy at Prague University under Franz Exner, who introduced him to the Herbartian school. From there he entered a seminary in preparation for the priesthood, but finding that he lacked the vocation he returned to university in Prague. There he continued with philosophy and began reading law, then switched to mathematics and natural sciences with a view to becoming a teacher. After spells of teaching in several *Gymnasiums* (grammar schools), he received in 1878 a call to the chair of pedagogy, psychology, and ethics at Prague University. It was a period when the Habsburg monarchy was under considerable pressure for greater autonomy from several national groups. Accordingly, the educational system in Bohemia was divided into German and Czech sections. Although German-speaking, Lindner opted to join the Czech side in an effort to bridge the divide, a move resented by most of his Austrian colleagues and not uniformly welcomed by the more extreme Czech nationalists. He wrote a 'Textbook of empirical psychology as an inductive science' that went into numerous editions, and, following his mentor Herbart, a text on pedagogy. He also published a rather curious little book entitled *The problem of luck* (1868), an odd title for a work that was essentially a critique of capitalist society, said to restrict the life-chances of the poor. Like his choice of opting for the Czech side, it testifies to his left-radical outlook.

Lindner's 'psychology of society'

The book of interest in the present context has as title of the second part 'Fundamentals of social psychology'. Lindner was widely read and was influenced by a range of contemporaries such as Herder, Lazarus, and Lotze. He himself took his lead from Herbart, who figures most prominently in his *Ideas for a psychology of society as foundation of social science* [Sozialwissenschaft] (Lindner 1871).

The work consists of three parts, the first headed 'Society as a social organism', with the sub-title 'Physiology of society'. This already indicates that Lindner adopted the organic analogy popular during the second half of the nineteenth century – as will be more fully discussed in due course. At the outset he sketched the rise of civilisation from a hypothetical primitive starting point where, in an extraordinary flight of fancy, early people are likened to mindless plants. Then major institutions are surveyed such as the economy (organisation of trade), government (organisation of power), and language as the organisation of mental exchanges. Society is compared with a natural organism, characterised by a dense network of exchanges, both material and mental. Thus collective economic activity is equated with the vegetative sphere of the social organism, and telegraph wires with the nerves. The capital city is likened to the head, the government machinery within it to the small brain, but cultural institutions such as the sciences, arts, etc. to 'the large brain' – definitely an academic's-eye view!

The specifically psychological aspects are dealt with in part two, while the third part is concerned with the purposive activity of society and has the sub-title 'Political psychology'. The second part is the key one here, its title being 'Society as *vorstellendes* being', the term referring back to Herbart's *Vorstellungen* discussed above. Broadly it refers to the sum total of mental processes. It is the sub-title 'Fundamentals of social psychology' that breaks new ground.

In his introduction to the three parts, Lindner cites Herbart's dictum to the effect that psychology cannot confine itself to isolated humans, and states that Herbart thereby opened up the prospect of moving from individual to social psychology. Lindner describes the task of social psychology as that of 'deriving from the mutual effects [*Wechselwirkungen*] of individuals in society the phenomena and laws of social life'. Like many of his contemporaries, Lindner was clearly much impressed by the regularities demonstrated by the pioneering Belgian statistician Quetelet (to be discussed further in chapter 4), for he referred to the 'relentless moral statistics' much debated at the time, which seemed to imply that the numbers of those who commit suicide or get married are predestined. He went on to say that 'The statistical data are an expression of societal conditions and facts, which demand an explanation as much as do individual ones. They indicate a system of interactions whose nature is partly physical [i.e. physiological] and partly psychological' (Lindner 1871, p. 13). In the tradition of the Enlightenment, Lindner assumed a psycho-physical continuity such that no sharp line could be drawn between the psychical and the material, both being equally subject to natural laws. Some of the assumptions underlying the whole thesis may be gauged from another paragraph that is cited at some length, since it is programmatic:

> The task of social psychology is the description and explanation of those phenomena that depend on the mutual psychic effects of individuals, and on which the total mental life of society rests. Society is nothing apart from individuals; hence its mental life cannot be other than that which occurs within the individual consciousness of its members. It follows, first, that the principles of social psychology have to be borrowed from the teachings of individual psychology. Yet that social psychology none the less has its own sphere different from that of individual psychology arises from the fact that the mutual psychological effects, which constitute its subject matter, can only be observed in society. Of course, the conditions of society are reflected in the consciousness of each individual.   (Lindner 1871, p. 14)

With all this toing and froing between the individual and societal poles, one senses considerable uncertainty on Lindner's part as to the epistemological status of societal mentality: are there or are there not psychic processes other than those of individuals? It is a dilemma similar to that faced later by Wundt. Lindner took no clear stand, often writing as though there *were* collective mental processes – for instance, he referred to 'societal consciousness'. Yet although his writing was not always consistent, on balance he seems to have decided against such a view. In any case, the whole scheme rests on analogies between individual and society of the kind originally suggested by Herbart. Returning to the analogy, it is also to be noted that the juxtaposition was between the individual and society-as-a-whole. It is true that intermediate levels such as the family are occasionally mentioned, but only to be dismissed as relatively insignificant. Another relevant question is what Lindner understood by the term 'society', and the answer is that, again like Herbart, he usually meant the *state*, perhaps wishing to dissociate himself from *Völkerpsychologie* concerned with the people (*Volk*). Moreover, he wanted to differentiate social psychology from economics and political studies. These, he submitted, deal only with 'the external side of the life of the state', while the deeper motives are the business of social psychology. In fact, however, Lindner had little to say about motivation in the second (social-psychological) part discussed here, relegating it to the third, concerned with politics. He also advocated cooperation between social psychology and neighbouring disciplines, notably anthropology.

In the 'Fundamentals of social psychology' Lindner noted that any one person lives within a narrow circle, has few direct relationships with society at large, and can only exert minimal influence on the social whole. Conversely, however, most of the practices, habits, beliefs, modes of expression, etc. which individuals fondly imagine to be 'their own' are in fact derived from society's *Vorstellungen*, convictions, or principles. Thus any news found in a paper is already coloured by 'societal consciousness'. This societal consciousness comprises those states of mind that are common to members of the society as a result of their interactions. However, a few pages further on he explained that the concept of a social consciousness, embodying the common states of mind of members of the society, is really a scientific fiction or, better, an ideal. Societal consciousness, he further maintained, is bound to be public, a necessary condition for the convergence of individual mental states. It manifests itself by words, deeds, and what Lindner called 'physiognomic expressions'. By this he meant national styles in, for instance, houses or dress, and symbols like flags or badges. Private states of mind could often in principle be made public, but in practice are not since they would lack a receptive audience. Yet at that point he is clear that social or, as he sometimes calls it, 'public' consciousness is not something that exists over and above individual consciousness.

How does this social consciousness come about? In seeking to account for it, Lindner fell back on what he called 'individual selfishness'. It is owing to such selfishness that society is characterised by conflicting interests. Following the Herbartian model, he argued that, as in individuals, conflicting opinions and attitudes are said to inhibit each other at first, and then combine in order to better resist further inhibitions. People compete in putting forward their own ideas, and in order for these to become public they must excite interest on the part of others. This is somewhat similar to what Gabriel Tarde was to write some two decades later about the spread of ideas in society; but while Tarde's exposition was lucid, that of Lindner remained obscure and often incoherent.

Lindner struggled, unsuccessfully, to delineate the relationships between individuals and society in accordance with Herbartian teachings. Surprisingly for someone with a radical cast of mind, he ended up by suggesting that what really matters for the functioning of society is a limited set of concepts, notably those of God, law, and freedom – in their absence, anarchy ensues.

In fairness it should be added that he modestly regarded social psychology as a project for the future, of which he merely claimed to have sketched the basic outlines. Yet while conceding in some places the provisional nature of his scheme, in others he did not hesitate to state that he was enunciating natural laws! A few years later his compatriot Schäffle pursued much the same theme, but did so from a broader basis.

Schäffle's pseudo-Darwinism

Unlike his predecessor Lindner, Albert Eberhard Friedrich Schäffle (1831–1903) was not primarily concerned with psychology. He was trained as an economist and became professor of politics (*Staatswissenschaft*) at Vienna University. Active in politics of the left and sympathetic to the ideas of the radical social democrat Ferdinand Lassalle, he served for a time as Austrian minister of trade. In his autobiography Schäffle explained that his broad interests in the social sciences arose from his dissatisfaction with the resort to facile slogans and the proclaiming of unfounded generalisations in the realm of party politics. He mocked the multiplication of binary principles such as 'order and freedom', 'aristocracy and democracy', 'individualism and collectivism' – this last dichotomy in fashion again within the social sciences (cf. Kim et al. 1994). Wishing to arrive at more secure foundations, he read Wundt's *Physiological psychology*, Fechner's *Elements of psychophysics*, and Alexander Bain. 'What fascinated me most was the literature on Darwinism, above all Darwin's and Häckel's own writings.' He was also familiar with Herbert Spencer (about whom more in chapter 5), but claimed to have found him too speculative, and preferred, as he put it, to rely on the solid ground of empirical facts. In spite of these protestations there are clear resemblances to Spencer in Schäffle's use of the organic analogy. This is indicated already by the title of his major work, *Structure and life of the social body: encyclopedic sketch of a real anatomy, physiology and psychology of human society* (Schäffle 1875–8). There is also a further sub-title which likens economic activity to the metabolism of the social body. Thus 'society' was for him synonymous with 'social body', and not just in a metaphorical sense, since he stated that 'the mental life of that body is a higher power of the individual mind'.

There is a certain resemblance to Lindner's views here, but it would seem that Schäffle developed his ideas quite independently from Lindner. Schäffle, like Lindner, strove to work towards an understanding of what both regarded as the natural laws governing the functioning of mind in society. But unlike Lindner, he was inspired by Darwin to propound his own theory of evolution that had little in common with Darwin's, being as extravagant as it was simplistic. There are, according to Schäffle, three evolutionary levels, ranging from the inorganic, via the organic, to the social. All three 'worlds', as he called them, share certain basic features upon which more complex ones are progressively superimposed. He mentioned a suggestion by Lotze that perhaps 'in each atom of the nerves there might be occurrences resembling our own sensitivities'. He pointed to the attraction and repulsion of atoms as indicating that, even in the inorganic world, the germs of later developments are to be found. In this connection he seems to have taken his cue from the more mystical writings of Gustav Theodor Fechner, who had viewed not only humans but plants, animals, stars, and the universe as a whole as having life and soul.

Even inorganic nature is said to be subject to evolution and also decay, as when celestial bodies collide. Thus there are structural homologies as one moves from the inorganic to plants and animals and thence to 'uncivilised humans'. The obvious implication is that only civilised humans are social, and it will be recalled that Lindner had taken a similar view. The apex of evolution is reached when all the elements of the inorganic and organic worlds enter into the social body. This is a process Schäffle called *Vergeistigung*, a term that could perhaps be glossed as 'mentalisation'. It is accompanied by increasing individuation, which entails becoming increasingly more conscious as evolution proceeds.

Schäffle had clearly been carried away by his enthusiasm for what he mistakenly believed to have been Darwinian evolutionism, and much of it will strike modern readers as little more than empty verbiage. It may well be asked what this has to do with social psychology, and his answer seems to be that it can be approached through an overarching principle of essential continuity:

> Nothing stands in the way of explaining the course of social movements in accordance with the laws of mechanics, and to find in human society a much more complicated play of the same movements and forces which already unfold in the organic and inorganic world – in transformations of simpler equivalents and correlations of the original elemental force which is indestructible as it is impenetrable.   (Schäffle 1875–8, vol. 1, p. 24)

Referring this time directly to Fechner's doctrine of the correlation between mental activity and 'psychophysical motions of the nervous organs', Schäffle contended that 'all mechanical and mental activity of the social body is to be viewed, like the visible movement of arms and legs ... a resultant of inner small and invisible patterns of physical and chemical processes'. Such preoccupation with 'mechanics' probably reflects Herbartian teachings.

In contrast to such lofty speculations, Schäffle did not have much to say about empirical methods at this point, though like Lindner before him he discussed 'moral statistics'. Much of the discussion is philosophical, but he recognised the value of a statistical approach, though rightly pointing out that it can only arrive at empirical generalisations rather than natural laws.

The issues considered so far were merely prolegomena to social psychology proper, dealt with under the following prolix heading: 'The psychic facts of social life and their connections viewed as a whole or the basic phenomena of the "mind of the people [*Volksgeist*]" as a general part of the fundamentals of social psychology.' It is explained that the starting point for this goes back to Herbart:

> All manifestations of individual mental life can be found again in society, unfolded as collective mental work ... Herbart was the first to recognise this dual aspect. Unfortunately only in general, since he repeatedly went past the open door of a special social psychology.   (Schäffle 1875–8, vol. 1, p. 392)

He then went on to discuss the parallels in some detail, following many others by showing how much of what people regard as their private life does in fact depend upon society. On the other hand, Schäffle claimed that the threads constituting the mental life of society itself are spun by individuals. Yet conversely, the patterns of relationships between thoughts, attitudes, or decisions within societal existence were said to be the same as those found within individuals. Memory in individuals corresponds to traditions in society, and is enshrined not only in symbolic form in books, newspapers and so on, but also in what we would call 'material culture', i.e. tools, machines, organisational practices, and so on.

Schäffle put forward an intriguing speculation concerning the possibilities of measurement in individual and social psychology respectively, that was prompted by Fechner's psychophysics. Schäffle started off with a scheme modelled on Fechner and set out schematically here:

A External stimuli → B Inner processes → C External responses

The argument runs as follows: in the case of individuals we can readily measure (A) and (C), while (B), consisting of changes in the nervous system, remains inaccessible. It is the reverse for the social body, where only (B) can be measured. This is far from obvious, and so the reasoning involved has to be elucidated by looking at how Schäffle described the three elements in the social case. The external stimuli (A) 'spring from natural and social life', too complicated for measurement. The inner processes (B) consist of symbolic exchanges, either direct or mechanically mediated, which, he asserted, are measurable. It is the external responses (C) that are 'the social-psychological effects which correspond to the magnitude of the inner feelings of individuals and thus are extraordinarily difficult to measure'. As soon as one examines the nature of these categories, the scheme falls apart, since most of them remain completely vague and as such obviously not measurable. None the less, the conclusion that what he called 'social psychophysics' requires different methods from individual ones is reasonable, though it does not follow from the argument.

Fechner's Law, which states that the 'strength' of a perception is proportional to the logarithm of the physical stimulus, led Schäffle to seek for social analogues. One example he gave concerns the relative value of money: ten florins would be for a domestic servant the same as 10,000 florins for a millionaire. Another is perhaps a *cri de cœur* from a disappointed radical politician: 'Experience shows that people who have long been oppressed seem to require a vast increase in stimulation before they become sensitive to efforts at improving their lot'!

Other proposed individual/social parallels are derived from Herbart as well as Fechner. It is stated that 'mental energy' is limited in both individuals and the collectivity, shown by the fact that the public mind soon gets tired – whatever that may mean. This is perhaps related to 'the law of mental contrast' in its social-psychological form. It boils down to the claim that 'the various manifestations of a people's mind [*Volksgeist*]' change constantly and even go to extremes in art, fashion, taste, and so on. Political parties await the most favourable moment in the swing of the pendulum, and thereby 'speculate on the law of contrast'.

Then there is the 'threshold phenomenon', whose discussion by Schäffle brings out sharply the weakness of his approach. According to it, not every idea enters into general consciousness (i.e. the consciousness of the central collective organs), let alone into the consciousness of all individuals. The central organs only become conscious

> of a small part of all the mental events of social life. As against that it has to be noted that in special cases any kind of event in social life can rise above the threshold of social consciousness. It needs only an exceptional increase in the psychophysical movement accompanying such events: alarmist newspaper stories, special appeals for help, lively demonstrations . . . to introduce excitements and movements – which otherwise do not pass the threshold – into the consciousness of the people and produce conscious reactions on the part of the central organs of the state and other central organs.   (Schäffle 1875–8, vol. 1, p. 403)

This is very much an extrapolation from Herbart. At a first superficial glance it might seem reasonable, but on closer inspection one finds several category confusions. While it is clear that 'general consciousness' is not identical with 'consciousness of all individuals', it is supposedly identical with that of the 'central collective organs', which remain undefined. Then there is reference to the 'general consciousness of the *Volk*' – how does this relate to individuals? But no doubt enough has been said to demonstrate the incoherence of the argument.

Much the same applies to the last two sections, in the first of which he asked the question 'Is there a *Volksgeist*?' This is an issue that was widely debated at the time, as has already been shown. From the lengthy and rambling discussion, which does not lend itself to a summary, my best guess is that Schäffle's answer, much like that of Lindner, was 'no and yes'. He probably did not believe in the existence of collective mind in a real sense. On the other hand he claimed that the *Volksgeist* is real in the sense of a complexly structured system of 'mental energies and tensions'. However, these energies are said to be distributed over all the elements of the social body, so as to 'unite individuals into a collective mental force'. So he can have his cake and eat it.

In sum, Schäffle sought to construct a social psychology from diverse sets of ideas: those of Herbart and Fechner, of Spencer (in spite of his denial), of Wundt, and what he imagined were Darwin's. His attempt to create a synthesis of all these ended up in rather a muddle. In hindsight it is surprising that his ideas were widely discussed for many years, and not only in German-speaking countries.

Waitz, a man in advance of his time

Here we retrace our steps to the period just before the mid-nineteenth century when Waitz had been active. Lindner had endeavoured to remain faithful to the ideas of Herbart, which proved something of an intellectual straitjacket. By contrast Waitz, who had originally been a student of Herbart, broke away from the teachings of the master to pursue his own lines. Waitz is important, since his work anticipated several themes that much later became incorporated into social psychology.

Theodor Waitz (1821–64) was an unorthodox Herbartian whose initial doctorate was in philosophy. What first attracted him to Herbart was that he saw in his teachings a third way between Feuerbach's crude materialism and Hegel's idealism. At the University of Leipzig he studied under Drobisch, one of Herbart's most devoted followers. Yet although himself an able mathematician, Waitz came to reject Herbart's mathematical approach to the subject. On the other hand he fully shared Herbart's belief that psychology should not ignore the social nature of humans, and also had a strong interest in the educational applications of psychology on which he later published extensively. He obtained a post at the University of Marburg, where he formed a close friendship with an outstanding physiologist, which gave him a taste for empirical work. Waitz died in the same year (1864) as the term 'social psychology' was first used by Cattaneo. While he had therefore not been in a position to use it, a good deal of his work certainly dealt with topics that are closer to modern social psychology than those treated by either Lindner or Schäffle.

Waitz on interpersonal relationships

One of his most important publications was entitled *Textbook of psychology as a natural science* (Waitz 1849). It was radically different from many such books appearing at that period, which tended to be philosophical, highly speculative, and rather woolly. By contrast his book was clear and precise, reporting mainly physiological experiments, especially with regard to vision and hearing. So the bulk of the book has evidently little to do with social psychology, but there is one relevant chapter headed

'The moral feelings'. It has already been explained that the term 'moral' long had the connotation of our 'social', and while the fashion then was to juxtapose individuals and the *Volk* or the state, Waitz – like some of the Scottish philosophers before him – was also concerned with what are now known as interpersonal relationships. However, there is no indication that he was familiar with the writings of Hume and Smith.

Apart from resort to some Herbartian language, the chapter on 'The moral feelings' reads rather like Adam Smith. Waitz began by saying that what is essential for the development of moral sentiments is that we have a *Vorstellung* – in this case an internal representation – of a certain 'other'. Together with our own attitude towards that person, this relationship exerts an extensive influence on our own thinking and willing:

> The person with whom we are in a relationship has become a force in our own mental life, which enhances or inhibits those sets of *Vorstellungen* which lead us to action, as long as the action has, or appears to have, anything to do with that person.   (Waitz 1849, p. 394)

If and only if that other person embodies the authority of social norms or the law, then obedience to that authority which overcomes one's own contrary inclination will in due course lead to what we would call the internalisation of moral standards.

Waitz was also in agreement with Hume and Smith that another source of morality is *sympathy*, which leads us to feel with others when they are troubled. Waitz reckoned that perceiving the suffering of others not only produces appropriate *Vorstellungen*, but elicits a physiological reaction; in this he anticipated, as had Cabanis, modern findings of neuropsychology. Curiously enough, he considered that having a physiological basis, such behaviour cannot really be considered moral. For him that applies to the relationship between mother and child, dictated by nature.

Waitz discussed the paralinguistic signs from which we infer the state of mind of other persons, and which often guide interactions even in the absence of speech. We create an image of the other person and a *Vorstellung* of that person's relationship to ourselves, which guides our actions towards that person. The early stages of sociality can be observed in children, who listen with rapt attention even to adult conversations largely unintelligible for them. But they can read the inner feelings and mutual relationships of the persons involved through their facial expressions and gestures. It took another century for these ideas to be further developed.

Waitz noted that we are all born into a particular social milieu with its own norms, according to which we come to be judged. Moreover, he was one of those, like Adam Smith, who anticipated George Herbert Mead on the development of the self:

> The inner mental content every one of us possesses only becomes fully objective when we view ourselves through the eyes of others. In the behaviour of others towards oneself one encounters from all sides one's own picture; for the behaviour of others in relation to oneself is substantially influenced by the image of one's own personality the others have formed.   (Waitz 1849, p. 403)

The vicissitudes of interpersonal relations are surveyed with remarkable insight, and some important principles such as reciprocity are discussed. There were of course no experiments, only acute observations. Yet that was true of much of the work by Heider, and also applies to modern 'discursive' social psychologists. Subsequently Waitz, in another major work, made an even more significant contribution with a bearing on social psychology.

Waitz on 'psychic unity'

Relatively late in his life – that was unfortunately rather short – Waitz turned towards anthropology and published the *Anthropology of primitive peoples* (1859–72) with the significant sub-title *On the unity of the human species and the natural state of humans*. It consists of six volumes, the last published posthumously, and an abbreviated version appeared in English (Waitz 1863). His reasons for turning to anthropology are to be found in the introductory pages. Physiology and psychology, he commented, are disciplines treating humans as isolated individuals and in fact as mere specimens of the species – a complaint frequently reiterated since. Ignoring differences, psychology also aims at universal laws and is unduly narrow:

> But the consideration of humans in their communal life is alien to these *Wissenschaften* [fields of study]. The whole sum of intellectual achievements, which resulted from the complex interactions of individuals and transformed societies extensively, falls outside psychology's horizon ... cultural history turns its interest exclusively on the collective life in society. The contribution it makes to the understanding of human beings is doubtless as essential as that yielded by the natural sciences.   (Waitz 1859–72, vol. 1, p. 5)

Although psychology sometimes gets close to such issues, he noted, it tends to retreat again in the face of the complex causal nexus involved that cannot be reduced to just 'psychological laws'. Hence Waitz turned to anthropology, admitting that it had in the past largely consisted either of abstract speculations, or of collections of exotica assembled haphazardly, therefore failing to provide any coherent picture. He advocated more systematic empirical approaches of the kind adopted in other sciences. Hence Waitz embarked upon the enormous labour of ordering and collating a mass of reports about peoples varying widely in their social organisation and technological levels, many being 'primitives'. He described their psychological features and their social lives, of course very different from those of Europeans.

Waitz's purpose in analysing ethnographic reports was to provide empirical evidence for his strongly held view that humans constitute a single species, with basically the same psychological characteristics. The enormity of such a claim, at a period when the inequality of 'races' was deemed by most people to be axiomatic, is difficult to appreciate in the twenty-first century. For instance, Carl Vogt (1817–95), a great German-Swiss naturalist after whom a street is named in Geneva, maintained that the differences between Germans and 'Negroes' were greater than those between two different species of apes; he put forward a theory about a missing link between 'Negroes' and apes, which he saw in microcephalous idiots. American 'savages' fared little better, and the consensus of most eminent scientists during the nineteenth century was that physical differences entail mental ones and signal biological inferiority.

Waitz himself was of course well aware of what he was up against, and mentioned the then prevalent stereotypes about the

> thoughtless Negro, the restless nomadic [native] American, or the cannibal South-Sea-islander. The primitive man stands in such striking contrast to the civilized man, that the latter in his vanity considers the former as belonging to a different species; that he [i.e. the 'civilized'] himself once occupied a similar position, he does not seem to take into any serious consideration.   (Waitz 1863, p. 260; cf. also Jahoda 1999)

Waitz challenged the prevailing assumption of a close association between physical and mental characteristics by showing in some detail the inconsistencies in the copious published data then available about cranial capacity, and the fact that intra-group variations tended to be ignored. He concluded: 'We are thus compelled to renounce the doctrine that the capacity of the cranium indicates the amount of mental endowment.' Waitz also resorted to a sophisticated argument that has stood the test of time, namely comparing intra-group with inter-group variability at the same or different times. He was not, of course, in a position to do so quantitatively, but in later sections sought to demonstrate a high degree of variability that throws considerable doubt on the assumption of fixed and permanent differences in potential. In this he anticipated the findings of modern genetics.

On the positive side, Waitz proceeded to examine what all humans, including the 'so-called savages' (a significant qualification), have in common, and what especially distinguishes them from animals. The obvious answer, given before by others like Buffon, was language: 'even the most barbarous nations possess a language with a more or less regular grammatical structure'. This common element, permitting all humans to express their thoughts, is far more important than any physical differences. Wherever travellers go, they find essentially the same modes of psychological functioning, the same human nature. Waitz further reviewed other specifically human features, including the desire for ornamentation, some form of collective or individual property rights, religion, and attachment to one's country and people. At this point he returned to the key role of language in a passage that reveals the influences of Herder and Humboldt:

> It is chiefly language which separates and unites mankind, by impressing the national character upon the individual, and the peculiar mode of thinking and feeling belonging to his stock, drawing thus closer the bonds which unite the individuals as a whole.   (Waitz 1863, p. 277)

Another line of argument involves a comparison between non-European 'races' and the lower classes in Europe, showing distinct similarities and sometimes even superiority in some respects of the former. Thus, he argued, it is a mistake to attribute differences in levels of civilisation directly to differences in mental endowment. Since, as Waitz believed, people have no built-in drive for intellectual progress, external influences must be involved; and in a later section he dealt at great length with a range of ecological and historical factors. In any case, given the great antiquity of the earth (which had been established by geologists in Waitz's time), a mere few thousand years of advance in civilisation is too short a period to judge the relative capacity of all humankind. Hence he regarded the available facts to be entirely consistent with what he termed 'the theory of the psychic unity of the human species'.

This slogan of 'psychic unity', sometimes wrongly attributed to others, is a phrase that has secured a permanent place in the vocabulary of the social sciences. Altogether, his treatment both of interpersonal interaction and of human differences marks out Waitz as an outstanding independent thinker.

4 France and Belgium: adventurous blueprints for a new social science

During the first half of the nineteenth century there began a movement of thought known as 'positivism', so named after Auguste Comte's 'positive philosophy'. Comte was an important figure, and Gordon Allport, one of the most prominent social psychologists of the twentieth century, regarded Comte as the founding father of social psychology. The term 'positivism' has acquired a wide range of meanings, but as used here it refers to a view initially articulated by Saint-Simon that social phenomena can be studied by the methods that had proved so successful in the natural sciences, which he called 'positive'. It was not a new idea, having been put forward during the Enlightenment, and merely the label was new. Saint-Simon regarded society as a kind of superorganism in which individuals and groups constitute what we would describe as a quasi-biological system. Somewhat similar notions can be found in German philosophers of the Romantic period such as Herder and Hegel, and later, in Britain, in Spencer. An alternative model of society as a 'mechanism' characterised most nineteenth-century economists.

The efflorescence of positivism was due to Comte, and became highly influential as the doctrine that all phenomena, social as well as natural, are subject to fixed laws. The first impact of positivism was greater in Britain than in France, since it was taken up there by a distinguished group of thinkers, while in France a more traditional metaphysics remained dominant. In spite of their strident advocacy of a *scientific* approach, Saint-Simon was little more than a dilettante and Comte, though better equipped, failed to keep track of scientific advances.

Quetelet, by contrast, was a distinguished astronomer and statistician interested in problems of society and social behaviour. A contemporary of Comte, he was a Belgian who looked for relevant empirical data and developed his theories in relation to them. Quetelet was not a member of the group of positivists in either France or Britain, but the effects of his work were long lasting in these countries, and also in Germany.

The social physiology of Saint-Simon

Henri Comte de Saint-Simon (1760–1825) had served in the American War of Independence, and during the French Revolution managed to make a small fortune by speculating in confiscated properties. His activities became known to the Republican Committee of Public Safety and he was imprisoned for eleven months, narrowly escaping the guillotine. On his release he was able to continue his property dealings during the Directorate, an anarchic period between the Terror and the advent of Napoleon. He amassed a large fortune, which enabled him to create a salon frequented by a catholic mixture of the old aristocracy, bankers, industrialists, artists, and scientists, the last of these the most numerous. That hectic atmosphere saw the gestation of his grand system, and in 1803, when already over forty, he published his *Lettres d'un habitant de Genève* (Letters from an inhabitant of Geneva). It was the first tentative exposition of his philosophy, but it already contained the essence of a thesis about a 'positive' transformation of society. By 1806 his great fortune had been frittered away through his lavish lifestyle, and he found himself in dire straits. For the rest of his life, devoted to the elaboration of his system, he had to struggle financially.

Before discussing Saint-Simon's ideas about human nature, at least some brief comments are necessary on his socio-political proposals, shaped by the experience of the Revolution and its aftermath, since they formed an integral part of his system. Underlying his theory of human society was his belief in the necessity of a transformation of the old class structure based on privilege, into a meritocracy chosen by innate ability. Being determined by 'physiology' as he conceived it, there would result a 'natural' class system in which behaviour and social action would be a function of assignment to occupational or professional roles appropriate to individual capacities.

The concrete details of his political scheme were rather bizarre. Traditional roles would be completely modified, with 'spiritual power' being taken away from the pope and wielded instead by scientists, while 'temporal power' would be removed from the hands of elites and transferred to property owners. He was no more willing to concede a political voice to the have-nots than Condorcet had been; and when he referred to *prolétaires* it was in the sense of an ignorant mob. Nevertheless Saint-Simon is often regarded as the originator of French socialism, because he sought to reorganise society scientifically and prophesied a transformation of the social world through industrial progress.

Towards the end of his life Saint-Simon founded the *New Christianity*, a somewhat odd religion in which God is universal love, revealing itself as mind and matter; and to this triad correspond the three domains of religion, science, and industry. This curious doctrine gained disciples in Britain as well as France, and Saint-Simonian Societies flourished for some time.

Having outlined the social framework envisaged by Saint-Simon, let me now turn to his 'positive' approach to human nature. He employed the term 'positive' in the sense it had been used by the *idéologues*, namely the abandonment of any search for 'first causes' and a focus on lawful regularities. In the early years of the nineteenth century only astronomy, physics, and chemistry were regarded as exact sciences, while the life sciences (in spite of their brilliant exponents like Buffon, Cuvier, and Lamarck) were still far from having received adequate recognition of their scientific status; and that applied *a fortiori* to the 'moral' or 'social' sciences.

Saint-Simon's ambitious aim was to work towards a system of 'positive' knowledge encompassing all fields of science, and he sought, unsuccessfully, for a single formula that would produce advances in both physical and social sciences. His dream was of all sciences becoming in due course an 'organic' whole. Unlike the German philosophers of the period for whom 'organic' had mystical overtones, Saint-Simon seems to have meant by it a unitary and coherent body of knowledge.

As far as the science of human nature is concerned, Saint-Simon in his *Lettres* had favoured the mathematical methods advocated by Condorcet, but later moved away from mathematicians, reproaching them with not having made a contribution to the solution of pressing social problems. Hence he turned towards the life sciences, reminding his readers that humans are organic bodies, so that it is legitimate to treat social relations as *physiological* phenomena. Such arguments were subsequently further developed in such writings as his *Mémoire sur la science de l'homme* (Essay on the science of man) (1813/1965), where he stated that the history of humanity can be studied scientifically. This history, he claimed, displays successive phases from polytheism via theism to 'physicism', a sequence later adopted in modified form by Comte. All sciences, he maintained, start by being conjectural and eventually become 'positive'. Once this has happened in all spheres of science, then science-in-general will become the new 'positive' philosophy. According to Saint-Simon, physiology, although on the threshold, did not yet merit being classed among the positive sciences. In his discussion he linked physiology with psychology: 'This [advance] will happen when physiology and psychology come to be based on observation.' In addition to a physiology of individual functioning, Saint-Simon envisaged a general physiology dealing with society, for him 'a veritable organised machine' or even, in another metaphor, 'a veritable BEING'. It is worth mentioning one of Saint-Simon's conjectures that has nearly come to pass. He argued that the ultimate stage in the reorganisation of society would be the disappearance of national boundaries and the establishment of a European union.

When Comte, born into the small bourgeoisie, joined Saint-Simon as his secretary at the age of nineteen, Saint-Simon was in his fifties. While the writings of Saint-Simon tended to be verbose and somewhat rambling, those of Comte reflect a sharp analytical mind. What they had in common was that their ideas were connected with the socio-political turmoil of the period in which they worked. Comte adopted essential parts of the Saint-Simonian thesis, and clarified and greatly extended it, subsequently claiming it to be entirely original.

Comte, messiah of science and religion

The life of a brilliant eccentric

The young Auguste Comte (1798–1857) was lucky to have become Saint-Simon's personal secretary in 1817. He had been born during the social chaos and political ferment in the aftermath of the French Revolution, and during his life saw no fewer than seven different political regimes and numerous insurrections. This probably accounts for his blueprint for a 'positive' political system (Comte 1853/1876) that would remedy the prevailing disorder. It could not be achieved through violence and required a firm but benevolent dictatorship. The place of women in his utopian society would have been a modest one, since according to him 'biological analysis presents the female sex, in the human species especially, as continually in a state of perpetual infancy'. This attitude was in contrast to that of John Stuart Mill, who regarded women as equals and pleaded for their emancipation.

During the Napoleonic regime Comte had been admitted to the elite Ecole Polytechnique, where he studied mathematics and science. In spite of his brilliance, he was expelled for leading a student rebellion. Afterwards he was only able to eke out a meagre living by private tutoring, until he joined Saint-Simon. However, being very different personalities, their relationship became increasingly acrimonious and it ended in 1824. A year later he met and married a young prostitute. The marriage was a stormy one, yet lasted with some interruptions until 1842, when he had completed the final volume of the famous *Cours de philosophie positive*. In spite of his prodigious output Comte remained short of money all his life, making it necessary at times for his wife to support him by her former trade. He was also helped by well-wishers from Britain, notably the circle of Mill and Lewes, but was less than gracious in acknowledging such support. Comte seems to have regarded it as merely his due from those he regarded as his disciples, a view not shared by the benefactors themselves.

After his wife had left him, Comte had a passionate affair with Clotilde de Vaux, an impoverished aristocratic woman, who died after two years.

4   *Auguste Comte (1798–1857)*

This shattering experience transformed his outlook from a severely intellectual to an unctuously sentimental one. Positivism was to become the
religion of humanity, and one of Comte's last works was a 'Positivist
Catechism'. Its bizarre rules included the daily worship of a woman, and a
ritual touching of parts of the head specified according to phrenological
teachings. The outer forms of his new religion in many ways reflected the
Catholicism of his parental background, whose doctrines he had abandoned while still quite young.

   Altogether Comte was not an attractive character and he has been
dubbed 'as pathological an egocentric as ever strutted the stage in a
Strindbergian madhouse'. Yet it cannot be gainsaid that he was a giant
figure on the nineteenth-century scene, inspiring many of the outstanding
intellects of his time.

The nature of 'positive philosophy'

Comte's energy was remarkable: in spite of an interruption of two years
when he had a suicidal breakdown, he published the six volumes of his
Cours de philosophie positive between 1830 and 1842, and it was this work
that established his fame. Mill read the first two volumes and wrote to
congratulate him. In the first chapter one finds the well-known 'Law of the
three stages':

> This law is ... that each branch of our knowledge passes successively
> through three different theoretical conditions: the Theological or ficti-
> tious, the Metaphysical or abstract, and the Scientific or positive. In
> other words, the human mind, by its nature, employs in its progress three
> methods of philosophising, the character of which is essentially different
> and even radically opposed.   (Comte 1855/1974, p. 25)

This general sequence, it is important to note, was attributed to a universal property of the mind, since 'the phases of the mind of a man correspond to the epochs of the mind of the race'. Thus the child is a theologian, the youth is a metaphysician, and the adult is a natural philosopher. On the historical scale this progress is not uniform, and the attainment of the positive stage varies in different fields of knowledge. The order of such attainment is itself a lawful one, and hence there is a necessary hierarchy of the sciences. The five fundamental ones are astronomy, physics, chemistry, physiology, and 'social physics', the last being the most complex and at the apex of the hierarchy.

Comte regarded psychology as illusory, the last remnants of the theological stage, which fails to study the physiological basis of intellect. It was curtly and rather sarcastically dismissed on the grounds that its single method of introspection is invalid, because the mind cannot split itself into observer and observed. Psychology was therefore treated as part of physiology, which made sense for Comte since he was a believer in phrenology.

Comte regarded society as a collective organism, and for him this was no mere analogy. He contended that both individual and the collective organisms display a structural and functional harmony through the smooth interactions of its parts, which jointly act upon and react to the environment. The main difference between the individual and the collective organism is that the former remains relatively invariant, while the latter can progress if guided by scientific principles and has a wider range of functions. This conception of society as an organic entity anticipated the views subsequently adopted by Herbert Spencer and further elaborated by others.

The study of society and of social behaviour, the highest and most complex field of scientific knowledge, was to be the subject of 'social physics', further subdivided into 'social statics' and 'social dynamics'. This terminology is somewhat reminiscent of Herbart, though there is no indication that Comte was familiar with his work. 'Social statics' is concerned with social relations and generally the conditions of existence in any society, while 'social dynamics' focuses on progressive development. Needless to say, the above is merely a crude summary to convey the essentials. Other aspects of Comte's approach also need some mention, notably his conception of basic aims. As we have seen, the first characteristic of the *Positive philosophy* was that it regarded all phenomena as subject to invariable natural *Laws*.

> Seeing how vain is any research into what are called *Causes*, whether first or final, our business is to pursue an accurate discovery of these Laws, with a view to reducing them to the smallest possible number. By speculating upon causes, we could solve no difficulty about origin and purpose. Our real business is to analyse accurately the circumstances of phenomena, and to connect them by their natural relations of succession and resemblance.   (Comte 1855/1974, p. 28; emphasis in original)

The term 'cause' in the above passage refers to metaphysical notions, rather than to the way the term is now used in the social sciences. Moreover, as was not unusual at that time, his concept of 'laws' remained unclear. Comte's discussion of the methods whereby his aims could be achieved was more interesting. One is of course observation; but he pointed out, rightly, that observation is impotent without a theory to guide it; and he regarded 'positive science' as that guide. However, he maintained that in so complex a sphere as social physics, static observation is inadequate in the absence of some knowledge of 'the laws of social solidarity', and thereby circularity arises. Comte's curious attempt to escape this dilemma was to suggest that one should start with 'positive speculation', whatever was meant by that.

Several other possibilities were mooted. One is what he called 'indirect experimentation', an approach pioneered by physiologists and still a powerful tool today. This refers to the use of pathological cases for the purpose of understanding normal biological functioning. Comte proposed that the same could be done in relation to social phenomena by examining cases of *social* pathology: 'These disturbances are, in the social body, analogous to diseases of the individual organism'; it was a literal application of the 'organic analogy'. Finally, Comte pointed to several other types of comparisons: between animal and human societies, and also between different human societies, both synchronically and especially across historical periods. The latter resembles J. S. Mill's more fully developed 'inverse deductive method', yet nowhere did Comte consider the issues of evidence and proof, as was done by J. S. Mill in his *Logic*. The only data he ever presented were historical ones, drawn from a fairly narrow range and constantly recirculated. He held out the prospect of sociological laws, yet supported his views with little more than abstract arguments.

In this connection it is worth stressing that Comte was apparently concerned with 'laws' in the sense of fixed regularities, and in spite of his mathematical background was not interested in probability and statistics. Paradoxically, he declared throughout his writings his admiration for Condorcet: 'From the outset of my career I have never ceased to represent the great Condorcet as my spiritual father.' A few lines later he bemoaned 'my unfortunate connection in early youth with a depraved charlatan'. This unkind gibe refers to Saint-Simon. Yet he only cited Condorcet's work on *Outlines of an historical view of the progress of the human mind* and never mentioned Condorcet's efforts to apply probability theory to social affairs. Comte also displayed a lack of interest in the work of Quetelet on the application of statistics to social data. Yet he must have known about Quetelet's (1835/1869) use of the expression 'social physics', for it led Comte to invent the term 'sociology' and substitute it for what he himself had previously called 'social physics' – probably so as not to be regarded as a mere follower.

One might perhaps concede that some of Comte's themes, dealing for instance with social relations and the conditions of social consensus, bear at least a distant relationship to aspects of what later became social psychology. All the same, it is hard to understand how Allport (1954a) came to describe Comte as the founding father of the discipline. It is of course true that Comte's *œuvre* made a powerful impact, and that his advocacy of a scientific approach to social and societal issues accords with the dominant values of Allport's version of social psychology. None the less, his choice of founding father seems rather odd (cf. Samelson 1974).

Comte's dismissal of psychology as a separate subject contrasts with the opposite stance taken by his fellow countryman Victor Cousin (1792–1867), who held that psychology is a philosophical discipline based on the very introspection Comte decried. Cousin believed that one could thereby gain insight into human minds in general and perhaps even the 'Infinite Mind' – the last clearly a 'spiritualist' notion. Cousin was liberal in his political outlook, which temporarily blocked his career. Thereafter, however, he achieved the kind of worldly success for which Comte had striven in vain, so that there were personal as well as academic grounds for their mutual dislike. Cousin's training had been literary and philosophical, and he knew little about natural science. Rejecting the inheritance of the *Lumières* as materialistic and immoral, the 'spiritualism' he advocated remained dominant in France during the first half of the nineteenth century. Consequently Comte for a long time had few backers in his own country, and was even denounced by a bishop as holding impious doctrines. He found a more responsive audience in Britain, especially in Mill and his circle.

Social science modelled on astronomy: the 'moral statistics' of Quetelet

It will be recalled that Comte must have known about the work of Adolphe Quetelet (1796–1874), Belgian astronomer and professor of mathematics, but he did not mention him. Perhaps this was because in his book *On man and the development of his faculties*, sub-titled *An essay on social physics*, Quetelet (1835) had praised Cousin, Comte's arch-enemy; in the second edition (Quetelet 1869) *Social physics* became the main title. In between, he published a work entitled *On the social system and the laws governing it* (Quetelet 1848) which further elaborated his ideas about humans in society. Quetelet was a distinguished scientist who was held in high esteem by his peers, among them Sir John Herschel (1792–1871), president of the Royal Astronomical Society. Like Comte, Quetelet wanted to break away from the prevalent philosophical speculations, but unlike Comte he tried to lay the foundations for an empirical approach, using his skills as a statistician. Yet in order to achieve that, he had to create a model of the functioning of society and the role of individuals within it.

Quetelet began with the question as to whether the actions of individuals are subject to any laws. The problem in trying to answer it is that individuals vary so widely – in their personality, character, intellect, and so on – that one could not get anywhere if one attempted to take account of such differences. So he decided to treat them as 'accidental' and therefore to ignore them. This meant that he left individuals as such out of account, considering them only as part of a series of larger units, up to humanity as a whole. He concentrated on common elements resulting from social influences, reiterating an old refrain:

> In order to know how far our will is enmeshed in the social system, let us consider the least of our actions . . . as well as the social rules we have to take into account in our relations with the external world. Our dress, our walks, our speech, our pleasures, the hours of our meals, and even those of our sleep, are fixed by others rather than ourselves.   (Quetelet 1848, p. 71)

Moreover, he went further by postulating that each social system will produce an *homme moyen*, an 'average' individual type stripped of all 'accidental' variations. His account of social systems will be presented first, followed by the method he pursued in trying to capture social phenomena empirically.

On the 'social body'

The task he set himself was that of researching the 'laws' governing the social body, but it soon becomes evident that for him the meaning of the term 'law' was context-bound:

> the laws concerning the manner of being of the social body are not essentially invariable: they can change with the nature of the causes that gave birth to them: thus the progress of civilisation has necessarily produced changes in the laws relating to mortality, as they must also influence the physical and moral aspect of man.   (Quetelet 1835, vol. 2, p. 15)

It is therefore clear that what he termed 'laws' refers here to regularities such as mortality rates, and elsewhere to some fundamentals of social relations. The latter were evidently meant when he declared as his aim the scientific study of 'the vital phenomena presented by the social body'. The term 'body' is to be taken more or less literally, since he also referred to the physiology of that body, which can have illnesses and is liable to change within certain limits. For Quetelet there existed different kinds of social bodies in a hierarchy, humanity being the ultimate one. At that level, he maintained, human free will is entirely eliminated, and there are laws as immutable as those ruling the starry heavens – the same image as that employed by Herbart. However, Quetelet's main focus was on the intermediate level of the 'nation', whose physical, moral, and intellectual development has to be studied. As has already been noted, the 'organic analogy' – in this case the concept of the 'social body' as a quasi-physiological entity – was not confined to Quetelet and was common during the nineteenth century.

A second and quite distinct kind of analogy is to be found in his work, which explains its title of 'social physics'. That analogy is between social and physical systems, both subject to natural law in the strict sense. As already indicated, Quetelet on several occasions drew parallels between social and cosmological systems. Both are said to be subject to a universal 'principle of equilibrium'. This was not merely a theoretical postulate, but something he wanted to demonstrate empirically: 'No science, up to the present, has investigated the principles of equilibrium and of movement, and especially the principles of conservation which exist between the different parts of the social system.' There are, according to him, constant and variable forces operative in societies. The constant ones are what we would call the ecology: climate, the configuration of the landscape, water courses, and so on, which respectively favour or hinder the work of civilisation and are also responsible for the rise of different human races. Social forces making for stability are traditions and customs, while those producing changes are mainly 'collective opinions', apt to be capricious. In the best-organised societies these forces cancel each other out and an equilibrium prevails. However, it is a moving equilibrium and the centre of gravity proceeds in a straight line towards a better future – like most of his contemporaries Quetelet believed in inevitable progress, signalled by the advancement of science. The mechanical model underlying this scheme is evident, and the role of the individual in this kind of process is necessarily limited. Humans, unlike animals, are capable of modifying their conditions of life; and this in part accounts for the 'perturbations' in the social body which affect the equilibrium, but only within certain relatively narrow limits. Hence the seeming paradox 'that social phenomena, influenced by man's free will, proceed from year to year with more regularity than those phenomena influenced purely by material and chance causes'.

In addition to such general principles, social bodies such as nations are characterised by their own particular systems. The individuals composing such social bodies are heterogeneous, which results partly from innate and partly from accidental causes, and this applies to both physical and moral attributes. Yet the distribution of such characteristics is itself lawful, which makes an analysis possible. The aim was to find the physically, morally, and intellectually 'average person' in different nations, which typifies them. Such a quest, as will be shown, is problematic.

The empirical studies

Quetelet had to make use of such statistical data as were available to him, and these were most abundant for what he called 'physical qualities'. They included birth and mortality rates (that had long been collected), population sizes, heights and weights at different ages, and rates of physical illness. Here only the investigations relating to 'moral and intellectual qualities' will be considered. The tabulations served a dual purpose: the maximum frequency or peak of the distributions sometimes indicated the 'average man', while breakdowns by age, sex, and sometimes other variables defined the so-called 'accidental causes'.

At the outset Quetelet noted that while physical measures are relatively straightforward, no one had previously attempted to measure the others, and he discussed the difficulties involved. As an example he took 'courage', and demonstrated that it would be impossible to get a large enough sample of acts of courage that were strictly comparable in terms of their situational aspects. He speculated about the possibility of measuring memory, and of assessing the degree of foresight prevalent in different populations if one had adequate data about banks and other savings institutions.

As regards intelligence, he argued convincingly that one can only judge that in terms of the works or acts produced by it. He chose to compare in the first instance the number of dramatic works written in England and France, broken down by age of the authors. He further computed the expected number that would have been produced if the authors had not died. The outcome was not very illuminating, e.g. talent develops between thirty and thirty-five years and goes on until the fifties, and English authors were found to have been somewhat more precocious. But as he himself recognised, other factors could account for this. He also tried to make qualitative comparisons by assigning scores from one to three, according to his own judgements of relative merits, with similarly inconclusive results.

He further compared rates of mental illness in several countries by age and sex, carefully distinguishing between madness and idiocy, and working out the ratios between the two. These varied considerably across countries, but no conclusions were drawn because of the association then existing between idiocy and the mountainous nature of a country. It was later discovered that the reason for this was that the absence of iodine in the water resulted in thyroid deficiency, leading to cretinism.

Temperance and its opposite were also investigated. Charles Babbage (1791–1871), famous for his 'difference engine', a predecessor of computers, provided Quetelet with data on the number of drunks apprehended by the police in London in 1832 according to sex and month of the year. Quetelet noted the high proportion of women (two for every three men), but the fact that the incidence was highest during the last quarter of the year is hardly surprising.

The major part of the investigations dealt with crime, no doubt because ample data were available, making possible sophisticated analyses, even including curve-fitting. A large number of variables were cross-tabulated, including age, sex, literacy, countries, regions, seasons of the year, types of crime, trends over years, and even 'apparent motives'. There would be no purpose in going into details, but the best-known outcome, that exerted a powerful influence on subsequent students of society, will be conveyed in Quetelet's own words:

> Thus, as I have occasion to repeat already several times, one moves from one year to another with the sad perspective of seeing the same crimes reproduced in the same order, and attracting the same punishments in the same proportions ... the greater the number of individuals, the more the single individual will becomes obliterated and allows general facts to predominate, facts which depend on causes, facts according to which society exists and preserves itself.   (Quetelet 1835, vol. 2, p. 247)

These findings were cited in Henry Thomas Buckle's *History of civilization in England* (1857–61) which became very popular, and it was through Buckle that Quetelet's studies became known in Britain and Germany. From that source they became known to John Stuart Mill, who in the *Logic* commented on them at some length, including the following passage:

> What act is there which all would consider as more completely dependent on individual character, and on the exercise of individual free will, than that of slaying a fellow creature? Yet in any large country, the number of murders, in proportion to the population, varies ... very little from one year to another and in its variations never deviates widely from a certain average. What is still more remarkable, there is a similar approach to constancy in the proportion of these murders annually committed with every particular kind of instrument.   (Mill 1843/1879, p. 533)

Coming back to Quetelet, it will have been noticed that in the empirical sections of the work there is hardly any reference to the 'average person', and she or he is merely a ghostly presence. Yet in the final discussion he declared that he had ascertained the physical and moral development of *l'homme moyen* and the modification that 'average' creature undergoes as a result of various influences. One might be tempted to regard the 'average person' as an anticipation of the 'modal personality' approach pioneered by Cora Du Bois (1944), but this would be erroneous. For Quetelet that figure was variously an ideal type, a 'centre of gravity' for a particular population, a 'normal' person, or the centre of a distribution. Thus he wrote that '*L'homme moyen*, in effect, is in a nation what the centre of gravity is in a body', and proposed that this figure is involved in all the phenomena of societal equilibrium and movement as well as having some remarkable properties. Thus '*l'homme moyen* represents at the same time all that is great, beautiful, and good'. In sum, the concept is an unholy mixture that will not stand close scrutiny. Its weakness was pointed out by Herschel in his introduction to the second edition (Quetelet 1869).

In the concluding pages of that work Quetelet claimed that his researches had demonstrated the perfectibility of humans, and predicted that the effect of advancing civilisation will be progressively to narrow the limits of variation of human beings. In other words, the human world will become increasingly uniform.

With the wisdom of hindsight the flaws of Quetelet's theoretical scheme have become glaringly obvious. In part they clearly result from the influence of his training in astronomy, which led him to postulate quasi-mechanical relations inappropriate for the social sciences. But his empirical work, a model of its kind, stimulated a fashion for 'moral statistics' in several countries, not always as rigorously treated as by the master. For instance one of his followers in Germany, Adolph Wagner, published a book on *The regularity of seemingly chance actions from the point of view of statistics* (1864). He somewhat arbitrarily ransacked official statistics, producing masses of tables into which he read regularities that were not always there. Yet there were enough solid findings confirming the existence of some important trends.

The impact of the social-statistical investigation was considerable. Positivists and materialists hailed the results, which seemed to confirm the lawfulness of human conduct, while opponents saw in them the threat of determinism to human freedom of the will. Much of Quetelet's phrasing did imply a form of determinism. For instance, he referred to a 'disposition to crime' normally distributed in the population in the same way as the heights of army recruits. It was an issue Durkheim had to face in his famous study of suicide, and is also related to the claim that there are or can be social-psychological 'laws'. The philosophical debate itself is beyond the scope of the present discussion.

5   Britain: logic, evolution, and the social in mind

A group of prominent 'positivist' thinkers introduced Comte's ideas to Britain. They included John Stuart Mill, George Henry Lewes, and Alexander Bain. Mill's initial enthusiasm cooled markedly later, and in particular he disagreed with Comte on the treatment of psychology. The same was true of Lewes, though he otherwise remained a very dedicated follower. Herbert Spencer, whose system resembled Comte's in some important respects, never was a follower, but to his considerable dismay was widely regarded as having taken Comte as his model. None the less, Spencer has usually been described as one of the positivists in the wider sense, and was closely connected with both Mill and Lewes.

Among those mentioned above, Alexander Bain (1818–1903) was not a central figure, but was sufficiently prominent to merit at least a brief account of his position. Bain held the chair of logic at Aberdeen University, though lecturing and writing mainly on psychology. He was introduced to Comtian philosophy by Mill, and in turn recruited converts at Aberdeen. Yet while accepting the basic philosophical tenets of positivism, as a psychologist he rejected Comte's views on the subject. In his influential writings Bain seldom touched on social aspects of psychology, but it is worth recording that in *The emotions and the will* (Bain 1859/1899) he criticised Adam Smith by asking these questions: 'Where does the impartial spectator get his standard? Where does he find the rules that he is impartially to interpret?' These questions were raised in relation to the validity of various theories of morals, notably 'intuitive' versus 'rational', and it was unfortunate that he was led thereby to decry one of Smith's most fruitful contributions.

While Bain's psychology focused mainly on individual processes, Lewes was interested in the role of what he called the 'social medium', which together with physiology fashions the functioning of the human mind. Hence he, rather than Comte, deserves to be recognised as one of the forerunners of social psychology.

The positivists discussed here formed a close social network of mutual support. Why this was needed has been hinted at in the preceding chapter, but perhaps requires some elaboration. In the context of much of the nineteenth century the opposite of 'positivism' was 'spiritualism', based on traditional theological and ethical doctrines. 'Spiritualism' was a reaction in Europe against Enlightenment and revolutionary values, and 'positivism', which regarded any kind of metaphysics as futile, was perceived as a threat by established authorities. So it will be understood that 'positivism' was not a neutral term, but presented a challenge to the intellectual *status quo* analogous to the even more powerful Darwinian one.

Although the several figures discussed here shared a great deal of common ground, their approaches to what might in a broad sense be called social-psychological themes differed considerably.

John Stuart Mill on the methods of the social sciences

Mill on Comte

Mill's father, James Mill, had been a friend of Jeremy Bentham and a member of the group of 'philosophical radicals' who were active in social and educational causes. James Mill's (1829) *Analysis of the phenomena of the human mind* propounded the 'laws of association', which provided psychological support for utilitarianism. James Mill subjected his son John Stuart (1806–73) to an upbringing that has become legendary: Greek at age three, Latin at eight, logic at twelve, and political economy at thirteen. Kept away from his peers, his main relaxation (?) was a daily walk with his father, in the course of which he was questioned about what he had learnt. It is likely that this severely constricted early environment accounts for a mental crisis he suffered in 1826 and which left him depressed. He was saved from becoming a permanent emotional cripple by his friendship with Harriet Taylor, wife of a merchant, who in 1830 was the first young woman he had met outside his family circle. He married her in 1851 after her husband had died.

Shortly before meeting Harriet Taylor, Mill first came across an early essay by Comte expounding a preliminary version of the 'Law of the Three Stages', which impressed him. It was this essay, he later wrote to Comte, that had helped to free him from the Benthamism of his father. Mill first heard about the *Cours de philosophie positive* in 1838, and having read it was generous in his praise. Although disagreeing with some of Comte's views, he nevertheless strongly recommended the *Cours* to his friend Alexander Bain.

Mill had scant regard for the later religious turn of Comte's writings and published a balanced critique of his general positivist thesis (Mill 1865). One of his main objections was to Comte's contention that any psychology must always be part of biology. Mill, by contrast, argued that much of psychology constitutes a set of concepts that cannot be accounted for in terms of biology. Yet his reservations did not prevent Mill, always fair-minded, from giving credit to Comte in his *System of logic* (Mill 1843/1879).

In that work Mill expounded the methods used in the 'hard' sciences, setting out the fundamental tenet that the only basis for faith in the natural sciences is the knowledge that the laws governing the universe

5   *John Stuart Mill (1806–73)*

are necessary and constant. Then he went on to ask 'Why should this be less true for human nature?' Mill's introductory remarks on this topic rather cautiously suggest what in the table of contents is put quite bluntly: 'The backward state of the moral sciences can only be remedied by applying

to them the methods of Physical Science, duly extended and generalized.'
As already mentioned, the model of physics had already been widely put
forward during the eighteenth century, persisting well into the twentieth.

Mill on psychology

As against Comte, Mill affirmed that there *is* a science of mind, in other
words a psychology. In discussing its problems, Mill concentrated largely
on individuals. He opposed the 'metaphysicians', then still much in evidence, who maintained that thoughts and feelings are beyond the scope of
science. Any 'facts' are potentially subject to laws, even if such laws are yet
to be discovered. Moreover, not all sciences are exact, and he instanced
meteorology. People's mental processes and actions are also dependent on
causes, even if owing to their complexity they are not as yet, and may never
be, entirely predictable. Psychology is concerned with 'the uniformities of
succession, the laws ... according to which one mental state succeeds
another'. It should be noted that this refers to processes taking place *within*,
as it were, a single person's head. The possibility of one mind causing
something in another mind is not considered, so that in this formulation a
social psychology is excluded by definition.

There was only one major context in which he touched upon social
aspects, and that was when he put the case for a future 'science of the
formation of character', which he called 'ethology' (not to be confused
with what we now understand by this term, namely the study of animal
behaviour). Mill postulated a division such that psychology was to be the
science of 'the elementary laws of mind', while ethology should deal with –
presumably subordinate – laws of the formation of character. While such
laws were necessarily uniform, the contexts in which they operated would of
course vary. This implies that ethology would be about *differences*, both
individual and collective.

Mill had nothing substantive to say about ethological laws, but discussed ways in which they might be investigated. In this, as in psychology
generally, he followed his predecessors in ruling out experiments, but he
discussed the possibilities and limitations of observations. One of his
examples is cited below:

> What is obtained, even after the most extensive and accurate observa-
> tion, is merely a comparative result; as for example, that in a given
> number of Frenchmen, taken indiscriminately [i.e. randomly], there
> will be found more persons of a particular mental tendency, and fewer
> of the contrary tendency, than among an equal number of Italians or
> English, similarly taken ... Since, therefore, the comparison is not one of
> kinds, but of ratios and degrees; and since in proportion as the differ-
> ences are slight, it requires a greater number of instances to eliminate
> chance ...   (Mill 1843/1879, vol. 2, pp. 454–5)

He noted that environmental factors of various kinds, such as differences in government, customs, educational systems, etc., could account for the differences in characters. These were not envisaged as necessarily permanent, as implied in Mill's reference to gender differences. His views on this topic were markedly different from those of Comte and later Spencer:

> A long list of mental and moral differences are observed, or supposed to exist, between men and women: but at some future ... period, equal freedom and an equally independent social position come to be possessed by both, and their differences of character are either removed or totally altered.   (Mill 1843/1879, vol. 2, p. 456)

Finally, ethology would be concerned not merely with individual characters, but also with 'national and collective' ones. All this is somewhat reminiscent of David Hume's less ambitious essay on 'national characters' (cf. p. 40); it is a topic that had been of interest long before Hume, and was to be taken up again in social psychology.

More generally, Mill reviewed various methods of the physical sciences and discussed the extent to which they might be applicable in the 'moral' ones. On the whole his conclusions tended to be rather pessimistic, unduly so with hindsight. For example he considered the Method of Difference, which requires 'two instances, which tally in every particular except the one which is the subject of inquiry'. Given his belief that experiments are not feasible in psychology, he regarded that only as a theoretical possibility. However, this is precisely what is done at present when two groups are selected at random, with one being assigned to a treatment.

As a possible alternative he mentioned the Indirect Method of Difference, 'which instead of two instances differing in nothing but the presence or absence of a given circumstance, compares two *classes* of instances respectively agreeing in nothing but the presence of a circumstance on the one side and its absence on the other'. He illustrated its hypothetical use with the case of economic policies of nations. What we would call the independent variables were protectionism versus free trade, and the dependent one the level of prosperity. Again he noted that prosperity might have arisen from other causes so that the method is bound to be inconclusive, and that cannot be denied in principle. However, if one has at the outset a hypothesis about likely causal relationships, the method can be valuable for testing (but not 'proving') it. For example Dasen (1975) proposed that modes of subsistence are likely to influence cognitive development in certain ways. He proceeded to apply appropriate tests in cultures differing in many respects except that the mode of subsistence was primarily agricultural, and also in one where it was mainly hunting; and the predicted relationship was found.

None the less, Mill's wide-ranging survey of the possibilities and drawbacks of various methods is still instructive. In particular it is worth noting a distinction drawn in his discussion of what he called 'the laws of mind', that still seems relevant. He divided these laws into two types, one abstract and universal, the other resting on 'the truths of common experience, constituting a practical knowledge of mankind ... Such familiar maxims, when collected *a posteriori* from observation of life, occupy among the truths of the science the place of ... Empirical Laws' (Mill 1843/1879, vol. 2, p. 448). He went on to state that 'empirical laws' refer to a uniformity 'which holds true in all instances within our limits of observation, but is not of a nature to afford any assurance that it would hold beyond these limits'. Such a distinction is relevant for social psychology. As has become clear from recent neuropsychological studies, there are certain pan-human 'laws' governing social relationships. An example would be Adam Smith's 'sympathy', or as it is now often called 'empathy', i.e. the ability to enter into the feelings of others. By contrast, it is likely that many of social psychology's generalisations, whether or not based on experiments, constitute 'empirical laws' in Mill's sense. Their range of application may be limited by a number of factors, cultural variations being one of the most important. This is of course not to question the value of intra-cultural studies, but merely points to the fact that one has to be aware of their possible limitations.

Spencer, pre-Darwinian evolutionist

Mill had been favourably disposed towards the original positive philosophy, and also adopted quite deliberately some of Comte's vocabulary, such as 'social statics' and 'social dynamics'. Spencer did so more or less accidentally, and thereby made difficulties for himself, being accused by supporters of Comte of plagiarism. It was also claimed that he had copied Comte's approach, which riled him greatly since he was opposed to most of it. On the other hand the accusation is understandable, since there are a number of parallels between the grand systems of Comte and Spencer. They shared the ambitious aim to produce an overarching scheme of, respectively, 'positive' and 'synthetic' philosophies. Spencer agreed with Comte that 'Sociology is a science in which the phenomena of all other sciences are included'; whence Spencer's rather unrealistic recommendation that aspiring sociologists should study both the abstract (i.e. mathematics and logic) and concrete (e.g. astronomy, geology) sciences, so as to learn broad analytical principles and form appropriate habits of thought. Spencer was more inclined than Comte to grant psychology the status of a science, but he agreed with Comte in treating it as a division of biology, coming between and mediating the transition from biology to sociology.

Their disagreements were numerous. Spencer criticised the 'Law of the Three Stages' and the corresponding classification of the sciences; he did not accept the kind of mental determinism underlying the Comtian system, and did not believe in the 'historical method' which Mill had found stimulating. In his autobiography Spencer (1904) claimed that in 1851, when *Social statics* was published, he had not yet read any Comte. In any case, Spencer added, Comte had been concerned with *human conceptions* and so his account was relativistic, while he himself focused on the *external world* so that his own account was objective and absolute. No false modesty there!

A self-made man

Perhaps his confidence stemmed from the fact that he came from a relatively modest background and was largely self-educated. Herbert Spencer (1820–1903) was born in Derby and educated informally by his father, a schoolmaster, and then by an uncle. The scientific and mathematical training he had received from them was sufficient to qualify him as a railway engineer. Thereafter he entered journalism, and published *Social statics*. Its content was political and popular, as indicated by the sub-title referring to 'the conditions essential to human happiness'. Shortly afterwards an inheritance enabled him to give up his job and devote himself exclusively to scholarship. Spencer always remained a bachelor, living modestly. In his later years he suffered from extreme insomnia and depression, becoming ever more of a recluse – yet that did not affect his prodigious output.

Spencer on evolutionary processes

He elaborated an evolutionary framework before Darwin, and evolution was for him a master key for all the areas of knowledge he dealt with. It is of course true that there were many prior evolutionary theories, but Spencer's formulation was original. Evolution, for him, involved the twin principles of increasing structural *differentiation*, i.e. specialisation of functions, and increasing *integration*, i.e. increasing coherence, interdependence, and coordination. The source of the inspiration for this scheme came from the embryologist Karl Ernst von Baer (1792–1876), whose work subsequently led to the concept of 'recapitulation' in psychology.

In illustrating this scheme Spencer referred within the biological sphere to primitive organisms, 'undifferentiated aggregates of protoplasm' capable of very little movement and largely at the mercy of their environment. Evolutionary changes result in a differentiation whereby the original uniformity gives way to parts specialised for particular functions related to each other in a coherent structure. The same, he argued, is true of societies. Like others of the period, he believed that primitive tribes are characterised by an assembly of individuals 'with no dependence on one another'. With increase of size there comes division of labour with differentiated activities, and permanent social structures emerge, which become more and more highly organised. He thus saw a close parallel between animal and human evolutionary processes, though he made no attempt to relate this to the psychological features of humans.

Generally, Spencer's writings on psychology as such are of little interest in the present context. His *Principles of psychology* (1855) is concerned almost exclusively with individual minds, barely touching upon social aspects of human behaviour. Spencer acknowledged that humans are gregarious and viewed sociality as deriving from sympathy, which is involved in the development of morality and what he called 'the higher social sentiments'. But this topic constitutes only a tiny and marginal aspect of the work, and it is his evolutionary thought that is most relevant.

Spencer equated evolution with progress, declaring 'Progress is not an accident, but a necessity. Instead of civilization being artificial, it is a part of nature; all of a piece with the development of the embryo or the unfolding of a flower.' When Spencer referred to evolution in such contexts he meant Lamarckian evolution in the sense of the inheritance of acquired characters. Modern evolutionary psychologists would agree with Spencer that civilisation is part of nature, but would deny that its development follows a predetermined direction.

Another general principle enunciated by Spencer on the same theoretical basis is that life constitutes a continuous *adaptation* of the organism to changing circumstances. This applies at all the different levels from biology to sociology, the latter dealing with societies as 'superorganisms'. The adaptations effected by parents are passed on to their offspring and are, in his telling phrase, 'made organic'. Thus better-adapted behaviours become cumulative, thereby leading to progress.

What Spencer regarded as the necessary connection between biology and sociology was justified by him in a set of arguments that can be reduced to a syllogism:

1   All social actions are actions of individuals.
2   All actions of individuals are governed by the laws of life in general.
3   Therefore the correct interpretation of the actions of individuals requires a knowledge of the laws of life in general, i.e. biology.

When presented in this bare form, it is evident that the premises are flawed and hence also the conclusion.

A second line of argument advanced by Spencer was that in both individuals and society as a whole one can discern the phenomena of growth, structure, and function. This led him to state: 'That there is a real analogy between an individual organism and a social organism, becomes undeniable when certain necessities determining structure are seen to govern them in common' (Spencer 1873/1894, p. 330). This 'organic analogy' exerted an immense fascination on numerous nineteenth-century thinkers, and the passage below shows how far it was pushed by Spencer:

> Out of great social centres emerge many large clusters of wires, from which diverge at intervals minor clusters … just as the main bundles of nerves on their way to the periphery, from time to time, emit lateral bundles … Moreover, the distribution presents the analogy that near chief centres these great clusters of internuncial lines go side by side with the main channels of communication – railways or roads – but frequently part from these as they ramify; in the same way that in central parts of a vertebrate animal, nerve trunks habitually accompany arteries, while towards the periphery the proximity of nerves and arteries is not maintained: the only constant association being also similar in the two cases; for the telegraph wire which accompanies the railway system throughout every ramification, is the wire which checks and excites its traffic, as the one nerve which everywhere accompanies an artery, is the vaso-motor nerve regulating the circulation in it.   (Spencer 1885, vol. 1, p. 525)

Yet after going into all this detail, Spencer was at pains to emphasise that it is only an analogy, showing structural similarities to biological entities. For instance, both organisms and societies grow, and, as they do so, increase in structure and become differentiated. What has to be understood is that Spencer's organic analogy, which stresses the similarity between organic and societal processes, was regarded by him as an exemplification of higher-order laws governing all kinds of phenomena.

In the *Principles of sociology* (1885) Spencer proposed that the life course from birth via maturity to death falls under the rubric of *organic* evolution, while *superorganic* evolution concerns the co-ordinated actions of many individuals and their outcomes. The transitional boundary region between organic and 'superorganic' evolution was said to be cooperation between parents, and as usual during the nineteenth century the family was the only small group mentioned before jumping to larger units from tribes to modern states. The relationship between a large social unit and its individual members was seen as an interactive one, serving to produce optimal adaptation to the environment:

> As soon as a combination of men acquires permanence, there begin actions and reactions between the community and each member of it, such that either affects the other in nature. The control exercised by the aggregate over its units, tends ever to mould their activities and sentiments and ideas into congruity with social requirements; and activities, sentiments, and ideas, in so far as they are changed by changing circumstances, tend to re-mould the society into congruity with themselves.   (Spencer 1885, vol. 1, p. 11)

Furthermore, Spencer maintained, each society at each evolutionary stage has its own suitably adapted mode of feeling and thinking. It was an idea later more fully developed by Lamprecht (see chapter 7). The implication is of course that these modes are subject to change. Spencer also insisted that action is determined by feelings rather than cognition: 'Rational legislation ... which is derivable only from a true theory of mind, must recognize as a datum the direct connexion of action with feeling.'

Although Spencer's evolutionism has been eclipsed by that of Darwin, the magnitude of his achievement must be recognised. He demonstrated the power of a developmental analysis using a single overarching principle, and showed the importance of adaptation not merely to the natural but also to the social environment. He was undoubtedly one of the intellectual giants of the nineteenth-century scene. Other great figures who came after him, such as Baldwin or Durkheim, were either followers or critics – none could afford to ignore him. In his history of psychology, Flugel paid him an eloquent tribute, claiming that 'The *Principles of Sociology* definitely and irrevocably introduced the concept of evolution into anthropology, social psychology, and sociology itself ... Spencer's *Principles* may be justifiably looked upon as the first book on "Social Psychology" as now understood' (Flugel 1933, p. 140). Curiously, Flugel's comment came at a time when evolutionary thought in social psychology was actually in sharp decline, being superseded first by behaviourism and then by cognitivism. It was not until the twenty-first century that an evolutionary social psychology once more took the stage.

Lewes on 'the social factor' in mind

While Spencer had elaborated his own evolutionary theory and then amalgamated it with the vastly more epoch-making one of Darwin, Lewes was writing at a time when Darwinism already dominated the intellectual horizon. Most histories, when dealing with social psychology, devote little if any space to George Henry Lewes (1817–78), and if he is mentioned at all he is usually regarded as just a minor figure compared with stars like Comte, Mill, and Spencer. Yet in one respect he outshone all of them, and that was in his efforts to draw attention to and elucidate the 'social' in psychology. Comte had simply dismissed psychology; Mill sprang to its defence but, with the exception of his 'ethology', saw it as a science focused on individuals and governed by universal laws. Spencer referred only in general terms to the relationship between individuals and society, without seeking to link this in any way to psychology.

A colourful life

Lewes had a wide range of interests and talents, and was a populariser in the best sense of the term of new ideas in many fields, through articles in the most respected journals of his time and a series of books. These included a *History of philosophy*, biographies of Robespierre and Goethe, and a work on Spanish drama, and he was also the author of a successful play. Hence Lewes is most widely known as a man of letters, and this was also the main perspective from which his biography was written by Ashton (1991). However, Lewes was also a competent scientist, who published on marine biology, and during a stay at Munich was invited by the Academy there to collaborate with the renowned chemist Justus von Liebig. The discussions on hunger and thirst in Lewes's *The physiology of common life* (1860) led to Pavlov abandoning his theological studies and switching to physiology. Given such versatility, it is understandable that the list of Lewes's friends reads like a *Who's Who* of the arts and sciences. It includes names like Robert Browning, Thomas Carlyle, Charles Darwin, Leigh Hunt, Thomas Huxley, Alfred Tennyson, and others of that ilk.

Lewes's personal life was distinctly unconventional. Radical in outlook, he supported the 1848 revolutions in Europe. At home, he shared his wife Agnes with his friend Thornton Hunt. When Agnes had a second child with Hunt, it proved too much. He met and moved in with Marian Evans, later known as George Eliot (1819–80). They collaborated and stayed together for the rest of his life. Had it not been for George Eliot, his last – and in the present context highly relevant – posthumous volume on psychology might never have seen the light of day.

Already in his twenties Lewes had read widely in French philosophy, and it was probably the writings of Comte which originally aroused Lewes's interest in issues related to sociology and psychology. In 1842 the young Lewes, armed with letters of introduction by Mill, visited Paris. There he met both Comte and Cousin, and, as already explained, the views on psychology of these two men were diametrically opposed: for Comte psychology was part of biology; for Cousin psychology was allied with philosophy and dealt with the soul.

Lewes sided with Comte, and in later polemics vigorously argued against 'the spiritual hypothesis'. In 1846 he went to Paris again and, unluckily, called on Comte the day after Clotilde de Vaux (see p. 74) had died. Her subsequent elevation by Comte into a secular saint within his 'Religion of Humanity' alienated many of his former followers. This was true of Mill's critique, already mentioned, in which he also objected to Comte's categorisation of psychology as part of biology – an objection by then also shared by Lewes. Moreover, Lewes was also sceptical about phrenology, which for Comte had been the physiological key to individual psychology. Thus although Lewes published *Comte's philosophy of the sciences* (1853), a translation with commentaries, he had become considerably less enthusiastic by the time his own text on physiology appeared six years later. Lewes's writings on psychology came towards the end of his life, in the five volumes of his *Problems of life and mind*, the last of which was published posthumously. Since they ranged widely and rather discursively, the emphasis here will be on his treatment of the 'social', including the considerations which led him to regard it as equalling physiology in importance.

Lewes's evolutionary approach to psychology

In the first volume Lewes began by setting out the old problem of the nature of the differences between animals and humans. His discussion being informed by Darwinism, he started with similarities and, following Spencer, argued that since animals and men have similar structures, these must have similar functions.

> That animals have sensations, appetites, emotions, instinct, and intelligence – that they exhibit memory, expectation, judgment, hope, fear, joy – that they learn by experience and invent new modes of satisfying their desires, no philosopher now denies. And yet the gap between animal and human intelligence is so wide that Philosophy is sorely puzzled to reconcile the undeniable facts.   (Lewes 1874, p. 152)

He reviewed some earlier suggested explanations which proposed contrasts such as a rational versus a 'vegetative' soul, or instinct versus reason, rejecting them as mistaken since such sharp dichotomies violate the principle of evolutionary continuity. The question remains of how a difference of degree became transformed into one of kind. Animals are said to be intelligent since their behaviour is adaptive, but they have no 'intellect', which presupposes the ability to manipulate verbal and other symbols. This notion that language, indispensable for abstract thought, is what makes us human is certainly not original and goes back a long way.

Another answer Lewes gave relates to the distinction between 'Feeling and Thought: the one belonging to the Animal Organism, the other rising out of this and out of the Social Organism'. Here one encounters an ambiguity, if not confusion, which indicates that Lewes operated with the 'organic analogy', probably following Spencer. The analogy recurs on several occasions, such as the one below:

> If man is a social animal, which is undeniable, the unit in a living whole, just as any one organ is the unit of an organism, obviously his functions will be determined not only by his individual structure, but also by the structure of the Collective Organism. The functions of the liver, or of the kidneys, are determined partly by their structure, partly by influences from other organs. Man's individual functions arise in relation to the Cosmos; his general functions arise in relations to the Social Medium; thence Moral Life arises.   (Lewes 1874, p. 159)

Some comments on the terminology are indicated here. 'Cosmos' at that time could also mean 'an ordered system of ideas'. The Social Medium is said to be 'constituted by the education of the race and the individual'; elsewhere it is taken to consist of beliefs, opinions, institutions, and so on.

y 'education' is meant more than schooling – it refers to the products of
çio-evolutionary processes, which will be one of the necessary determi-
\ts of the functioning of individual minds.

he evolutionary process envisaged is again a Lamarckian one, involving 'inherited experience' which modifies the structures and these in turn
create dispositions to behave in certain ways. Differences in the experiences of past generations are sources of individual as well as collective
variations. The stress on the social did not imply for Lewes that the animal
side has disappeared or become suppressed. 'Both the Intellect and
Conscience are products of the animal impulses and social impulses acting
and reacting' (1874, p. 174), though without language and society there
could be neither intellect nor morality. While processes of mutual influences are often couched in dispositional terms, at other times a quasi-
mechanical connection is suggested: 'Intellect and the Conscience are
social functions; and their special manifestations are rigorously determined by Social Statics – i.e. the state of the Social Organism at the time
being – which they in turn determine.'

The 'social' as an integral part of the human mind

In the final volume he returned to the topic, devoting a chapter to 'the
social factor'. Much of it goes over ground already covered, but then there
is also a decisive shift in the manner in which the social is envisaged. In
contrast to that of animals, human knowledge is regarded to a large extent
as the result of collective experience embodied in language. Ideas are
active, and any one of them determines the reception of others, which
have to be made congruent with the whole system of thought. This is
clearly the notion of apperception derived from Herbart, and perhaps
foreshadows Festinger's dissonance theory.

Another passage advocates resort to history, which provides information about a society's traditions encompassing its religion, art, and
science. 'It is therefore to History and the observation of man in social
relations that we must look for data which may supplement those of
Introspection and Physiology.' Experiment is said to be necessary, and
Comte's point about disease as experiment is mentioned. History may also
be regarded as a kind of natural experiment, showing the mental variations arising out of changing social conditions, and beyond that displays
the course of mental evolution.

In an insightful comment Lewes suggested that since people differ more
in their social relations than in their basic psychological constitutions, one
should look towards the former in seeking to account for differences. Social
relations can also help us to understand uniformities: 'Men living always in
groups co-operate like the organs in an organism.' By referring to 'groups'
he touched upon a key element mostly ignored by his predecessors.

It will be seen from what has been said so far that many of Lewes's arguments are borrowed, mainly from Comte and Spencer, and he lacked the analytical skill of Mill. But as has already been indicated, there is at least one crucial exception: while his predecessors acknowledged the importance of social factors, they viewed them as merely impinging on the individual from outside, without affecting basic psychological functioning. Lewes went further, as shown by the key passage below:

> Biology furnishes both method and data in the elucidation of the relations of the organism and the external medium; and so far as Animal Psychology is concerned this is enough. But Human Psychology has a wider reach, includes another important factor, the influence of the social medium. *This is not simply an addition*, like that of a new sense which is the source of new modes of Feeling; it is a factor which *permeates the whole composition of the mind.* All the problems become complicated by it.   (Lewes 1879, p. 71; my emphasis)

It is an intriguing question how he gained this understanding, which marks him off from most of his contemporaries. Perhaps the influence of George Eliot may have been an important factor. She was apt to incorporate aspects of the scientific debates of the period in her novels, and it obviously had to be done within a context of social interaction.

In the earlier volumes of the *Problems* the social aspects had formed a relatively minor part of his discussions, and were therefore apt to be overlooked by his readers. This failure to gain the recognition he felt he deserved was a source of considerable disappointment for Lewes. In 1877 he published some articles based on his work in progress, in which he stressed the key role of 'the social factor'. G. C. Robertson, then editor of *Mind*, and Alexander Bain responded rather negatively and questioned his claim to originality. In a letter to Robertson, Lewes wrote indignantly: 'Can you give me the titles of books and essays you seem to refer to as having preceded me in the discovery of the social factor in Psychology?' (cited in Ashton 1991, p. 271). From the fact that Robertson referred to Spencer in reply, it is obvious that he had not grasped what Lewes had been trying to say.

It might be added that new ideas seldom emerge in total isolation. If he had been aware of it, Robertson might have quoted in response to Lewes's challenge the passage below, published a few years before Lewes, and expressing the same basic position. One of its authors was Steinthal – famed together with Lazarus for the first version of *Völkerpsychologie* (cf. chapter 3):

> But it is necessary also to note the fact that vegetative and animal life . . . remains entirely within the individual. By contrast, human thinking, feeling and acting, indeed the whole of psychic life, only becomes reality in social intercourse. As soon as it is a question of human psychic life, one must not forget for a moment that according to experience it can

only come into existence in a human community.   (Steinthal and Misteli 1871, p. 108)

In specifying that the human mind is inherently and necessarily social rather than just physiological, such statements go well beyond the ancient tag that humans are social animals. It was an insight whose implications were slow to be fully realised, and even when social psychology had become firmly established, much of it confined itself to the study of one-way social influences impinging on individuals from the outside.

6 France: crowd, public, and collective mentalities

The latter part of the nineteenth century saw the rise in France of several important social theories. Some of these were closely related to the aftermath of disorders during and after the Revolution of 1789 and the Commune of 1871. These were dramatically presented by Taine, and coupled with rapid social and political changes resulted in a fear of the 'masses' by the intellectual elite. Prominent among these was Le Bon, whose 'crowd psychology' had a powerful impact. During the same period Tarde also wrote about crowds in less sensational terms, and analysed the emergence of 'publics'. An equally significant contribution by Tarde was his discussion of what he saw as the key role of 'imitation' in interpersonal relations and the social system as a whole. He also described his approach as dealing with social psychology.

In parallel with these developments Espinas, inspired by Darwinism, explored the continuities between animal and human societies. He was led to conclude that in both a kind of collective consciousness can be found. Basing his work to some extent on that of Espinas, without following all the way, Durkheim put forward his theory of 'collective representations'. In direct opposition to Tarde, whose analysis began with relations between individual persons, Durkheim's approach was 'top-down'. He held that social ideas and values exist independently of individuals, and that these 'collective representations' exert an all-powerful influence on the members of a society. Durkheim's theory was highly influential and continues to be discussed.

Lastly there was Hamon, a somewhat eccentric figure who took a position that was extremely radical for his time. However, he anticipated some ideas that later came to be adopted in social psychology.

The origins of 'crowd psychology'

There has long been an interest in the nature of crowds. Alcuin (c. 735–804), adviser to Charlemagne, wrote in a letter to the emperor that 'the riotousness of the crowd is always very close to madness'. Attempts to explain crowd behaviour systematically did not begin until the nineteenth century, and it is unlikely to have been an accident that 'crowd psychology' emerged when it did. This is because historical conditions favourable to crowd formation coincided with the expansion of psychology and sociology. During the century after the Revolution of 1789 France experienced a number of episodes of social unrest, resulting in the main from industrialisation and the consequent aspirations of the working class to improve their economic status and participate in government. Initially this was expressed in movements like Saint-Simonism (cf. chapter 4), and later socialism and communism. After the fall of Napoleon the monarchy was restored, and during King Louis-Philippe's reign a revolution broke out in 1830 when there was bitter street-fighting in Paris. In 1831 and 1834 there were strikes of silk-workers in Lyons, both of which needed large-scale intervention by the army to suppress them. In 1848 a series of popular uprisings took place in several western and central European countries, some inspired by discontent of the middle and to a lesser extent working classes, and others by a demand for national independence. In France it was mainly a case of social discontent, and as a result of the uprising Louis-Philippe was forced to abdicate. Louis-Napoleon, third son of the great Napoleon, was elected president of the Second Republic and in 1852 assumed the title of Emperor. In 1870 he unwisely declared war on Prussia and suffered a crushing defeat.

Following this humiliating defeat there was an uprising of Parisian Republicans from March to May 1871 that has become known as the Commune. The Second Empire had collapsed, and Adolphe Thiers, who had been critical of Napoleon III's policies, became chief of a provisional government located at Versailles. The revolutionaries established a Central Committee, formed a National Guard, and converted some of the regular army to their side. The Committee organised elections and, remarkably, nearly half the adult population of Paris turned out to vote.

The resultant assembly consisted of a mixture of intellectuals, artisans and workers, and violent fanatics. Gradually it became dominated by a group of ultra-radical Jacobins, who not only reintroduced the revolutionary calendar but began to arrest anybody suspected of disloyalty, taking hostages, and suppressing the churches. For a period only skirmishes took place on the periphery. There followed the 'bloody week' from 21 to 28 May, when full-scale combat ensued against the regular army sent in by Thiers. A desperate defence against overwhelming odds, street by street on the barricades, proved ultimately fruitless.

Women played an active part throughout, at first in the running of schools and other social services, and dealing with the distribution of food, which had become scarce. They also served on the barricades, first as auxiliaries providing first aid, and when things became critical even becoming combatants. There circulated a (fictitious) story that there were 'petrolières', groups of women who set buildings alight with petrol. What is certain is that numerous buildings were destroyed by fire. Just before the end came, all the hostages were executed.

The insurgents paid a heavy price. While the regular army suffered fewer than a thousand dead, at least 20,000 communards were killed and some 30,000 arrested. One should add to this toll an unknown number of dead who were victims of the repression carried out by the leaders of the Commune. Altogether it was a terrible struggle which left an indelible mark on the minds of the French intellectuals of the period. They had been faced with the threat of the disintegration of civil society as they knew it, and this gave rise to a deep fear of 'the mob' which profoundly influenced the theories of mass behaviour of the period.

Chronicler of horrors

One of the outstanding historians of the Commune, Hippolyte Taine (1828–93), was also something of a psychologist. Born in Vouziers, he came to Paris in 1841 to go to a famous Lycée where he proved a brilliant student. He enrolled in the Ecole Normale Supérieure, where he also excelled, just after the 1848 Revolution; but he was not universally liked, owing to his sharply critical spirit. In particular, he despised the philosophy of Victor Cousin, who had been Comte's pet enemy. Owing to his unconventional views he failed his examination. None the less, he found a teaching position at a provincial college, but was dismissed when he refused to express the gratitude and respect for the emperor Louis-Napoleon that was expected from all the staff. Undaunted, he moved back to Paris and prepared not just one but two doctoral theses, on sensations and perceptions respectively. They were judged unacceptable as being too controversial, which left him dismayed. For the next fifteen years he turned to literature, though he still remained keen on science, and especially psychology. This he combined with a passionate interest in political polemics. Even after the setting up of the Third Republic he had to struggle against prejudice. One of his academic opponents declared that a candidate would disqualify himself if he cited the authority of Taine on any historical question. In 1885 a fatal illness, probably syphilis, was diagnosed and he spent his last years in painful misery.

His interest in psychology is manifest in a work with the title *On intelligence* (Taine 1870) in which he analysed it in terms of 'sensations'. He claimed that only a thin line separates normal cognition and perception, which are attuned to external reality, from the delusions of the psychotics. He had planned to follow this by another volume on the emotions and the will, but was deflected from this by the advent of the Commune, which filled him with dread. He foresaw a repetition of the horrors of the French Revolution, its anarchy and barbarism, and determined to write a history of its bloody course. He saw the Commune as a plot by foreigners and fanatics that would make life unsupportable, and departed to Oxford, where he received an honorary degree before returning later to embark on his archival research. Taine did not regard this as an abandonment of his psychological work, since for him history was applied psychology.

Taine felt that the Enlightenment had been a disastrous aberration, in which abandonment of sound tradition for the insane pursuit of lofty but unattainable ideals had loosened all civilised restraint. In any case, he argued, some groups in society are more civilised than others, especially the nobility and the highly educated; moreover, women have more low animal instincts than men. During the Revolution crowds consisting of the dregs of society, lacking any civilisation, lost all their restraints.

The pages of *The Revolution* (1878) are filled with blood-curdling accounts of the actions of the mob.

> Foreigners, Italians, bandits, are mingled with the peasants and artisans, and expressions are heard and acts are seen which indicate a *jaquerie* [peasant revolt]. The most excited said to the bishop 'We are poor and you are rich, and we mean to have all your property.' Elsewhere, the seditious mob exacts contributions from all people in good circumstances. At Brignolles, thirteen houses are pillaged from top to bottom, and thirty others half-pillaged. At Aupt, M. de Montferrat, in defending himself, is killed and hacked to pieces. At La Seyne, the populace, led by a peasant, assemble by beat of drum; some women fetch a bier, and set it down before the house of a leading bourgeois, telling him to prepare himself for death, and that they will have the honour of burying him.   (Taine 1878, vol. 1, p. 18)

Taine attributed some of the vilest deeds to the effects of alcohol – 'They kill and they drink and kill again.' He likened the perpetrators to the Iroquois, the American tribe then believed to have been savage cannibals: 'At La Force, Madame de Lamballe (a friend of the Queen) is cut to pieces. I cannot transcribe what Charlot, the hairdresser, did with her head. I merely state that another wretch, in the Rue Saint-Antoine, bore off her heart and ate it' (vol. 2, p. 226). It is not possible to say how far such accounts were veridical. There is no doubt that terrible things happened, but many of Taine's sensational reports seem to be based on hearsay. At any rate, the graphic recitals of robberies and murders carried out by revolutionary crowds provided ample material for the crowd theorists, and Le Bon later used some of it to underpin his arguments.

Before Le Bon: Fresenius and Sighele

The term 'crowd psychology' now usually evokes the name of Le Bon, who initially claimed to have been the first in that field, a claim he later had to tone down. It is easy to show that a good deal had been written on the topic before him, and there has been some controversy about how much Le Bon borrowed from others. In particular, Le Bon's friend

Gabriel Tarde – about whom more later – had written on 'crowds', and so had Sighele, who accused Le Bon of plagiarism.

Even before Sighele, a German scholar whose work was occasioned by the 1848 European revolutions proposed that the time had come to establish a 'psychology of crowds' (Fresenius 1866). He distinguished three main kinds of collectivities: the chance assembly of roughnecks; people living together; and those sharing ideas and beliefs. This last comes close to what Tarde later came to call 'the public'.

The first kind, 'crowds', was again sub-divided into the passive and the active crowd. The passive crowd gains satisfaction from mere togetherness. It gapes, makes cheap jokes, is cowardly, lazy, and so on. When a crowd is frightened, panic results. By contrast the active crowd becomes conscious of the power of large numbers and in blind fury engages in acts of violence. The explanation offered by Fresenius for the criminal tendencies of the active crowd is basically individualistic, referring to the personalities of the people composing the crowd. However, Fresenius also put forward the notion of the diminution of personal responsibility in the presence of others, which is much the same as that adopted about a century later by Zimbardo (Haney et al. 1973). An effect is also attributed to the general atmosphere, being in a 'mass' resulting in a combination of impudence and cowardice. Fresenius raised the question of how it is possible for an active crowd to commit a cruel murder, and his answer was:

> No single one really wants to do the deed; but every one feels himself goaded by the fury of the whole crowd to maltreat the victim. He is keen to show himself in tune with the others, but at the same time hiding behind them so as to escape any personal responsibility.   (Fresenius 1866, p. 128)

This anticipates the notion of 'crowd contagion' that later played a large role in discussions of crowd behaviour. It should also be noted that he applied the term 'crowd' to organised groups, a practice then common and often revealing the authors' political orientations.

The two later figures who gained far more prominence in this sphere were Sighele and Le Bon, both of whom claimed priority. Scipio Sighele (1868–1913) was a follower of Cesare Lombroso (1836–1909), Italian physician and criminologist. Lombroso was famous at the time for his notion that crime is hereditary. He also held that crowds consist largely of unsavoury characters tainted by inborn delinquency, or led by such. In 1891 Sighele published a book on *The criminal crowd*, subsequently expanded in a second French edition (1901). It begins with a lengthy quotation from Spencer, to whom he ascribed the axiom 'that the principal characteristics of human society correspond to the principal characteristics of humans', a view also shared by Comte, Schopenhauer, and Espinas. Now if that is true, he suggested, the equation should hold not only for society as a whole, but for its constituent parts; and that is

manifestly untrue. Pointing to differences between social classes in education, language, dress, modes of life, etc., Sighele argued that they all
possess not merely general human attributes, but those of their particular
subgroup as well. Then he went on to ask whether or not the psychological
laws governing the behaviour of individuals also hold for groups of
individuals, and replied in the negative. Sighele cited the example of juries,
who are often said to arrive at nonsensical verdicts.

> Well, what do all these facts prove, and so many other similar ones
> which everybody has been able to observe for themselves? They prove
> simply this: that twelve intelligent men who have good sense can make
> a stupid and absurd judgement. *Hence an assembly of individuals can
> give a result opposed to that which each of them would have given on
> his own.*   (Sighele 1901, p. 9; my emphasis)

No real attempt was made by Sighele to explain this mysterious phenomenon, which he compared, in Spencerian style, to unexpected chemical
reactions in the cells of which an organism is composed. One is reminded
of the notion of 'group polarisation', fashionable in social psychology
during the 1970s. It was claimed at that time that after discussion group
members become more extreme in their judgements. Anyway Sighele,
impressed by what he thought he had found, proposed that in addition
to a psychology concerned with the individual, and to a sociology which
deals with society as a whole, there should be a collective psychology
focusing on gatherings of people like juries, parliamentary assemblies,
theatre audiences, and such-like.

Somewhat inconsistently, Sighele affirmed that Spencer's principle is
valid in *homogeneous* groups, breaking down only in *heterogeneous* ones,
and the outstanding case of the latter is the crowd, 'because it is composed
of individuals of all ages, both sexes, all social classes ... all degrees of
morality and cultivation', and it is also clearly non-organic (in the sense of
society resembling an organism) since it comes into being suddenly and
without prior arrangement.

The bulk of the volume is devoted to an analysis of the nature of the
crimes committed by crowds, and the dangers crowds present. Given such
views, it is hardly surprising that Sighele was suspicious of parliamentary
assemblies. At the same time, he was not oblivious to the socio-political
transformations that were taking place:

> Once the individual was everything, in politics as in science. Today the
> individual is in decline; in politics in the face of that collective being
> which is public opinion, and in psychological science in the face of that
> collective being which is the crowd.   (Sighele 1901, p. 22)

Evidently Sighele was well aware that 'the age of the crowd' had dawned,
as Le Bon later put it, and for him all kinds of radical social movements or
trade unions constituted 'criminal crowds'. In his role as an expert in

jurisprudence, Sighele helped with legal 'reform' in Italy, which in effect entailed the drafting of repressive legislation.

There are many similarities between Sighele's and Le Bon's accounts of crowds. For instance, Le Bon criticised Spencer in much the same way as Sighele had done; like Sighele, he also made use of a chemical analogy. But there are also significant differences, and Sighele's contribution was eclipsed by the remarkable success of Le Bon's work.

Le Bon on the stupidity and menace of crowds

Coming from a solidly bourgeois but provincial family, Gustave Le Bon (1841–1931) – like many French people to the present day – was anxious to escape from what he felt was a backwater. In 1860 he arrived in Paris and underwent a medical and broad scientific training, qualifying as a doctor. However, he yearned for a more glittering career and decided to become a writer on scientific topics, in the vain hope that this would gain him academic recognition and a prestigious post. Le Bon was not a modest person, and as an old man in 1922 wrote to Einstein claiming to have discovered relativity before him!

Le Bon was a prolific writer with wide interests, including anthropology and Darwinism, which in his time had made a belated impact in France. One of his major works was *L'homme et les sociétés* [Man and societies] (1881), redolent with the then popular craniology and the influence of race on the evolution of peoples. Le Bon took over from Spencer's *Principles of psychology* the concept of 'reflex', viewed as the means of adaptation of an organism to its environment. If a reflex is useful, it gets transmitted as a (Lamarckian) inheritance and Le Bon accounted in this way for intellectual endowments. He also postulated emotional reflexes, which he regarded as survivals from more primitive stages of humanity, and which are most prominent in people lacking in reason. It is only among civilised people that reason plays a significant role, and modern urbanism and industrial life are apt to wear away the behaviour patterns that have evolved over historical periods and produce a tendency to regress to more primitive behaviour. He sought to illustrate this with reference to the excesses witnessed during the Paris Commune, spectacles which had also prompted Taine's attempts to understand crowd behaviour; but Taine's approach was more descriptive than explanatory.

Apart from the more general factors postulated by Le Bon, he believed in the enduring effects of race, which he tended to equate with 'nation'. He also had strong views about female inferiority, declaring that

> All the psychologists who have studied the intelligence of women ... recognise today that they represent the most inferior form of human evolution and are much closer to children and savages than to adult civilised man.   (Le Bon 1881, vol. 2, p. 157)

6   *Gustave Le Bon (1841–1931)*

He went on to say that women's emotional nature brings them close to monkeys, or even to more inferior mammals. Such views about the effects of race and the status of women were not unusual among his contemporaries.

By the time Le Bon wrote the book about crowds he had become very interested in hypnotism, and attended lectures on it. The distinguished neurologist Charcot, working at the Salpêtrière hospital (where Freud came to learn from him), and Bernheim at Nancy were rivals who varied in their interpretation of the phenomena. Yet both contributed to making scientifically respectable what had been a rather mysterious curiosity. Le Bon was impressed by the power of hypnotic suggestion which, he believed, accounted for the influence orators were able to exert over their listeners, and also explained how leaders could dominate a crowd. This was the theme he pursued at length in his *Psychologie des foules* [Psychology of crowds] (1895), which made him famous. It went through numerous editions and was still reprinted several times in the twentieth century.

In its first chapter he proclaimed the 'psychological law' of the mental unity of crowds. Like Sighele, he maintained that the crowd is a great leveller, however diverse the characteristics of its members might be. He compared this to a chemical process, whereby elements combine and form a new substance whose properties are quite different from those of its components. In a crowd the conscious personality is submerged, and archaic tendencies, normally unconscious, take over.

> Whoever be the individuals that compose it, however like or unlike be their mode of life, their occupations, their character, or their intelligence, the fact that they have been transformed into a crowd puts them in possession of a sort of collective mind which makes them feel, think, and act in a manner quite different from that in which each individual of them would feel, think, and act, were he in a state of isolation ... The psychological crowd is a provisional being formed by heterogeneous elements which for the moment are combined.   (Le Bon 1895/1966, p. 27)

In the crowd people regress into an earlier evolutionary stage and become barbarians, governed only by instinct. Intelligence declines, while feelings persist, and crowds are not necessarily criminal – they may embrace a lofty ideal. It all depends on the suggestions to which they are exposed by their leaders. Charismatic ones are able to capture the collective mind of the crowd by a kind of hypnotic suggestion and shape it at will. Given how Le Bon regarded women, it is not surprising that he likened the mentality of crowds to that of women. Thus crowds are said to be impulsive, lacking reason and critical judgement, and being dominated by emotions.

Le Bon's conception of a 'crowd', like that of Sighele, was very wide, as his classification indicates. He divided them first into hetero- and homogeneous. The heterogeneous ones are sub-divided into anonymous ones (street crowds) and non-anonymous ones (juries, parliamentary assemblies). Homogeneous crowds include political and religious groups, castes (e.g. military, priestly), and social classes, differing in degree of organisation. Le Bon's discussion was confined to the features of heterogeneous crowds.

Le Bon's ideas and values have to be seen against the background of the situation in France in the period in which he lived. As already noted, the nation was divided along religious, political, and social lines. The defeat by Prussia signified external weakness, and the trauma of the Commune had affected the whole of his generation. He was anti-radical and especially anti-socialist, distrusting democracy and its institutions, and declaring that 'the era of crowds' had arrived. Yet he also recognised that the clock could not be turned back, and had to accept that an extended franchise had come to stay. At the same time he had little respect for collective decision-making, as is evident from the following passage:

> The decisions affecting matters of general interest come to by an assembly of men of distinction, but specialists in different walks of life, are not sensibly superior to the decisions that would be adopted by a gathering of imbeciles ... In crowds it is stupidity and not mother-wit that is accumulated.   (Le Bon 1895/1966, p. 29)

He expounded at some length the irrationality of juries, which are swayed by such irrelevant factors as noble birth, celebrity, or beauty in women. In this he was no doubt largely correct; but his portrayal of juries as mindless collectivities is somewhat impaired by his account of the tricks which a counsel had to employ in order to bring around two 'obstinate' jurors. Similar considerations apply to parliamentary 'crowds', said to be very open to suggestions by prestigious leaders. However, he had to concede that on issues where their local interests are prominently involved, deputies' minds are hard to change.

The criminality of crowds received a great deal of attention from Le Bon, and he stressed what he called the 'absolute unconsciousness of the acts of the crowd'. By this he meant that such acts do not result from deliberate decisions, but arise more or less spontaneously in a highly charged atmosphere. The story below, which Le Bon culled from Taine, refers to the storming of the Bastille during the French Revolution:

> The murder of M. de Launay, the governor of the Bastille, may be cited as a typical example. After the taking of the fortress the governor, surrounded by a very excited crowd, was dealt blows from every direction. It was proposed to hang him, to cut off his head, to tie him to a horse's tail. While struggling, he accidentally kicked one of those present. Someone proposed, and his suggestion was at once received with acclamation by the crowd, that the individual who had been kicked should cut the governor's throat.
>
> The individual in question, a cook out of work, whose chief reason for being at the Bastille was idle curiosity as to what was going on, esteems, since such is the general opinion, the action is patriotic and even believes he deserves a medal for having destroyed a monster. With a sword that is lent to him he strikes the bared neck, but the weapon being somewhat

blunt and not cutting, he takes from his pocket a small black-handled knife and (in his capacity of cook he would be experienced in cutting up meat) successfully effects the operation.   (Le Bon 1895/1966, pp. 160–1)

This episode is an instance of the diminished feeling of personal responsibility already noted by Fresenius, and named 'de-individuation' by Zimbardo. It will be noted that the suggestion in this case came from 'someone', i.e. another member of the crowd rather than a leader.

It is easy to pick holes in many of Le Bon's arguments, but that would be beside the point. The important fact is that his work made an enormous impact – Allport (1954a, p. 35) described it as 'Perhaps the most influential book ever written in social psychology'. Le Bon sent a copy to Mussolini, who used his ideas extensively, and not merely in expounding fascist ideology; he also found it useful for addressing adoring 'masses'. It is not clear whether Hitler had any first-hand knowledge of Le Bon, but the arguments in *Mein Kampf* certainly do closely reflect Le Bon's ideas, such as the description of crowds as 'feminine' and characterised by feeling rather than reasoning. In the German translation of Le Bon's book the phrase *Massenpsychologie* was used, and 'mass psychology' thereafter became for a period synonymous with 'social psychology' in the German literature.

It is interesting that Le Bon's ideas were received rather differently in America. While social scientists there accepted the view of the suggestible and irrational nature of crowds, they did not agree that elected representatives constituted crowds and they retained their faith in democracy (cf. King 1990). By contrast, both Sighele and Le Bon were fearful of democracy, though conceding that its progress was unavoidable.

Tarde: crowd versus 'public'

A somewhat similar view was taken by Gabriel Tarde (about whom more below), a friend of Le Bon who was also concerned with crowds. However, in his book *L'opinion et la foule* [Opinion and the crowd] (1901/1989) Tarde avoided Le Bon's lurid tone and differentiated the crowd from what he called 'the public'. For Tarde crowd psychology and behaviour are produced by an assembly of people in close physical proximity at a given time and place who share emotions and beliefs, which instigate their joint action. By 'public', on the other hand, he understood a set of people of any size who have sufficient unanimity of ideas and beliefs to have a tendency towards common action but are widely dispersed in space. There have always been crowds throughout history but, as Tarde pointed out, 'publics' are a modern phenomenon. He maintained that 'the formation of a public presupposes a far more advanced mental and social evolution than the formation of a crowd. The [reading] public consists of a large number of individuals who daily and simultaneously are exposed to information, entailing suggestion at a distance; and in the intense social life of urban communities this leads to imitation and amplification of opinions.' However, he noted that while one can only be a member of a single crowd, one can be part of several publics depending on one's varied spheres of interest. Hence in modern society the social bond is not organic, as had often been previously proposed, but consists of a community of miscellaneous ideas and sentiments.

'Publics' are made possible by the advent of newspapers, and subsequently, one might add, by other media not yet in existence at the time Tarde was writing. He was in two minds regarding the implications of this development. On the one hand, he argued, the members of a public are in relative isolation when they make up their minds on an issue and have more opportunity for rational reflection. On the other hand he mentioned the fact that news, simultaneously disseminated in a sensational fashion, may have effects somewhat resembling what can happen in a crowd. If he had lived in the age of television he would probably have been even more concerned about the power of non-rational persuasion. In any case, his analysis of opinion formation in a public, which included personal conversations, constituted a distinct advance. Curiously, this aspect of Tarde's theory received rather less attention in France than in America. The prominent sociologist Robert Park wrote a PhD dissertation at Heidelberg University entitled *Masse und Publikum*, later published as *The crowd and the public* (Park 1904/1972).

Tarde on 'imitation' as the key to social behaviour

Tarde's contribution to the emergence of a social psychology has been largely and unjustly forgotten. He was one of the first to entitle a book *Etudes de psychologie sociale* [Studies in social psychology] (1898), and, as we shall see, he strongly influenced the nascent social psychology in America. Tarde was an important transitional figure, who moved beyond the dichotomy of a largely physiologically oriented individual psychology versus a sociology abstracted from individuals of the kind espoused by Durkheim. As he himself noted, Comte's was a 'social physics', Spencer's a 'social biology', and what was needed was a 'social psychology'.

Gabriel Tarde (1843–1904) came from a family who had abandoned their aristocratic background, and his father was a judge. He received a classical education in a school run by Jesuits, and resented the severe discipline to which he was subjected. He studied law, but also read widely in philosophy, mathematics, and the social sciences, including Spencer and J. S. Mill. A salient influence was the economist and mathematician

Cournot, and in particular Cournot's (1861) book on the relationships between fundamental ideas in science and history, examining the manner in which knowledge is transmitted. It was this work which inspired him to adopt the concept of 'imitation' as the cornerstone of his theoretical edifice. As a provincial magistrate he also became interested in criminology, criticising the 'Italian school' founded by Lombroso and publishing extensively in this field, as well as in statistics and sociology. He lectured frequently on all these topics in a variety of institutions, and in 1899 was appointed professor of modern philosophy at the prestigious Collège de France.

Tarde on imitation as the key to social life

In comparison with Durkheim, Tarde elaborated a wide-ranging theoretical framework that went far beyond the limited objectives of sociology and was similar in scope to Spencer's vast scheme. Central to it was the notion that social processes have to be analysed in terms of what might be called inter-mental activities of sets of associated individuals. Such activities take three main forms, namely repetition, opposition, and adaptation. He saw these not merely as a foundation of sociology, but as a kind of cosmic philosophy. This trinity was probably derived from Hegel, but more importantly it was also influenced – like many contemporary writings – by Darwinism. In his case, however, what he took from it were the notions of 'opposition' and 'adaptation' which he used in a manner very different from Darwin, whose fundamental ideas he seemingly failed to understand. While recognising the value of the concept of natural selection, he went on to say: 'Its efficacity is essentially negative, its virtue of eliminating damaging varieties ... is no longer contested, but it is less and less regarded as having a truly creative power.' He also preferred the term 'transformation' to that of 'evolution'.

   It is of course neither possible nor necessary here to go into the details of his grand scheme and a few brief indications will suffice, beginning in reverse order with 'adaptation'. Tarde saw the panorama of history as one of gradual change towards ever more efficient adaptation and social harmony. Thus 'opposition' becomes ever more benevolent, starting with crude conflict, softening to competition, and then discussion. It was an optimism typical from the Enlightenment onwards, which ended abruptly with the First World War. Opposition can also be internal to the individual, in which case there exists a state of what Festinger called 'dissonance', entailing conflicting ideas, beliefs, wishes, etc. For Tarde, it was not purely internal, but always related to the individual's social milieu; and the resolution could take three forms: rejecting the social model, accepting it and abandoning conflicting elements, or some sort of compromise.

It is with the third principle, of 'repetition', that we come to his enduring contribution, at the core of which lies 'imitation'. This is not to say that the notion of 'imitation' as a potent factor in social life was a novel one, and its prevalence has already been noted. What Tarde did was to show in detail *how* imitation functions in society and *what* its far-reaching consequences are. In order to avoid misunderstanding, it should be said at this point that Tarde really operated with the twin concepts of *invention* and imitation, for without the former there could be no change or transformation. Hence invention is bound to be prior to imitation, and they jointly constitute basic social phenomena which lie at the root of any social action.

In Tarde's most famous book, *The laws of imitation*, first published in 1890, he claimed that the twin concepts can already be discerned in the animal world, even at the level of insects. In support he cited observations of the behaviour of ants made by Espinas. According to Espinas, migrations are not the result of some collective instinct. Rather, an individual ant detaches itself and taps its neighbours, waving its antennae in seeming invitation to follow. Imitation then takes over, leading to a collective movement. Tarde did not hesitate to compare ants directly with humans in this respect: 'M[onsieur]. Espinas has said expressly that the works of ants can very well be explained in terms of "individual initiative followed by imitation". That initiative is always an innovation, an invention equal to our own in boldness of spirit.' However, matters are clearly more complicated in the human case and this will now be surveyed in more detail, beginning with 'imitation'.

According to Tarde, imitation can be conscious or unconscious, the outcome of reflection or spontaneous, and voluntary or forced. The onset of imitation is internal when, say, an idea, custom, or whatever is implanted in the mind and becomes accepted – the conditions of acceptance will be considered below. There will then gradually follow external manifestations in terms of behaviour, words, and/or actions, which become integrated into the person's behaviour repertoire. Within society, imitation tends to proceed from those higher in social status downwards. The 'law of geometric progression' refers to the remarkably speedy dissemination of fashions of various kinds, rumours, etc. through waves of 'repetitions' spreading ever wider. There is also the law of 'internal versus exotic', which proposes that the familiar is more readily imitated than the strange. The 'laws of imitation' themselves, when reduced to their bare bones as is done here, will hardly seem exciting. But the really innovative aspect of Tarde's thought, for his time, was the notion that imitation is an *inter-individual* process and entails communication between persons. Its simplest form is that of the dyad, and it can go up to a vast network. Hence Tarde's definition of a social group as either 'a collection of beings imitating each other or, without imitation, they resemble each other and their common features are old copies of the same model'. In order to appreciate how innovative such a conception was, one has to look back at his predecessors. Since the writings of Condorcet (group decisions) and Adam Smith (sympathy), none of the many scholars discussed in the previous chapters paid much if any attention to the details of *interactions* between individuals. For Tarde, by contrast, the personal relationship entailed in imitating each other constitutes the fundamental building block of society. Let us now turn to the second of the key concepts, namely 'invention', which Tarde used broadly to cover ideas, practices, technical innovations, and such-like. An invention generally consists of a novel recombination of existing ideas, and the greater the pool of ideas in society, the greater the chances of novelty emerging. An 'inventor' may put forward something new, but of course it would not necessarily be accepted and imitated. On the contrary, there will nearly always be obstacles to the abandonment of established ideas, and ways of doing things. Moreover, there is competition between novelties:

> A discovery, an invention appears. There are two facts to note: the increases in acceptance, through propagation from one person to another; and the decreases it undergoes if another discovery or invention having the same objective or meeting the same need is encountered. This encounter gives rise to a logical duel.   (Tarde 1890/1895, p. 167)

It must be remembered, of course, that Tarde was writing before the advent of the mass media and large-scale advertising, but the principle is clear. The 'logical duel' is said to take place first at the intra-personal level (in the sense of conflicts between ideas *within* an individual's mind), and then at wider social levels.

In sum, imitation and invention were for Tarde the keys for the understanding of social behaviour and thereby also of society. Imitation, he proposed, plays a role in society analogous to that of heredity in organisms and he regarded it as instinctive. In the final analysis he saw imitation as more fundamental than invention, for 'All inventions and all discoveries are thus compounds which have as their elements prior imitations.' Tarde's work, as will be shown, had a considerable influence on the then emerging American social psychology. While imitation in Tarde's sense has not featured much in twentieth-century social psychology, it has moved recently into the foreground in evolutionary psychology.

A radically different approach to social theory was developed by Durkheim, whose fame was more enduring than that of Tarde. British social anthropology was at one time dominated by Durkheimian analyses, and Piaget's studies of the emergence of moral concepts in children were in part designed to question Durkheim's thesis on morality. Durkheim in turn owed a considerable debt to the writings of Espinas on the social behaviour of animals, which reflect the impact of Darwinian theory.

Espinas on animal societies

Victor-Alfred Espinas (1844–1922) came from a provincial family of the minor bourgeoisie. After a local school he went to the prominent Lycée Louis-le-Grand in Paris, where his exceptional abilities were recognised. From there he enrolled at the Ecole Normale Supérieure where he was highly regarded by some professors, while he upset others by his adventurous ideas to the extent that he was not allowed to graduate for several years. From 1867 he spent a decade teaching at schools in various parts of France, spending his leisure time in observing animals and collecting notes on their behaviour. He was keenly interested in evolution and later entered into a correspondence with Darwin.

The turning-point in his career came with the outbreak of the Franco-Prussian war, during which he enlisted in the National Guard. It may have been the regimented military life, coupled with the trauma of the defeat, that led Espinas to speculate about the nature of human societies and their relation to the animal world. He read Spencer and, together with the prominent psychologist Théodule Ribot, translated Spencer's *Principles of psychology*. He was taken with Spencer's organic analogy, and made extensive use of it in the thesis which he submitted to the faculty of philosophy at the Sorbonne. His main contention that there is a relationship of continuity between animal and human societies was not well received. The examiners, much to Espinas's dismay, regarded it as dealing with comparative psychology; but what he had wanted was to demonstrate an approach linking biology with sociology rather than with the psychology of individuals. Eventually the work was published in 1877 under the title *Des sociétés animales* (Animal societies), and a second edition came out in 1878.

Espinas took the view not only that there is a continuity between animal and human societies, which is orthodox Darwinian doctrine, but that this also entails a collective, supra-individual consciousness. Referring to Comte's view of society as an 'immense organism', and what he called the complementary ideas of Spencer and Schäffle, Espinas suggested that they had not taken their arguments far enough. Biologists, he observed, have always perceived an affinity between organisms and societies, and between the social organisations of insects and humans. He gave numerous examples, citing for instance the great physiologist Claude Bernard (1813–78), whose organic metaphor closely paralleled that of Spencer, or Ernst Haeckel (1834–1919) who had written:

> The cells which compose a living organ can thus be compared to the citizens of a state among whom some fulfil one function, and others another one; this division of labour and the consequent organic perfection allow the state to accomplish certain tasks that would be impossible for isolated individuals.   (Cited in Espinas 1878, p. 93)

This kind of comparison, it may be noted, was frequent at that time and need not imply a collective mind of any sort. However, in the course of a lengthy discussion which does not lend itself to a succinct summary, Espinas made that jump. Just some of his arguments, many of which deal with animal societies, can be briefly illustrated. According to him, social relationships in animal as well as human societies pre-suppose representations, which imply thought, and this in turn implies consciousness.

Collective acts may become habitual, thereby no longer requiring awareness. Social acts in animals and humans are partly intentional and partly spontaneous, and the difference between these is only a matter of degree. Both animal and human collectivities 'form a single unit governed by the same laws that are those of biological evolution'. A society is not a mechanism, as had been suggested by some, but an organism; and the societies of the higher mammals are closely similar to those of 'the most degraded human societies' – both have a collective consciousness. This observation can be understood in the light of the then still common belief that the 'inferior races' are closer to apes than to civilised humans. At any rate, according to Espinas, every individual consciousness is part of a superior one. The conclusion is that 'a society is truly a living being, but distinguished from others in so far as it is above all constituted by a consciousness. A society is a living *consciousness*, or an organism of ideas' (Espinas 1878, p. 530). Elsewhere Espinas suggests that there is in all living beings an innate preference for being with other members of the same species. In higher ones this takes the form of sympathy, and like Adam Smith he maintained that beyond the family it is sympathy that holds a society together.

In common with other group-mind theorists, Espinas skirted around the issue of the precise nature of the unit to which he attributed conscious-ness, and provided no criteria whereby one could distinguish social units which share a consciousness from others that do not. A similar problem arises in the theories of Durkheim, who described the work of Espinas as fundamental for sociology.

In the course of developing his arguments, Espinas referred to observa-tions of animals which provided ammunition for crowd theorists. The example previously cited of the migrations of ants is a case in point. Crowd theorists maintained that the same process occurs in crowds: the leaders of crowds take the initiative for action and are followed by the rest.

Even more relevant is the account Espinas gave of the diffusion of emotion across a collectivity. He cited the case of wasps and hornets which, without any observable communication, collectively attack any intruder. He went so far as to state that it is a general law that the perception of an emotional state in others produces the same state in the mind of any observers. This holds not just for insects, but for higher mammals, including humans from children to adults. As far as higher mammals and humans are concerned, Espinas's hunch is to some extent supported by recent studies in neurophysiology. According to him, the intensity of such emotional contagion rises directly in proportion to the number of those present, and he even proposed a formula for quantifying emotional arousal. As examples of this process among humans, he cites the way theatre-goers are collectively moved, and how the audience of an orator can be carried away. This notion of 'emotional contagion' was crucial for crowd theorists, and owing to Espinas they were able to claim that it has profound biological roots. While such a claim is not completely unfounded, it was carried by them to excessive lengths.

Durkheim, Tarde's powerful rival

As already noted, Espinas also helped to inspire the work of Emile Durkheim (1858–1917), who continues to be held in high esteem as one of the outstanding figures of the social sciences. Apart from Espinas, Durkheim was also influenced by Comte and Spencer, and commented favourably on the work of Schäffle, indicating that he must have felt comfortable with the organic analogy. But he was not prepared to take it as far as had Spencer or Espinas, wishing to maintain a sharp distinction between biological organisms and societies.

Durkheim was born in Epinal (in Lorraine) into an orthodox Jewish family of modest means. His father was a rabbi, as were his grandfather and great-grandfather, so it is not surprising that he was expected to follow the family tradition. He studied for a while in a rabbinical school, but soon decided that it was not for him. None the less, he retained all his life a fascination for religion in general. His early background no doubt shaped his character, which was stern and puritanical, with a strong sense of duty. At the age of twelve he experienced the French defeat in the Franco-Prussian war, which may have contributed to his patriotism.

Durkheim moved to Paris, having been successful in gaining a place at the Ecole Normale Supérieure. During his three years there he encountered a number of other students destined to become famous, including Pierre Janet who became a leading French psychologist. It may have been their influence that led Durkheim finally to abandon Judaism. After graduating he was awarded a scholarship to visit German universities, and there he met Wilhelm Wundt, who was at that time preparing a book on ethics in which he anticipated a good deal of what was later to become his *Völkerpsychologie*. Durkheim was greatly impressed, though not wholly uncritical. On his return he was appointed to a teaching post at the University of Bordeaux, and in 1902 he was called to the Sorbonne in Paris, where he remained.

Durkheim's scientific sociology

His aim was to contribute to the establishment of such a sociology, and to carve out for it a specific realm, namely the 'social'. Society was for him a reality *sui generis*, over and above its constituent individuals. Just as the properties of a cell cannot be derived from those of the chemical elements composing it, so those of a society cannot be derived from individuals. Society is characterised by a *conscience collective* (collective consciousness) consisting of commonly held sets of ideas, beliefs, and values arising from past social interactions and forming a coherent system independent of individuals. As such, 'collective consciousness' is a social *fact*, having its own reality outside individual consciousness, and therefore capable of coercing individuals. He took over from Espinas, and considerably elaborated, the notion of 'collective representations', which specify the shared components of the *conscience collective*. He viewed collective representations as impinging on individuals, governing their thought, beliefs, and social behaviour. This formulation has had an enormous impact on the social sciences.

It was eagerly adopted by an older generation of social anthropologists – cynics might say as a valuable labour-saving device. This is because if 'society' imposes upon all of its members the same ideas, beliefs, and customs, then more or less any member of that society would be equally able to serve as an informant for eliciting the dominant values, beliefs, and customs characterising the society. This assumption of homogeneity has been shown to be unfounded (e.g. Wassmann 1995). On the other hand, Durkheim inspired Moscovici (1984) to produce an updated version which drops that assumption, and which as 'social representations' has become a flourishing field of research in – mainly European – current social psychology. Thereby Moscovici has created an approach to social psychology which is closer to sociology than to mainstream experimental social psychology, yet at the same time departed from Durkheim's view that most of psychology is an integral part of sociology. In order to appreciate this, it is necessary to understand Durkheim's conception of psychology.

Durkheim's postulate that there exists a supra-individual level of social reality, a kind of collective mind which almost exclusively determines social ideas, beliefs, and actions, left little room for psychology, confining it to dealing with purely individual functioning according to what he called 'organico-psychic' factors. Now it must be remembered that in Durkheim's time 'scientific' psychology was largely experimental and physiological, focused on individuals. Such social psychology as there was he characterised as being 'nothing but a word designating all kinds of vague and imprecise generalities, without any definite object' (Durkheim 1901/1947, pp. xviii–xix). Thus he virtually absorbed social aspects of psychology into sociology and, as will be shown later, there followed much discussion as to where exactly social psychology belonged.

It would be wrong to leave the impression that Durkheim was only a theorist who made a take-over bid for social psychology. In his classic empirical study of suicide (Durkheim 1897/1952) he followed the 'method of concomitant variations' advocated by Mill, and thus was probably the first to have applied what is now known as multivariate analysis. He noted that:

> there exists a multitude of social phenomena which occur throughout society, but which take on diverse forms according to geographical location, occupation, religion, etc. The kinds of social phenomena whose variations are determined in this way included for instance crime, suicide, birth rate, marriage rate, savings rate, etc.   (Durkheim 1901/1947, p. 133)

In contrast to Quetelet, who had treated many kinds of variations as accidental and focused mainly on regularities, Durkheim sought to explain differences causally. He interpreted variations in suicide rates in terms of his concept of *anomie*, i.e. becoming detached from the social bonds that hold society together and give meaning to life. The prevalence of *anomie* itself he saw as a function of the above-mentioned variables, though he also believed that the social circumstances of a whole society may incline it towards a particular level of suicide rates. This is a crude summary of a complex argument intended to be purely sociological. However, as Lukes (1973, p. 215) aptly commented, Durkheim was 'by implication proposing a social-psychological theory about the social conditions for individual psychological health'. While this is true, it must be remembered that Durkheim's message was also that 'each people has *collectively* an inclination of its own to suicide' (Durkheim 1897/1952, p. 305, my emphasis).

The radical manner in which Durkheim opposed any explanations of social facts in terms of individual psychology led to accusations of materialism, reductionism, and anti-psychological bias. He complained that his views had been misrepresented, and the revised edition of his book on suicide sought to refute such allegations:

> in separating social from individual life, we in no way contend that social life has nothing psychological about it. On the contrary, it is evident that it consists essentially of representations. Only collective representations are of an entirely different nature from individual ones. We see no objection to saying about sociology that it is a kind of psychology, as long as one takes care to add that social psychology has its own particular laws, which are not those of individual psychology.   (Durkheim 1897/1952, p. 352)

Thus Durkheim was prepared to accept that his sociology was a form of social psychology, since collective representations are mental in character.

However, for him these were fundamentally different from individual ones, in some sense existing over and above individual persons and governing their social behaviour. This resulted in a clash between his theoretical position and that of his contemporary, Gabriel Tarde.

> Let us go back to the elementary social pair ... of two persons ... of whom one acts mentally on the other. I maintain that the relationship between these two persons is the unique and necessary element of social life, and that it always consists at the outset of an imitation of the one by the other.   (Tarde 1898/1999, vol. 4, p. 59)

Such a view is the diametrical opposite to that of Durkheim, for whom social facts were collective in character, impinging upon individuals from an overarching set of collective representations. According to him, the aggregation and combination of individual minds gives rise to 'a psychic entity of a new type' and it is this entity that has to be studied. Consequently he laid down the famous rule that 'The determining cause of a social fact has to be sought among antecedent social facts and not in the states of the individual mind' (Durkheim 1901/1947, p. 109).

For about a decade Durkheim and Tarde conducted a sometimes rather ill-tempered debate, which turned on the fundamental question of how social phenomena should be approached. Prominent figures like Comte or Spencer had maintained a sharp dividing line between sociology and individual psychology. Others, like Herbart and most of his followers, postulated a parallel between individual psychology and the functioning of society. None of them, however, was much concerned with the principles governing the social behaviour of individuals, and this also applied to Wundt. It should also be noted that in Tarde's dispute with Durkheim the issue was not one of psychology versus sociology, since the boundaries were still fluid and Tarde regarded himself as a sociologist. Social psychology as such had not yet emerged as a distinct discipline, and was in due course to be claimed by both.

Hamon, an odd man out

Lastly, among the late nineteenth-century writers in France there was one who seems to have had little connection with his distinguished contemporaries and ploughed a lone furrow; but he had interesting ideas, that will be briefly outlined. Auguste Hamon (1862–1945) was a colourful figure in the positivist tradition, who regarded himself as a scientist. Politically he was on the extreme left, which led to encounters with the police. He published extensively, an important example being his *Psychology of the professional soldier: studies of social psychology* (1894). In it he analysed the effects of life in the professional army on the mentalities of both officers and the (oppressed) enlisted soldiers. According to him, ordinary soldiers acquire a 'slave mentality' of unquestioning obedience. Officers, used to being obeyed, fail to recognise the limits of their authority and behave in a manner that is effectively criminal. Lubek and Apfelbaum (1989), in an illuminating essay which throws a fascinating light on Hamon's colourful personality, suggest that he anticipated some modern ideas. His interpretation of the impact of military life resembles Goffman's analysis of 'total institutions' and Zimbardo's conclusions about the effects of anonymity and depersonalisation on behaviour. Moreover, Hamon's refusal to separate his scientific work from his political views makes him a forerunner of 'critical social psychology'. Hamon saw the 'sociological sciences' as the remedy for social ills, notably criminality, which was a salient preoccupation of the period.

It will be apparent from the above that in France the emergence of social-psychological ideas was fused with sociological ones, and both have to be seen against the background of radical social and political changes. As will be shown in the next chapter, the situation in Germany was rather different.

7   Germany: in the shadow of Wundt

During the second half of the nineteenth century Germany was the country in which the most rapid advances in psychology were made. One could cite a long list of distinguished names, among them Helmholtz, Weber, and Fechner, who laid the foundations of physiological psychology. Ebbinghaus, pioneer of the experimental study of memory, was inspired by Fechner. In a second-hand shop in Paris he came across a copy of Fechner's *Elements of psychophysics*, which gave him the idea of applying experimental methods to the 'higher mental processes', hitherto regarded as beyond the scope of experiment. The best-known name is no doubt that of Wundt, who came to divide psychology into an individual psychology that can be studied experimentally, and *Völkerpsychologie* dealing with the higher mental processes in their historical and cultural contexts. By the end of the century Wundt's laboratory had become the Mecca to which fledgling American psychologists flocked.

One of Wundt's colleagues, the historian Lamprecht, sought to use social psychology for a novel and supposedly scientific approach to history. The enthusiasm for an 'explanatory' and scientific psychology was not shared by Dilthey, a friend of Wundt, who thought that it impoverished the reality of human life. In this he was a forerunner of certain recent trends in psychology. Lastly, the insightful contributions of two other German scholars of a more sociological orientation will be briefly discussed.

The towering figure of Wundt

The first *Völkerpsychologie* of Lazarus and Steinthal was little known outside Germany, but with Wundt's international reputation the fame of his *Völkerpsychologie* spread. This is not to say that many people understood the term, let alone read all the massive ten volumes; but writers in other countries wanted to refer to it, and so the problem of a suitable translation of the term arose. In English this was done in a whole variety of ways, including 'ethnic psychology', which Wundt had specifically excluded and assigned to ethnology. The most common translation is 'folk psychology' – which is close, although 'folk' has the wrong

7   *Wilhelm Wundt (1832–1920)*

connotations. Next in frequency is 'social psychology', which Wundt himself had at one time considered using, but rejected as being too close to sociology. Hence it is perhaps not surprising that he is often regarded as *the* pioneer of social psychology, though such a notion is highly questionable, as will become apparent from the discussion of his ideas.

Wilhelm Wundt (1832–1920) was born in a small provincial town, the youngest son of a Protestant minister. In his autobiography Wundt claimed that the theme of *Völkerpsychologie* had run as a constant thread through most of his life, and traced this interest back to his youth:

> The earliest topic I had in mind was a general history of religions. Bringing out what the various religions had in common appeared to me a question well worth an effort of research. Later the other one that also came to mind was the general course of world history ... the idea underlying these fantastic projects was that of a comparative study of the mental products of man, in which the highest and most mysterious ones played a dominant role.   (Wundt 1920a, p. 199)

During the years 1845–51 he went to grammar school at Heidelberg, then enrolling as a medical student at Tübingen University. He became bored with that course, which consisted entirely of book-learning, and transferred after only a year to a chemistry course at Heidelberg University. There he undertook his first piece of laboratory research that was actually published; it dealt with the effect of salt deprivation on the chemical composition of his urine. Since there was then no physiological laboratory at Heidelberg, he carried out all kinds of procedures, including vivisections, in his mother's kitchen. In these difficult circumstances he undertook further research for his dissertation.

In the summer of 1856 he moved for a semester to Berlin University, where he did postgraduate work. He then obtained the post of laboratory assistant to Hermann von Helmholtz (1821–94), distinguished physiologist and physicist, in the newly established Physiological Institute at Heidelberg University. After nearly seven years with Helmholtz he became professor of inductive philosophy at Zurich University, then a relatively new and modest institution housed in an old building with only a few lecture rooms and no library. It was while in Zurich that Wundt began to lecture on *Völkerpsychologie*, and this may well have been connected with the fact that Lazarus had been appointed professor of *Völkerpsychologie* at Berne University in 1860.

Wundt's call to the chair of philosophy at Leipzig University came in 1875, in rather curious circumstances. Owing to internal disputes the chair had remained vacant for ten years, and the appointment of an experimentalist to the chair was a daring innovation. During the first few years Wundt's teaching was confined to philosophy and psychology, and experimental work did not begin until 1879.

During that period Wundt's views regarding the character of psychology underwent progressive modifications. Given his background, it is not surprising he treated it initially as closely allied with the natural sciences. But increasingly he shifted towards a position where it was also related to the *Geisteswissenschaften*, a term usually, though not altogether accurately, glossed as 'arts and humanities'. He was of course familiar with the writings of Herbart and the Herbartians, including the first version of *Völkerpsychologie*, and these undoubtedly influenced his thinking.

Early origins of his *Völkerpsychologie*

When early in his career Wundt was planning a book on experimental psychology, he decided to supplement this with a discussion of 'the mental products of the social life of peoples'. This became a substantial part of the second volume of his *Lectures on the human and animal mind* (1863), in which the main concern was with *Sitten*; this term covers both customs and morals, and for brevity will be referred to as 'customs'. Wundt pointed out that the development of customs cannot be studied in the consciousness of single individuals – one must look for it in the historical life of peoples. Yet as will be seen, in this and subsequent writings Wundt always returned to the individual as the primary focus.

Since he believed that uncivilised peoples were close to their origin and had undergone little development, he began with civilised peoples, among whom he regarded 'great men' – founders of religions and reformers – as having had a powerful influence, and where customs become embodied in laws. However, he later made the rather obscure statement that customs are not invented, neither by individuals nor simultaneously by the collectivity. Rather they are said to arise from an instinctive tendency, prompting everybody to adjust their behaviour to certain norms. Customs cannot be innate, since they change in the course of historical development and coincide with the beginning of society. But, Wundt went on to argue, what arises from the common life cannot be original, since the individual exists prior to society. As we now know, that was a fallacious argument.

Already in that early work Wundt explicitly dissociated himself from the approach to *Völkerpsychologie* adopted by Lazarus and Steinthal. While they, in the Romantic tradition, were pursuing the *Volksgeist* (spirit of the people), he was concerned with understanding individual consciousness and its laws. When it came to the discussion of what he called 'a-historical' peoples and the explanation of their backwardness, Wundt fell back on the old notion that extremes of temperature are usually unfavourable to moral culture. The influence of climate is readily explained: in the far north conditions are so harsh that the natural state of the peoples is one where the vices of crude gluttony and drunkenness prevail, coupled with sloth; and they live in dirty conditions. Much the same faults are attributed to people of the tropics, though for the opposite reason: nature provides everything in abundance, so they are shy of any effort. He also drew on the contemporary travel literature, presenting highly unflattering portraits. For instance, South Sea Islanders are said to appear mild and gentle at first, but closer acquaintance reveals traits of wild cruelty and beastly crudity: 'In the South Seas human flesh is a privilege of the well-to-do just as with us the daily roast in the kitchen.' It should be added that Wundt later felt embarrassed about what he had written along these lines, declaring it a 'youthful sin'.

Towards the final version

Twenty years later Wundt began lecturing regularly on *Völkerpsychologie* in Leipzig, and by then had arrived at a rather different formulation of the concept. The lectures were popular, attracting students from a wide range of disciplines. Not long after they had begun, a prominent philologist savagely attacked Lazarus and Steinthal's *Völkerpsychologie*, and by implication also that of Wundt. He maintained that all psychological processes take place within the individual mind, so that *Völkerpsychologie* is a false abstraction. Wundt was stung into a reply, in the course of which he distanced himself even further from Herbart as well as from Lazarus and Steinthal. He sought to make out the case for a *Völkerpsychologie* at least partially independent of individual psychology. Defining mind as the sum total of all inner experiences, he pointed out that many experiences are shared within a community, especially language and mythical representations. So why should there not be a kind of collective mind, and why should it not have the same reality as the individual one? In a later part of his defence he retreated from this full-blown 'group-mind' concept, stating that the key problem of psychology is that of mental development in the historical sense. In the course of that development individual and collective mutually affect each other, and the changes at the collective level are no less lawful than individual ones. Wundt's notion of the 'collective mind' was not very different from Durkheim's 'collective representations'. Yet although Wundt certainly knew Durkheim's work, he did not refer to it.

What aspects of the collective mind are then most amenable to study? Wundt excluded history, art, and sciences on the grounds that they are too specialised, so that three major areas remained, namely language, myth, and custom. It is these, he affirmed, which are mental products, in whose fashioning specific psychological laws are involved. It was to these three that the bulk of the monumental ten volumes of his *Völkerpsychologie*, which appeared between 1900 and 1920, were devoted.

The contents of these volumes are varied, and of course do not lend themselves to any summary. The first volume deals, among other things, with expressive movements and the language of gestures, considered by Wundt to be universal modes of communication which form the basis of all human social life. Although this function of language had long been recognised, the detailed analysis presented was novel and constituted an outstanding contribution. The volume on art includes many interesting observations on the development of drawing skills in children, and the psychology of child art in general. By contrast, in the volumes on myth and religion one finds numerous detailed accounts of myths, rituals, and religious forms, interpreted in a highly speculative manner. Even where the section sub-heading includes the word 'psychology' – as in 'The psychological development of the forms of prayer' – there is little in the text that would be seen as such nowadays.

There are two main reasons why it is difficult to illustrate Wundt's argumentation about the processes supposed to underlie the supernatural: he operated with concepts that are now unfamiliar, and his language is often well-nigh untranslatable. Moreover, a brief account has to omit the subtleties and is liable to make him appear simplistic, which he certainly was not. None the less, I shall try to convey at least the flavour of his arguments as well as of his style, beginning with a passage about the putative origins of funeral rites:

> The disposal of the corpse ... apparently originated initially from the fear of the demon into which the soul of the deceased is transformed, and which torments the survivors by nightly appearances or illness, or causes other kinds of trouble. As long as the corpse lies unburied, it also remains

> living in memory: it appears as a dream image or is viewed as a wander-
> ing ghost.   (Wundt 1910, vol. 4, part 1, p. 153)

Wundt then added that 'inner perceptions' lead at that stage of culture automatically to new forms of funeral rites, which on the one hand serve to subdue external powers and on the other re-establish the inner peace disturbed by associations. The beliefs described are drawn from various ethnographic reports, selectively cited in order to find support for the dubious assertion that 'fear' was the motive for burials. Yet at least the argument is clear, which is by no means always the case. Below is a passage about the alleged psychological basis of magic.

> Affect and will belong closely together in the psychological structure, in such a way that the occurrence of willing itself is everywhere only a manifestation of affect. The course of such an emotional episode is impeded by its own final effect, namely the act of will. The emotional excitement then fades away to a quieter mood. In this manner the magical act consists regularly of these two components. [Either strong emotions or striving for success in terms of wealth or love generate the idea of an external force.] Affect and will, these two firmly intermeshed basic motives, dominate all magical acts and ideas of magic.   (Wundt 1910, vol. 4, part 1, pp. 272–3)

If you, the reader, fail to understand this passage, you are not alone. It took me more than an hour to grasp the meaning of what were two long encapsulated sentences, and to break them down for (partial) translation. Perhaps this is one of the reasons why no one has so far ventured to translate all ten volumes. What is clear, however, is that 'magic' is viewed as the result of purely intra-psychic processes, a view totally unacceptable today (cf. Vyse 1997).

It is also curious that the massive ten-volume work contains few general theoretical statements about *Völkerpsychologie*. The most extensive treat-ment of its nature and method is to be found in the *Logik der Geisteswissenschaften* (1908). There it is formally defined:

> We shall call *Völkerpsychologie* the field of psychological investigations relating to those processes which, owing to their conditions of origin and development, are tied to mental collectivities. Since the individual and the community are interrelated concepts which presuppose each other, this name does not indicate a field whose content is totally separate from individual psychology; rather it indicates an abstraction which complements the study of individual psychology.   (Wundt 1908, vol. 3, p. 226)

This definition suggests that Wundt wrestled with the problem of the relationship between individual and *Völkerpsychologie*. The curious for-mulation about *Völkerpsychologie* being an 'abstraction' from individual psychology might be noted, since it is not evident what that could mean. The extensive passage cited below is even more obscure:

from the outset it is out of the question that one could come across any general psychological laws in *Völkerpsychologie* that are not already completely contained in the laws of individual consciousness.

In so far as *Völkerpsychologie* can find any psychological laws of independent content, these will always be *applications* of principles valid for individual psychology. But one can also assume that the conditions of mutual mental interaction will bring out new and special manifestations of the general psychic forces that could not be predicted from the mere knowledge of the properties of individual consciousness; these again will augment our insight into the functioning of individual mental life. Thus only individual psychology and *Völkerpsychologie* together constitute the whole of psychology ... just there, where the experimental method reaches its limit, the methods of *Völkerpsychologie* provide objective results ... As in the interpretation of its findings *Völkerpsychologie* must necessarily fall back on individual psychology; the latter is certainly the more general discipline, while the former has more of an applied character. But this relationship is here, as in many other cases, substantially modified by the following fact: in order to achieve a complete solution of its tasks, notably in the sphere of the higher mental functions, individual psychology already uses certain results of *Völkerpsychologie* in order to make inferences concerning the laws of individual consciousness.   (Wundt 1908, vol. 3, pp. 227–8; emphasis in original)

Wundt's dilemma, evident from these highly convoluted arguments, is that he wanted to assert at least two things that do not seem readily compatible: (a) individual and *Völkerpsychologie* are equally important and complementary parts of a unified whole; and (b) yet ultimately it is individual psychology that is more fundamental, and *Völkerpsychologie* somewhat derivative. Moreover, underlying Wundt's reasoning was his belief that neither higher mental processes, nor collective ones, are amenable to experiments and can only be tackled by the comparative method.

In the *Logik* Wundt also discussed in some detail the aims of *Völkerpsychologie* and its relation to other disciplines. Wundt believed that during the early periods of humanity psychological processes, both individual and collective, were relatively uniform. Under the influence of changing conditions, and of particular forceful personalities that began to emerge, a progressive differentiation set in. Consequently collective phenomena such as art and religion began to take on a variety of distinctive forms. Once that has happened it is no longer the variable superficial aspects, but rather the underlying, most general mental content that reveals the universal *völkerpsychologische* (adjective) determinants. The task of *Völkerpsychologie* would then be that of teasing out these common determinants (by which he may have meant something like what we call the higher mental processes) from historical records and ethnographic reports.

History, by contrast, is concerned with understanding singular events, and for this purpose it has recourse to psychology as an aid to the interpretation of historical phenomena. Yet according to Wundt,

Völkerpsychologie cannot fulfil that purpose; only individual psychology, which deals with the actions of particular persons, can do so. He saw *Völkerpsychologie* as a fundamental body of general theory which would serve as a guide for the *Geisteswissenschaften*, comparing it with the 'causal science of mechanics' in relation to the natural sciences. This was an aim that was not, and could not have been, achieved. As regards the other purpose, namely to advance an understanding of higher mental processes, Wundt's scepticism has turned out to be unjustified and they have been extensively studied by means of experimental methods.

The corpus of Wundtian theories was transmitted to American psychology by Titchener, who was not greatly interested in *Völkerpsychologie* and perhaps regarded it as a kind of aberration. Hence little attention was paid to it outside Germany, and even there it was discussed only for little more than a decade after Wundt's death. It was rediscovered during the latter part of the twentieth century, and was then sometimes proclaimed as having been the origin of social psychology. From the preceding sketch it should be clear that such a claim is unfounded. Wundt's ideas bore little if any resemblance to what has become social psychology, nor were they even mentioned by the early social psychologists. On the positive side, his contention that beliefs, norms, customs, and so on, have been shaped by social interactions over historical time was an important and novel idea. But he never moved beyond this very general statement to consider the nature of such interactions. One is therefore led to wonder how Wundt came to be seen as the father-figure not only of experimental psychology, where such an acclaim is fully merited, but also of social psychology. It probably had something to with the fact, noted above, that *Völkerpsychologie* was often translated as 'social psychology'.

Lamprecht's 'social psyche'

Wundt's suggestion about the value of psychology for history, an issue much debated at the time, was taken up seriously by his historian colleague Lamprecht, who gave Wundt's approach a positivist twist. The period around the end of the nineteenth century saw something of a turmoil among German historians who were debating what their aims and methods should be, an episode known as the *Methodenstreit* (quarrel over methods). In that context the possible role of psychology as an aid for historical studies was discussed, and this in turn entailed the question whether or not psychology is a natural science. In Dilthey's view – about whom more shortly – much of psychology is, or should be, a *Geisteswissenschaft* or humane discipline, while Ebbinghaus strongly argued that it is a science.

The dominant trend among traditional historians at that time was to see their subject as a descriptive and interpretative/hermeneutic one, concerned with the actions of particular 'heroic' figures. Supporters of this kind of conception of history felt that a scientific psychology was of little use to them. By contrast, Lamprecht's ambition was to create a scientific approach to history, with social psychology (he actually used the term) as the chief tool. This did not endear him to his elders, especially as he was rather vain and arrogant.

Karl Lamprecht (1856–1915) studied medieval history at Göttingen (where he met Waitz), and later was also a student at the University of Leipzig, where he first encountered Wundt as his examiner in philosophy. In 1878 Lamprecht left Leipzig, but he returned there in 1891 to take up a post, which made him a younger colleague of Wundt. Both men were at that time embattled, which drew them together. Wundt's immense reputation received a jolt when two of his most outstanding students, Oswald Külpe and Hugo Münsterberg, left to take up critical positions concerning some of Wundt's main teachings, and were joined by Ebbinghaus in the claim that the causes of all mental phenomena are physiological.

Lamprecht's ambition to make history scientific resulted in his being branded a materialist, then a grave accusation. It was not a reproach that could possibly have been addressed to Wundt, and so a wish to repudiate the label may have been a factor in Lamprecht's adoption of many elements of Wundt's *Völkerpsychologie*; but he used them in a less coherent and far more deterministic manner. In a provocative article signalling his conversion (Lamprecht 1896/7), he contended that psychology is central to the study of history because it is concerned with psychic causality and the laws of mental processes which drive historical changes.

In the years that followed he elaborated these views in typically dogmatic fashion. Thus in a book on historical method (Lamprecht 1900) he maintained that the *Geisteswissenschaften* deal in the same way with mental events as the *Naturwissenschaften* (natural sciences) deal with physical ones. Similarly, following Wundt, he proposed that 'an inductive psychology has to be the basic science of mental phenomena just as mechanics is for the physical ones'. According to him, historical phases and events are essentially of a psychic nature, so that any cultural stage is paralleled by a collective psychic state. This he called a diapason, characterising any given period and pervading all mental functioning described as 'socio-psychic', and thereby also all activities. Lamprecht sought to demonstrate that cultural stages succeed each other in a definite order, displaying increasing differentiation in a manner reminiscent of Herbert Spencer's social evolutionary scheme. Each period has what he called a '*soziale Psyche*', dominated by specific factors such as religion or individualism. Transitions from one stage to another arise from increasing disequilibrium of psychological functioning through new stimuli, increasing uncertainty of feeling states, until a new 'dominant' emerges. Then the 'socio-psychic mechanism' becomes stabilised again.

Later in his career Lamprecht cast around for some way of validating his lofty ideas empirically, and thought that he had found it in child psychology, considered in the light of the 'biogenetic principle'. As already mentioned, this notion stemmed from the work of the German naturalist Ernst Haeckel, who had put forward the so-called 'biogenetic law' which states that ontogeny, in the sense of the individual's embryological development, is a concise and compressed recapitulation of phylogeny. Lamprecht assumed that this holds not merely for embryology but also for post-natal development; and he wrote with complete confidence:

> [that] one will be able to establish a sequence of stages of psychogenetic development valid for children all over the world; as regards the higher of these stages, it will be possible to order the character of the known phylogenetic, and that means cultural, stages of development; this will be done to the extent that one can allocate ethnographic material and folklore to a sequence of relative stages of development.   (Lamprecht 1912, p. 137)

He conceived the idea that this could be done by making use of drawings. At that time there was considerable interest in the development of drawing skills among children; and ethnographers frequently put a pencil into hands that had never held one. Lamprecht argued as follows: each stage of culture is characterised by a pervasive mental diapason, hence any psychological measure should be as good as any other. Given, moreover, the alleged parallels between individual and cultural stages of development, he believed that by comparing the drawings of 'primitives' and children, one could determine the evolutionary stage the former had reached. It was an ingenious though of course misguided method (cf. Jahoda 1991).

Lamprecht was an admirer of Darwin and came to view biology as the model for a scientific history, which led him to refer to 'the biology of the historical mental life'. Lastly it should be mentioned that the old analogy between individual and collectivity was taken for granted when he proposed that the course of historical development 'resembles the course of the psychic mechanisms of the single individual since the socio-psychical laws, as is well known [sic], are nothing other than applications of lawful regularities based on individual psychology'. It was a principle he believed Wundt to have enunciated, though it has been explained above that Wundt's position was less straightforward. In any case, Lamprecht advocated a *Sozialpsychologie* as a key tool for understanding historical changes.

Generally, Lamprecht's grand theories have not stood the test of time, but his idea of a relationship between history and social psychology did find successors. The two founders of the French historical school of the *Annales*, Lucien Febvre and Marc Bloch, were both familiar with Lamprecht's work, agreeing with him that historical periods are characterised by particular 'mentalities'. For more recent discussions of such issues see Gergen and Gergen (1984).

While Lamprecht's ideas about a social psychology were rather vague and confused, in at least one respect he was later vindicated as against his numerous critics among historians. His rejection of an exclusive focus on personalities, in favour of a concern with prevailing social and economic conditions, in due course won the day. His social psychology has lapsed into well-deserved oblivion.

Dilthey: against the tide

The latter part of the nineteenth century is generally viewed as the beginning of psychology's establishment as an empirical science and the gradual, often reluctant, wider acceptance of that claim. Dilthey was initially among the first of those who afforded such recognition of the subject as a science. Yet later he became convinced that this is true only of some psychology, and perhaps not of the most important kind. Wundt, who had formulated his *Völkerpsychologie* in order to overcome the limitations of a purely experimental/physiological approach, was sympathetic, but most others were not. They wanted psychology to be seen as a 'hard' science, as did Scripture, one of Wundt's American students, who proposed that the 'new psychology' should be modelled on physics. Hence the stance adopted by Dilthey in his mature years was not popular among contemporary psychologists.

The gradual move away from empiricism

Wilhelm Dilthey (1833–1911) was born in the small town of Biebrich am Rhein. His father and grandfather were somewhat unconventional Calvinist pastors, and he was expected to follow them. Accordingly, he enrolled as a theology student at the universities of Heidelberg and then Berlin. He studied philology under Jakob Grimm and his interests widened in the direction of the methods of humanistic disciplines. He found much of the teaching of theology arid and pedantic, which led him to abandon formal theological studies. When Dilthey encountered the work of Friedrich Schleiermacher, theologian and philosopher who developed hermeneutics, he became fascinated by Schleiermacher's thought, which remained a prominent influence for the rest of his life.

While in Berlin he met Lazarus, founder of the first version of *Völkerpsychologie*, and began to work with him at the time when the seminal issue of the journal outlining the project appeared. His initial enthusiasm was subsequently tempered by doubts about the speculative nature and diffuseness of the venture. Attracted by the more concrete empiricism emanating from France and Britain, Dilthey determined to acquaint himself with the natural sciences. He became a pupil of Helmholtz, studied Fechner's *Psychophysics*, and attended lectures and laboratory courses in physiology in Basle. It is important to know that when he came to reject the natural sciences as the main model for psychology, he did not do so as an ignorant and prejudiced 'arts' man. Already during his earlier years he had read the writings of positivists like Comte and Spencer, and later Schäffle. He particularly admired J. S. Mill's analysis of the methods of the 'moral sciences', although he subsequently viewed it more critically. His immense erudition impressed William James when he met Dilthey in Berlin, though the fastidious James was taken aback by his somewhat unusual attire and behaviour at table – Dilthey was a dedicated scholar who cared little about externals.

During the 1860s he increasingly focused on psychology, and thereafter never abandoned the belief that it had a crucial role to play in the *Geisteswissenschaften* (humanities), though he changed his mind about the kind of psychology that was needed. When delivering his inaugural address in Basle in 1867 he had still maintained that 'It is necessary to know the laws which rule social, intellectual, and moral phenomena.' By 1882, when he succeeded to Lotze's chair in Berlin, he had turned away from positivism and empiricism.

Dilthey's stance in later life

Throughout his career Dilthey was concerned with the nature and aims of psychology. The position he had reached in his mature years is epitomised in his *Ideas concerning a descriptive and analytical psychology* (Dilthey 1894/1964, vol. 5). At the time there were those, like Ebbinghaus, who contended that psychology is a natural-science discipline and nothing else. There were also still philosophical idealists who denied the possibility of any psychology, since they believed the 'soul' to be beyond the reach of systematic study. Dilthey avoided both these extreme positions, proposing that there are two distinct aspects of the subject. One is the empiricist approach, essentially concerned with hypothesis testing by means of experiments. Dilthey accepted this as entirely valid, calling it 'explanatory psychology', which considers mental processes as consisting of causal chains. However, he pointed out some important limitations of such a conception. First, it is too atomistic, dividing consciousness into elementary sensations and feelings (taken to be manifestations of underlying physiological processes) in order to make it amenable to rigorous study. This ignores the fact that the acting self has a functional unity which eludes any approach that concentrates merely on the constituent parts. Moreover, it cannot tell us anything about the higher mental processes.

The latter is no longer valid, but the same cannot be said of the other objection, namely psychology's emphasis on the self-contained individual. This is a similar point, it may be mentioned in passing, as that still made at present by critics of the largely intra-individual focus of experimental social psychology. Dilthey characterised the notion that humans have a permanent nature which existed already prior to history and society – prevalent in much of Enlightenment thought – as a fiction. He had gained that conviction early on, when still involved with the *Völkerpsychologie* of Lazarus and Steinthal and the then emerging anthropology. At that time he had cited with approval Bastian's optimistic forecast that psychology would be the science of the future, concerned with humankind as a whole and dealing with individuals only within this broad context. In spite of later disappointments, Dilthey continued to hold on to his grand vision of a new kind of psychology as the key discipline for all humane studies. For this purpose he proposed a 'descriptive and analytical psychology', based on a recognition of the culture-historically contingent nature of humans. He singled out Waitz (cf. chapter 3) as one of his predecessors in this respect, and regarded Waitz's monumental *Anthropology of primitive peoples* as a partial realisation of his plan for a descriptive psychology.

The cornerstone of that psychology is the concept of *Erlebnis*, which may be glossed as 'lived experience', and constitutes a person's response to a situation. Descriptive psychology is in essence the systematic elaboration of common experience, irreducible to such entities as sensations. This is not to say that one cannot distinguish between various cognitive or affective functions, provided that they are analysed within the context of a unitary structural system. Dilthey's views in some respects resemble those of Giambattista Vico (1668–1744), who in a famous passage had enunciated the

> truth beyond all question: that the world of civil society has certainly been made by men, and that its principles are therefore to be found within the modifications of our own human mind. Whoever reflects on this cannot but marvel that the philosophers should have bent all their energies to the study of the world of nature, which, since God made it, he alone knows; and that they should have neglected the study of the world of nations, or civil world, which, since men had made it, men could come to know.   (Vico 1744/1948, paragraph 331)

In the same spirit Dilthey drew a fundamental distinction between *explanations* of physical phenomena and *understanding* ourselves and our fellows. In the former case we can establish causal relationships, but can never get at the underlying reality. Personal experience *is* its own reality, and we cannot get beyond it. In sum, as Dilthey has it, we *explain* nature but *understand* psychic life. The term 'understand' does not correspond exactly to the concept of *Verstehen*, central to Dilthey's theory. *Verstehen* refers not to comprehension in general, but to a particular kind of understanding relating primarily to human behaviour; hence the German word will be retained. Contrary to what has sometimes been suggested, it refers not to a method, but to a specifically human capacity. It was, for Dilthey, not merely intuitive, but a cognitive process dependent upon representations of mental content. Such representations may be at any level of abstraction, but they are ultimately anchored in the structure of experience.

Closely related to *Verstehen*, in the sense that it is the object of *Verstehen*, is 'meaning' (*Bedeutung*). This refers not only, or even primarily, to the apprehension of an expression, or of verbal or non-verbal symbols, but to a grasp of the significance of the relationships between life-events. Thus any particular experience becomes intelligible within that wider context of organisational unity. Dilthey regarded *Verstehen* as a kind of induction, albeit different from the usual sense of the term whereby a set of particular instances are generalised into a law. Instead, the instances lead to the recognition of a structure, a system of order in which the parts make up a unified whole. This is what he meant by saying that a descriptive psychology must be analytical.

Dilthey's position was violently attacked by Hermann Ebbinghaus (1850–1909), spokesman for 'scientific' psychology whose studies of memory have become a classic. He accused Dilthey of being inadequately informed about the 'new' psychology and of setting up straw men in order to knock them down. Dilthey's views, he contended, were nothing more than a mixture of vague generalities and trivia. In fact he had misunderstood Dilthey as dismissing all scientific psychology, which was certainly not the case.

Other critics were more moderate and made some telling points. In response to such criticism, Dilthey came to acknowledge that his original starting point, the description of inner experience, is problematic. There can be no pure, value-free, objective description based on introspection. This led him to place increasing stress on *hermeneutics* as a method for approaching the socio-cultural products of the human mind, an approach he owed to Schleiermacher. Hermeneutics began as an ancient method of interpreting (usually theological) texts, which had been widened by Schleiermacher into a more general theory of *Verstehen*. Hermeneutics is inevitably a circular process, as may be illustrated by the example of understanding a sentence. In order to grasp the meaning of a sentence, one must understand the meaning of the words composing it; but these words in isolation can have different meanings, depending upon the context. This is particularly clear when it comes to translation. Thus the German word *Geist* can mean spirit, mind, intellect, or in the plural ghosts, depending on the context. One could therefore say that the whole makes no sense without the parts, nor the parts without the whole. The same applies, for instance, to the interpretation of a work of literature, or to what influenced the thinking of its author. Logically it would seem that we must remain imprisoned for ever within the hermeneutic circle. In practice we break through it by moving alternatively from the parts to the whole and back again.

While hermeneutics is to some extent formalised into rules, Dilthey held that it also involves a certain intuitive element that contributes to

Verstehen; it allows us to gain insight not merely into individual minds, but into the nature of the human mind in general, and its historical transformations. I might here add a brief comment about later 'critical theorists' who carried Dilthey's ideas much further in an anti-positivist direction. Some, like Habermas, argue that Dilthey's account of hermeneutics is itself tainted by the empiricist influences to which he had been exposed. Thus the notion that hermeneutic interpretation can obtain direct access to the state of mind of the text's originator is fallacious: 'Hermeneutic knowledge is always mediated through [this] pre-understanding, which is derived from the interpreter's initial situation' (Habermas 1972, p. 310). This initial situation is a function of socio-historical background; therefore hermeneutics cannot achieve 'objective' knowledge, as Dilthey had erroneously supposed. While such a critique seems pertinent, it certainly does not mean that Dilthey remained unaware of the importance of socio-historical factors.

Poets like Goethe or novelists like Dickens are cited by Dilthey as more realistic when they locate their figures in concrete historical settings, than those psychologists who parade an abstract individual as a universal trans-historical type. They fail to appreciate that the life of an individual is tied to her or his social relationships within a given historical period.

Without going as far as Lamprecht, Dilthey agreed that there is a certain uniformity in the mental characteristics of people living in the same period – it being tacitly taken for granted that it is also the same place. Moreover, and here the preconceptions of Dilthey's own time show through, it is also a *civilised* place. Variations in character and mentality are also considered, and viewed as the result of differences in nationality, social class, sex, and so on. The comments on what we would call differences of gender are prefaced by a proviso:

> in our culture ... the fundamental [gender] difference is that women's feelings and thoughts are produced by the closely experienced relation to the family ... while the more objective and comprehensive, but also less immediate and deeply felt life of the man results from his occupational training.   (Dilthey 1894/1964, vol. 5, p. 236)

Such a division between genders was not taken as immutable, since Dilthey noted that the extent to which such differences are innate or due to upbringing and education remains an open question.

Generally, Dilthey advocated a 'developmental' approach, by which he meant *historical* development that created certain social conditions, and these in turn shape the broad structure of personalities. Variations are due to the particular socio-cultural conditions to which people are exposed, and so he treated humans as persons in a socio-historical setting. As such, he had something in common with modern supporters of 'critical', 'discursive', or 'constructionist' social psychology, who reject the traditional scientific ethos. The basic position most of them share (though varying widely in other respects) may be illustrated by a passage from Gergen, one of the original leaders of the secession:

> My attempt at that point (Gergen 1973) was to undermine the presumption that social psychology was a cumulative science, moving steadily towards the establishment of ahistorical truths, and to replace such an orientation with historically embedded and ideologically sensitive forms of inquiry.   (Gergen 2001, p. 51)

I have not come across any reference to Dilthey in the writings of 'critical' psychologists, presumably because he was not radical enough and accepted the legitimacy of 'scientific' psychology. However, a number of them do mention Vico (e.g. Ibanez and Iniguez 1997), who had drawn a sharp distinction between 'nature' and the human mind.

Two other visions of social psychology

The period also saw two brilliant scholarly contributions, one well known and the other largely forgotten. The first was by Georg Simmel (1858–1918), a highly original sociologist and social philosopher. He shared Dilthey's views on the methodological differences between *Geisteswissenschaften* and *Naturwissenschaften* and developed his own approach to the problems of interpretation in the social sciences. His aim was to break away altogether from the positivist and organicist theories of Comte and Spencer and to analyse various forms of social interaction. In a famous work praised by George Herbert Mead he showed how in metropolitan society numerous social relations are mediated by money (Simmel 1900/1978), and more specifically he discussed the role of money in the relations between the sexes (Simmel 1898). He was also the first to have introduced the concept of 'modernity', and wrote extensively about the dynamic properties of social groups (e.g. Simmel 1897–9). Simmel was of course concerned with 'natural' groups as distinct from experimental ones, which had not yet come into existence. He was interested in social psychology and discussed it on several occasions, as when he published a piece with the title 'On the nature of social psychology' (Simmel 1908). Some of his writings were translated and published in the United States, where they proved influential. The significant contribution of Simmel to the development of social psychology seldom receives sufficient attention, though he is of course recognised as a pioneer of sociology.

The other notable scholar was Franz Eulenburg, who was familiar with the work of Simmel; for instance he reviewed *The philosophy of money*. It is likely that he developed an interest in social groups from reading

Simmel. In his inaugural lecture at the University of Leipzig (1900), Eulenburg presented a clear and comprehensive exposition of what he called the possibility and the tasks of a social psychology. It begins with a concise historical sketch up to and including preliminary sketches of Wundt's *Völkerpsychologie*, discussing its limitations. In this connection he pointed out that the *Volk* (people) is only one of many social categories, and that Wundt had nothing to say about the manifold mental processes within them. Hence Eulenburg raised the question whether it would not be time to substitute something new and different in this sphere. He noted that '*Volk*' is essentially a historical category, and psychic processes mainly take place within smaller units and then spread through imitation, a notion he no doubt borrowed from Tarde. When one considers such concepts as 'authority', 'honour', 'property', and so on, they all depend on mutual relations between two or more persons. If we call people so related 'social groups', then the mental processes occurring within such groups may be termed 'social-psychological'. He then went on to offer a more formal definition: 'Social psychology comprises those mental processes that are conditioned by *the presence of a social group*, i.e. a plurality of individuals who exert mutual effects on each other' (Eulenburg 1900, p. 212; my emphasis). This contrasts with those usual in texts that follow Gordon Allport's (1954a, p. 5) classical definition where the stress is on the *individual*.

Eulenburg was also one of the very few at that time who considered methods, and put forward hypotheses that might be tested. Thus he proposed that there would be an inverse relationship between the size of a social group and the number of 'psychic elements' its members are likely to have in common. Admittedly, he presented only a schematic table to illustrate this idea. However, regarding methods he suggested the use of statistics for the study of social representations (*Socialvorstellungen*), giving a concrete example of comparisons between countries on the basis of statistics of types of literary output – possibly inspired by Quetelet. He grouped these into several categories of literary productions: theology and education, science, practical guides, and finally entertainment. Using data available for the Austro-Hungarian empire, he demonstrated that the proportions of these categories varied according to the main languages used within the regions of the empire. In sum, Eulenburg drew on a number of then available sources, such as Simmel's writings to which he referred, in order to construct a vision of a social psychology that came rather closer to what social psychology was eventually to become than the speculations of most of his contemporaries.

8 America: Darwinian social psychology crosses the Atlantic

During the last decade or so of the nineteenth century many psychologists had come under the influence of evolutionary theory. This was true of Wundt, and of the growing number of Americans who came to sit at his feet. William James, the famous pioneer of American psychology, was a contemporary of Wundt, and he also shaped his great work on evolutionary principles. Baldwin not merely embraced evolution, but made a significant contribution to its theory; unfortunately his brilliant career in the United States was cut short by an indiscretion.

George Herbert Mead, whose work was founded on both Wundt and Darwin, came to be published only posthumously in 1934. But his fundamental ideas had been formulated long before in lectures and papers. He would probably have deplored the fact that his message came to be misinterpreted, thereby making him an apostle of sociological social psychology in the twentieth century. In this connection it is important to understand that during the early period there was no clear distinction between these two versions of social psychology, and Baldwin, for instance, embraced both quite indiscriminately. Several sociologists at that time introduced important new concepts that were subsequently incorporated in 'psychological' social psychology. Finally it should be explained that in American as well as European writings of the period there was considerable uncertainty concerning to which discipline social psychology properly belonged.

William James and the 'social self'

William James (1842–1910) began by studying medicine at Harvard and interrupted his study to accompany Louis Agassiz, a famous naturalist but also a creationist and opponent of Darwin, on an expedition to South America. He later spent a year in Germany with Helmholtz and broke down with a depression that plagued him for much of his early life. According to R. J. Richards (1987), it was his reading of Darwin's *Descent of man* that marked his return to health. In 1885 he became professor of philosophy at Harvard and embraced the pragmatism of Charles Pierce. It is an approach which regards the meaning and truth of an idea to be a function of its practical result. In other words, it favours empiricism and is critical of any absolutism – all truths are provisional, and subject to revision. In 1889 James changed the title of his chair to psychology, and a year later he published his renowned *Principles of psychology*.

The passages most relevant in the present context are those dealing with what he called the 'social self', which he defined as 'the recognition [a man] gets from his mates'. He went on to say that *'a man has as many social selves as there are individuals who recognize him* and carry an image of him in their mind' (James 1891, vol. 1, pp. 293–4, emphasis in original). This general topic is developed at considerable length, and he commented that our interest in our selves must have come about by 'the survival of the fittest'. Later he returned to the social theme: 'I should not be extant now had I not become sensitive to looks of approval or disapproval on the faces among which my life is cast.' He suggested that the development of this sensitivity is the result of natural selection. These formulations are very much in the spirit of Adam Smith, apart of course from the evolutionary aspects. Yet the only reference given in a footnote is not to Smith but to John Locke. It has also been suggested that James's extensive and subtle disquisition on the self probably owed something to his brother Henry James, the novelist.

In the last chapter of the second volume of the *Principles* James reviewed those features of the mind that he regarded as being the products of evolution. These included instincts, of which he detailed more than thirty.

The rise and fall of Baldwin

While several of the characters who make their appearance in these pages have been largely, and sometimes undeservedly, forgotten, this is not the case with Baldwin. Although his fame was eclipsed for a period as a consequence of his premature departure from the academic scene, his valuable contributions have been recognised anew, especially with the recent advent of evolutionary psychology. Before that, he influenced both the prominent Francophone psychologists Pierre Janet and Jean Piaget.

James Mark Baldwin (1861–1934) initially intended to study for the ministry, but was inspired while at Princeton by the courses in psychology he attended in the 1880s. While most American colleges then taught an old-fashioned kind of 'rational' (i.e. metaphysical) psychology, he was exposed to the Wundtian conception of an empirical and scientific psychology, as well as to Darwinian evolutionary theory. His teacher was James McCosh, a Scot who managed to combine his strict Presbyterian faith with one in science, and who was familiar with the writings of Spencer and Darwin. At the end of his undergraduate studies Baldwin won a travelling fellowship to Germany, which he spent, like many other Americans, mainly at Wundt's

8   *James Mark Baldwin (1861–1934)*

laboratory in Leipzig. On his return he completed a PhD dissertation and was for some four years an instructor at minor theological colleges, using this time to translate a book by the great French psychologist Théodule Ribot and to write several psychological articles.

These contributions received sufficient acclaim to win him a position at Toronto, where he established what he himself claimed as 'the first psychological laboratory in the British empire'. Unfortunately his appointment was in the philosophy department, as was common at the time. Many of his colleagues were of an idealist persuasion and objected to what they regarded as his 'materialistic' view of mental life. Hence he was no doubt relieved when he was offered a post at Princeton, where he went in 1893 and remained for a decade. There he published in 1895 *Mental development in the child and the race*, in which he expounded the 'genetic' (corresponding broadly to our 'developmental') psychology that became his hallmark. The theoretical and philosophical foundations of his approach are expounded in his *Thought and things* (Baldwin 1906–11) and *Genetic theory of reality* (Baldwin 1915). These works later inspired Piaget's early studies, in which Baldwin is constantly cited.

Baldwin on social development

In the preface to his 1895 book Baldwin acknowledged that he had drawn on the ideas of Spencer, notably Spencer's views on development, both individual and that of the species as a whole. Likewise, Baldwin adopted Spencer's notion of 'adaptation' to both the social and the natural environment. He was rather less forthcoming in acknowledging his intellectual debt to Tarde as regards the role of imitation, though he used that concept in a rather different way. While Tarde had maintained that Darwin's theory was not relevant for social life, Baldwin elaborated an evolutionary biopsychology of individual and social development. He also introduced a relatively new empirical approach, namely the systematic observation of his children. However, unlike Piaget after him, Baldwin rarely reported his observations directly, confining himself to the theoretical inferences drawn from them, which makes his text rather dry. An exception will be cited later. Baldwin's aim was to describe the development of the child from the earliest period of mere 'blank sensations' and feelings of pleasure or pain to that of a social and reflective person.

As implied in the title ('the child and the race', where by 'race' he meant 'the human race'), Baldwin also wanted to show that there is a parallel between the stages of development of individual children, and those of the global historical changes in humanity at large. This notion stemmed from the so-called 'biogenetic law' already mentioned (p. 130). Better known as 'recapitulation theory' in psychology when extrapolated to postnatal development, it was popularised by Stanley Hall. Now discredited in that form, it will not be further considered, and the focus will be on Baldwin's interpretations of child development.

He distinguished several stages, a concept taken over from him by Piaget. The first is the purely 'affective' or inchoate, about which there was, for him, little to say. It should be interjected here that modern developmental psychology has now provided ample evidence that even the youngest infant cannot be described as 'inchoate'. The other stages are as follows:

projective: the infant is conscious of others but not of herself; people are objects;
subjective: also conscious of herself; people are special objects, active but arbitrary;
ejective: consciousness of other persons as similar to herself; they are 'social fellows'.

Such labels of course tell us little, and the question is how the movement through the stages proceeds. Baldwin's answer was that it happens as a result of imitation, triggered initially by physiological maturation:

> when the organism is ripe, by reason of cerebral development, for the enlargement of its active range by new accommodations, then he begins to be dissatisfied with 'projects', with contemplation, and starts on his career of imitation. And of course he imitates persons. Persons have become, by all his business with them and theirs with him, his interesting objects, the source of his weal or woe, his uncertain factors.   (Baldwin 1895, p. 336)

So far it is merely 'simple' imitation, but this process results in the crystallisation of a subjective self and the beginnings of 'persistent imitation' produced by an effort of will, and this in turn creates an awareness of other persons as similarly subjective selves: 'Both *ego* and *alter* are thus essentially social; each is a *socius*, and each is an imitative creation.' In the course of development one thus finds a range of increasingly complex forms of imitation, from crude 'subcortical' ones to those requiring intricate cognitive preparations. Concluding, he found imitation to be 'a true instinct, a race habit'.

Baldwin also saw suggestion, closely linked with imitation, as an important feature of development in which he again discerned three stages. The earliest, which he called 'physiological suggestion', related to specific sensory states, which is almost like a form of conditioning. For instance, perception of the cot comes to be associated with habits, i.e. falling asleep in this case; then repetition of the perception would tend to elicit the corresponding behaviour. This happens without any awareness on the part of the child, while in the next stage, that of 'sensori-motor suggestion', the child is conscious of the link. Lastly there is 'ideo-motor suggestion', of which there are different types, a major one being 'imitative suggestion'. This may be simple, as when a model is roughly imitated without any attempt to improve, e.g. copying a model to build a block tower, but being unconcerned whether or not it collapses. In *persisting* imitation the child displays an intention to emulate the model, according to Baldwin a key transition. A somewhat similar scheme was later put forward by Piaget, though he more systematically related the later stages of imitation to symbol formation (cf. Piaget 1950). In later social psychology Albert Bandura (e.g. 1965) also discussed children's imitation of a model.

Baldwin had a section entitled 'How to observe children's imitations' in which he included an example of his observations of the pretend-play of his daughters; part of this is reproduced below.

> On May 2, I was sitting on the porch alone with the two children . . . aged respectively four and a half and two and a half years. Helen, the elder, told Elizabeth that she was her little baby; that is Helen became 'mama'

and Elizabeth 'baby'. The younger responded by calling her sister 'mama' and the play began.

'You have been asleep, baby. Now it is time to get up' said mama. Baby rose from the floor, – first falling down in order to rise, – was seized upon by 'mama', taken to the railing to an imaginary wash-stand, and her face washed by rubbing. Her articles of clothing were then named in imagination, and put on, one by one, in the most detailed and interesting fashion. During all this 'mama' kept up a stream of baby talk to her infant.   (Baldwin 1895, p. 362)

The whole episode is described in close detail for another two pages. Baldwin then went on to explain that these were merely the raw facts, which could only be interpreted in the light of relevant background information about the rest of the family. He said that he was able to recognise the phrases used by the children, where they came from, and to what extent meanings had been modified in the play context, a process he called 'social heredity'. He then went on to list the psychological infer-ences that could be drawn from such a scene:

As for Helen, what could be a more direct lesson – a lived-out exercise in sympathy, in altruistic self-denial, in the healthy elevation of her sense of self to the dignity of kindly offices, in the sense of responsibility and agency, in the stimulus to original effort and the designing of means to ends.   (Baldwin 1895, p. 364)

Baldwin took the view that what he described as 'society games' could throw considerable light on what are now known as 'socialization pro-cesses', and in this he probably inspired and in any case was followed by Piaget. In his work on *The moral judgement of the child* – to be discussed more fully in chapter 12 – Piaget (1932) demonstrated the genesis of social rule-following in the course of children's games.

Baldwin's social psychology and modern neo-Darwinism

His next book (Baldwin 1897) actually had the sub-title *A study in social psychology*. In it he broadened his argument to deal with adult personality and social behaviour, seeking to show that much of what people regard as attributes of their particular self are in fact social products. 'I have first found them in my social environment, and by reason of my social and imitative disposition, have transferred them to myself by trying to act as if they were true of me, and so coming to find out that they are true of me.' Hence '*a man is a social outcome rather than a social unit*'. He criticised writers like Comte and Spencer for juxtaposing individual and society as though they were independent entities.

In the manner of Tarde, he proposed that habits, adaptive responses to novel situations, and the adoption of new ideas are largely mediated through the imitation of social models. Moreover, such a process is also said to account for the growth and modifications of cultural traditions in society at large. This is not to say, however, that Baldwin's views conflicted with those of evolutionary psychologists of his own or later generations. On the contrary, he tried to spell out the evolutionary implications of his scheme, by postulating a parallel between social and biological heredity, with the former complementing the latter. The individual is immersed from the outset in a social setting that shapes her as well as those around her: 'Everything that is learnt is copied, reproduced, assimilated, from one's fellows.' In so far as social groups, from tribes to nations, are internally homogeneous, there is competition and selection in the strict Darwinian sense of natural selection, and one finds here an analogy between social and biological processes. But there is a quite different mode of selection 'in social life, which operates by *conscious choice and imitation*'. What this means is elaborated in the following passage:

> In so-called 'imitative selection' ... the imitative propagation of ideas in society – we have a phenomenon for which biology shows us no analogies. What survives in this case is not individuals, but *ideas*; and these do not survive in the form in which the first thinker conceives them, but in the form in which society applies them. Again, their fitness is not in any sense a fitness for struggle; it is a fitness for imitative reproduction and application. And finally, they are not physically inherited, but handed down by 'social heredity' as accretions to the store of traditions.   (Baldwin 1897, pp. 182–3; emphasis in original)

There is a revealing phrase here, namely 'the first thinker', implying a recognition that not everything can happen by mere imitation. Baldwin sought to incorporate this into a broader scheme, once again comparing biological and social processes. In biology, he called the tendency of heredity to converge on the mean a 'generalizing force', while the variations on which natural selection acts constitute the 'particularizing' force. In society the particularising force is the innovative individual who produces variations, and this '*supplies the essential material of all human and social progress*'. According to Baldwin, one cannot really separate imitation and invention, since these are integral parts of the same cycle:

> This process of taking in elements from the social world by imitation and giving them out again by a reverse process of invention (for such a sequel proves invention to be: the modified way in which I put things together in reading the elements which I get from nature and other men, back into nature and other men again) – this process never stops.   (Baldwin 1897, p. 431)

He also noted that unless the innovation is one that finds acceptance within the culture, it will fail to exert any influence. Apart from the fact that he stressed evolutionary factors, Baldwin's scheme of social evolution is similar to that put forward by Tarde.

It is worth digressing briefly here to show how closely Baldwin anticipated a recent, albeit controversial movement in evolutionary psychology.
In Richard Dawkins's seminal book *The selfish gene* (1976), he proposed a
cultural replicator parallel to genes, as explained in the following rather
florid passage:

> The new soup is the soup of human culture. We need a name for the new
> replicator, a noun which conveys the ideas of a unit of cultural transmis-
> sion, or as a unit of *imitation* [which he calls '*memes*'] ... Examples of
> *memes* are tunes, ideas, catch-phrases, clothes fashions, ways of making
> pots or building arches. Just as genes propagate themselves in the gene
> pool via sperm or eggs, so *memes* propagate themselves in the *meme* pool
> by leaping from brain to brain via a process which, in a broad sense, can
> be called imitation.   (Dawkins 1976, p. 206; emphasis in original)

From this beginning the concept of *memes* has spread by imitation and
spawned a wholly new field of '*memetics*'. In some of its manifestations it
borders on the absurd, since a quasi-independent existence is sometimes
attributed to *memes* (cf. Jahoda 2002).

Returning to Baldwin, he argued in a manner similar to Dawkins that
there are some similarities, but also substantial differences between biological and social evolution. It was at the time when Baldwin was writing
these books that he conceived an idea about 'a new factor in evolution', by
which he meant the capacity of consciousness and intelligence to affect the
direction of evolutionary change. In a brief and somewhat oversimplified
way this may be explained as follows: supposing the environment of an
animal species undergoes changes. Those capable of learning new adaptive modes of behaviour will tend to survive and leave offspring, while
others will die out. Over generations the learning capacity will then be
built into the organisms. This theory can account for the transmission of
learned behaviour without having to fall back on Lamarckism. As frequently happens, Baldwin was not alone in putting forward what he called
the principle of 'organic selection' – Lloyd Morgan in Britain had much
the same idea about the same time. None the less it is still known as 'the
Baldwin effect', which gave rise to much discussion, though most evolutionary biologists now doubt that it plays a significant part in evolutionary processes.

The fall from a great height

While the work discussed above is most central in the present context,
Baldwin published a great deal that is relevant for social psychology, and
mention should be made of *The individual and society* (1899/1911), which
deals with social psychology in relation to other social sciences, and especially sociology. Altogether, Baldwin's achievements in several fields are
impressive. They include contributions to developmental and personality

psychology, as well as his anticipation by a century of what has become evolutionary psychology. He always stressed the importance of social influences from infancy to maturity, and during the period from about 1890 to 1910 he was one of the most highly regarded psychologists in America.

In 1903 he had left Princeton to take up an appointment at Johns Hopkins University. While there, in 1908, he was caught in a police raid in what Titchener called in a letter 'a negro dive' – in other words a black brothel. While this perhaps indicates a commendable freedom from prejudice, it could not be tolerated at the time by Johns Hopkins after it had become public knowledge, especially since Baldwin's own explanation was far from convincing: 'I foolishly accepted a suggestion made after a dinner to go to a house of a colored social sort and see what was done there.' Sacked from Johns Hopkins, his career in ruins, Baldwin went to live in Paris, where he was welcomed into distinguished intellectual circles and honoured by the prestigious *Institut*. After his death in 1934 he was said by Charles Ellwood to have been 'almost universally regarded as the leading American social psychologist'.

George Herbert Mead's distorted inheritance

The inclusion of Mead at this point requires some justification, since his main work appeared much later than the period being considered. However, it was published posthumously, and his ideas had crystallised long before. George Herbert Mead (1863–1931) was born in Massachusetts and started at Oberlin College where his father was a professor of theology. Originally destined for the ministry, he lost his faith and became an agnostic. He taught in primary school for a while, then worked for three years as part of a survey team on railway construction. Following the advice of a friend he then enrolled at Harvard to study philosophy and psychology. Royce, his philosophy professor, was a Hegelian, who impressed Mead even more than William James, one of whose children he tutored for some months in 1888. At the end of that year he went to Germany and attended Wundt's classes during the winter semester.

The following year he went from Leipzig to Berlin, where he studied physiological and experimental psychology with Ebbinghaus, and philosophy with Dilthey. Mead left Berlin in 1891 for the University of Michigan, where he had been offered an instructorship in philosophy and psychology. There he met the young John Dewey, who later achieved fame as a pragmatic philosopher and early on became interested in social psychology; they formed a lifelong friendship. Also in Michigan he met Cooley, who was working for a doctorate in economics. Cooley suggested that Mead should read Adam Smith, who was the source not only of Cooley's but also of Mead's elaboration of Smith's notion of the 'impartial spectator'.

In 1894 Dewey was appointed to the chair of philosophy at the University of Chicago, and Mead joined him there. After a decade Dewey left for Columbia, but Mead remained at Chicago for the rest of his life. In 1904, while Dewey was still at Chicago, John Watson became one of his students for a period. But Watson found Dewey's teaching uncongenial and switched to J. R. Angell, a more biologically oriented psychologist. Under Angell's supervision he completed a thesis on maze-running by rats. In 1908 Watson became a full professor at Johns Hopkins and in due course, as is well known, the pioneer and guru of radical behaviourism. Mead and Watson shared a concern with the biological roots of behaviour, but none the less followed widely divergent paths. While Watson wanted to cleanse psychology of such notions as mind, consciousness, and the self, which he regarded as mystical, these were precisely the topics of particular interest for Mead. Watson triumphed, and from having been the study of the mind, psychology became the study of behaviour and largely remains so to this day.

Mead's evolutionary social psychology

Although Mead wrote numerous articles, he never published a book. From 1901 onwards he gave an annual course called 'social psychology'. Fortunately the enterprising students who attended his class in 1927 smuggled in a stenographer to record his lectures, and together with the students' own notes this formed the basis of a posthumously published book. It was edited by the philosopher C. W. Morris under the title *Mind, self and society; from the standpoint of a social behaviorist* (Mead 1934); the label 'behaviorist' was not Mead's own, but was attached by the editor. Mead was a highly original thinker, who in his work sought to weave together several strands of modern thought. Philosophically he was a pragmatist in the manner of William James. Mead was also a Darwinian evolutionist, whose training in physiology ensured that he never forgot that humans are biological organisms, though emphatically not only that (Mead 1909). Moreover, he held that evolutionary processes not only occur within species but also apply to institutions and societies, a view that has come to the fore again in recent years (cf. Wheeler et al. 2002).

Among humans, characterised by a capacity for self-reflexivity and symbolisation, such societal evolution can be influenced by intelligent action based on scientific principles. Mead sought to avoid the Cartesian dualism of Wundt who, as has already been shown, struggled in vain to clarify the relationship between his physiological psychology and his *Völkerpsychologie*. For Mead there was no such vexing issue, since he focused on the *act*, and especially the communicative act, which for him was central to human existence. The act depends upon experience stored in the brain, and thus has a physiological root, but it also takes place in a *social context* that will affect its form. Thus Mead anticipated what more recently became known as 'dialogism'.

Like many other followers of Darwin, Mead made use of the concept of 'instinct' for dealing with biologically programmed aspects of behaviour. He left the issue of numbers and types of instincts open, and took no dogmatic stand in the later nature–nurture debate focused on instincts. He pointed out that the operation of instincts varies according to phylogenetic level. In animals they are relatively rigid and stereotyped, while in humans they are highly flexible, so much so that it is misleading to attribute any behaviour directly to instincts. Hence he suggested that the springs of action

> are best termed 'impulses' and not 'instincts', because they are subject to extensive modifications in the life-history of individuals, and these modifications are so much more extensive than those to which the instincts of lower animal forms are subjected that the use of the term 'instinct' in describing the behavior of normal adult human individuals is seriously inexact.   (Mead 1934, p. 337)

In spite of such disclaimers, Mead often did rely on 'instincts' when seeking to explain the origins and functioning of social institutions rather than the actions of individuals. For instance, in his study of justice systems (Mead 1917/18) he traced their beginnings to 'the instinct of hostility' or demand for revenge, and sketched the subsequent evolution of institutions from *lex talionis*, via medieval courts given to torture, to modern justice systems. The conclusion of his analysis of the evolution of punishment was that a system based on the instinct of hostility was socially undesirable. This is noted here only to exemplify the fact that Mead did at times employ arguments based on instincts, and his position in this regard was not always consistent. It came out particularly when he dealt with infant development, where he wrote: 'If there are instincts in humans, as in animals, they lie in the social environment, for the stimuli to which the infant responds are there.' On balance Mead stressed social factors much more frequently than biological ones, and his greatest contributions lie in that direction.

As many had said before him, what makes us human is language, a social product. But unlike most of his predecessors, he attempted to analyse the processes involved. He criticised Comte and other positivists for proposing that the study of individuals and societies could simply adopt the approaches that proved so effective in physics – a view that originally had also inspired Enlightenment thinkers and numerous nineteenth-century ones. They ignored the *reflexivity* of human intelligence and its capacity for symbolisation, which means that social life can take a great variety of different forms. Hence there can be no fixed formulae that lead to understanding, and it is only an evolutionary perspective that can free us from static accounts.

Mead on the social functions of language

Mead took as his point of departure Darwin's (1872) work on the expression of the emotions as elaborated by Wundt in the first volume of the *Völkerpsychologie*. Wundt there proposed that such expressions may be regarded as 'gestures' which are part of a social act. Thus in a dog-fight each 'gesture' acts as a stimulus releasing behaviour of one of the participants, which in turn leads to a response by the other, resulting in a sequence of reciprocal changes. It follows that, while Darwin had been content to deal with isolated expressions, Wundt argued that these were just part of a complex set of behaviours. In the case of humans a man may shake his fist at another, which signals not merely a hostile attitude but also some idea and intention. Being equipped with language, the gesture may be a vocal one with a certain meaning, thereby becoming what Mead called 'a significant symbol'. Such symbols function within a field of social behaviour which requires mutual adjustment, and they make this possible in an efficient manner by conveying *meaning*. It is only within the context of social relationships that such meaning is constituted. Such emphasis on 'meaning' was probably derived from Mead's studies with Dilthey.

Social relationships and communication, according to Mead, are also essential for the emergence of a reflexive self, which he described as a social structure resulting from social experience. He discussed the genesis of the self in childhood, though his account is not based on any systematic observations, as in the cases of Baldwin and Cooley. He placed much emphasis on pretend play, as did Piaget (1962) in relation to the formation of symbols, during which children rehearse social roles, and, like Piaget, on games. Unlike Piaget, however, Mead saw games as settings in which children have, as it were, to adopt the attitudes of the others involved so as to act appropriately. These, he asserted, are the conditions under which the self becomes an object to children. It is only in the social group that such a self can emerge, when the child puts herself into the position of others. In other words, children internalise the norms and roles within their community as a result of such interactions with adults as well as with other children, within the given social environment. Mead called what is so internalised 'the generalized other', which can be recognised as none other than Adam Smith's 'impartial spectator'.

The self is of course more than a bundle of internalised social roles, rules, values, and so on. Mead distinguished between the subjective 'I' and the social 'me': 'The "I" is the response of the organism to the attitudes of the others; the "me" is the organized set of attitudes of others which one himself assumes.' There is a complex interweaving between these two aspects of the self. Once again, although the vocabulary is somewhat different, much the same idea had been put forward by Adam Smith, as the following passage shows:

> When I endeavour to examine my own conduct, when I endeavour to pass sentence upon it ... it is evident that, in all such cases, I divide myself, as it were, into two persons; and that I, the examiner and judge, represent a different character from that other I, the person whose conduct is examined into and judged of. The first is the spectator, whose sentiments with regard to my own conduct I endeavour to enter into, by placing myself in his situation, and by considering how it would appear to me, when seen from that particular point of view. The second is the agent, the person whom I properly call myself, and of whose conduct, under the character of a spectator, I was endeavouring to form some opinion.   (Smith 1790/1984, p. 113)

Hence one of the best-remembered aspects of Mead's theory, like Cooley's use of the notion of 'sympathy', can be traced back to the Enlightenment. There is more continuity of ideas in social science than is usually realised.

After Mead's death, Blumer, a sociologist, took over his course on social psychology. He gave Mead's theory, whose evolutionary basis he did not fully understand, a different twist which departed from Mead's spirit. He re-christened it 'symbolic interactionism', a term which has stuck, and has become the rallying cry of a sociological version of social psychology. In 'symbolic interactionism' one of the main pillars of Mead's theory, namely the evolutionary foundation, dropped out altogether. In its new incarnation, the slogan of 'symbolic interactionism' has also sometimes been adopted by movements of opposition against positivist mainstream social psychology.

Contributions of sociologists

Cooley and his 'primary groups'

Well into the twentieth century many seminal ideas in social psychology were put forward by sociologists. Some of the expressions they coined have ceased to be technical and become part of the everyday vocabulary. One of these innovative sociologists was Charles H. Cooley (1864–1929), who followed in Baldwin's footsteps. His father was professor of law at the University of Michigan. His son entered the same institution, first as a student, then as member of the teaching staff, and he stayed there all his life. Compared with Baldwin he was a rather drab character, troubled by physical infirmities. His first publications were in economics, but with the appearance of *Human nature and the social order* (1902) he made his name as a sociological social psychologist. Cooley read Spencer, from whom he derived an 'organic' conception of society and mind. His attempt to counter the then frequent belief in an antithesis between the individual and society was probably borrowed from Dewey. He took a close interest in child psychology and the writings of G. Stanley Hall, its foremost American exponent at that time. Like Baldwin, he observed his own children and kept careful records. Again like Baldwin, though to a lesser extent, his outlook was influenced by Darwin, and the first section of his introduction to *Human nature and the social order* is headed 'The evolutionary point of view'. It is a point of view he developed more fully in a later work.

Cooley's considerable and largely unacknowledged debt was to Adam Smith. There is first Cooley's stress on the importance of 'sympathy', which of course was not new – Darwin had briefly referred to Smith in this connection. But Cooley's formulation rather closely echoes Adam Smith:

> Sympathy is a requisite to social power. Only in so far as a man under-stands other people and thus enters into the life around him has he any effective existence.
> Sympathetic influence enters into our system of thought as a matter of course, and affects our conduct as surely as water affects the growth of a plant.   (Cooley 1902/1912, pp. 107–8)

Secondly, the phrase by which he is well known is that of 'the looking-glass self', which he suggested has three main aspects: how we imagine we appear to other people; how we imagine they are reacting to us; and some kind of accompanying feeling, such as pride or dismay. This may be compared with the corresponding passage by Adam Smith:

> We suppose ourselves the spectators of our own behaviour, and endea-vour to imagine what effect it would, in this light, produce upon us. This is the only looking-glass by which we can, in some measure, with the eyes of other people, scrutinize the propriety of our own conduct.   (Smith 1790/1984, p. 112)

A few years earlier Giddings (1896, p. 122) had briefly mentioned Adam Smith's 'spectator' in relation to the social origins of moral qualities, saying that Smith 'went to the heart of matter'; but Cooley had read Adam Smith and certainly found the 'looking-glass' himself. At any rate, in this context Cooley discussed the social determination of the self, as had William James, Baldwin and G. H. Mead. In a sense he was rather sitting on a theoretical fence between, on the one hand, an evolu-tionary orientation and, on the other, regarding human nature as pre-dominantly determined by the social environment. It is a dilemma that has given rise to innumerable 'nature–nurture' debates over the years.

Cooley's truly original contribution is to be found in the third chapter of his *Social organization: a study of the larger mind* (1909/1912). In it he coined the phrase 'primary groups'. These are face-to-face groups such as families, neighbourhoods, or play-groups of children in which a feeling of social unity prevails: 'it is a "we"; it involves the sort of sympathy and mutual identification for which the "we" is the natural expression'. Finally, one can find in Cooley's later *Social process* (1918) a fuller account of his Darwinian ideas. There he attempted to apply the notions of natural selection and adaptation to an analysis of the functioning of society and of social change.

Giddings on 'consciousness of kind' and Sumner on 'ethnocentrism'

One encounters somewhat related ideas in the writings of Cooley's contemporaries. Thus the 'we' feeling referred to in relation to 'primary groups', vastly extended to distinguish at one extreme between the animate and the non-animate and at the other extreme between nations and races, was captured by Giddings's phrase 'consciousness of kind'. The American sociologist Franklin Henry Giddings (1855–1931) regarded it as the basic principle of social organisation. According to Giddings, it involves a set of four processes:

1   A person makes the judgement of another person an object of his thought;
2   At the same time he or she makes their own thought an object;
3   Finds that both are much the same;
4   Now acts with the awareness that others think as she or he does.

This seems a rather laboured way of saying that two or more people have similar ideas and values. More generally, the concept refers to our identification with and conduct towards 'those whom we feel to be most like ourselves', and such conduct 'is instinctively and rationally different from our conduct towards others, whom we believe to be less like ourselves' (Giddings 1896, p. 18).

Or again, it was William Graham Sumner (1840–1910) who coined the now common expression 'ethnocentrism' which he described as

> the technical name for [a] view of things in which one's own group is the center of everything, and all others are scaled and rated with reference to it ... each group nourishes its own pride and vanity, boasts itself superior, exalts its own divinities and books, with contempt on outsiders. Each group thinks its own folkways [read 'culture'] are the only right ones, and if it observes that other groups have other folkways, these excite its scorn ... the most important fact is that ethnocentrism leads a people to exaggerate and intensify everything in their own folkways which is peculiar and which differentiates them from others.   (Sumner 1907, p. 13)

In the 1880s Sumner clashed with the president of Yale, who objected to his use of Spencer's *The study of sociology* as a text for his students, on the grounds that it was atheistic and unscientific. The resulting furore over academic freedom made it into the national press. Sumner was something of a social Darwinist and, rather like Spencer, favoured *laissez-faire*. In sum, he was a sociologist who placed the greatest weight on economic factors in determining customs and social values generally. Cooley, by contrast, attempted a balancing act in which he sought to take account of both biological and socio-economic influences, though leaning more towards the latter.

Where does social psychology belong?

Around the turn of the century in America there was a tendency to regard social psychology as part of sociology. An example would be a sociological text by Small and Vincent (1894), which had as the heading of one of its chapters 'The phenomena of social psychology in general'. It was asserted that society is essentially 'psychical' in character, and accordingly social structures and collective activities have to be explained in 'psychic' terms. Social philosophers, it was stated, therefore usually consider sociology in psychological terms, but it is important to draw a distinction between individual psychology and social psychology

> which describes the phenomena that result from the combination and reaction of the cognitions, emotions, and volitions of associated individuals. Inasmuch as the latter manifestations are a higher integration of the products of Individual Psychology, they may be said to form the subject-matter of a *Super-psychology* or an *Ultra*-psychology.   (Small and Vincent 1894, p. 306; emphasis in original)

They then went on to criticise Schäffle (cf. chapter 3) for his claims about the analogies between individual and societal minds, arguing that social phenomena are more than mere sums of the products of individual minds. Generally, they were struggling to reconcile the statement that society is a 'psychic' entity with the claim that sociology remains independent of individual psychology, and the bridging concept for them was that of a social psychology, but one that would be part of sociology.

It will have been noted that Vincent and Small referred back to Schäffle, and such reliance on historical precedent was even more pronounced in Ellwood, a student of John Dewey. Ellwood published in his early years a monograph entitled *Some prolegomena to social psychology* (1901). In it he suggested that 'Social psychology is simply psychology in general applied to the interpretation of the life of the social group.' It becomes apparent from what follows that he often used the term 'social group' as synonymous with 'society'. He viewed society as a whole as 'acting', which according to him makes a social psychology possible. The whole discussion of that initial effort is bedevilled by the fact that Ellwood at one and the same time adopted the Herbartian analogy between individual and society, but also brought in aspects of Tarde's, Le Bon's, and Baldwin's theories, as well as acknowledging a debt to G. H. Mead. Then he declared that 'The beginnings of social psychology as a scientific discipline are to be found in the *Völkerpsychologie* of Lazarus and Steinthal.' It will be appreciated that this resulted in rather an unholy mishmash. The gist of his conclusion then was that social psychology constitutes an essential part of sociology, a view he later modified and presented in a more coherent manner (Ellwood 1917). Rival claims for 'ownership' of social psychology persisted for some time before it came to be shared between the two disciplines.

PART III

The twentieth century: towards maturity in America

9 Was 1908 a crucial date?

> [Social psychology is a young science] ... born with the new century
> marked by Wundt's (1900–20) *Völkerpsychologie* and the concurrent
> appearance of the first two textbooks explicitly called *Social Psychology*,
> one by a sociologist (Ross, 1908) and the other by a psychologist
> (McDougall, 1908).

The above statement by McGuire (1999, p. 325), far from being an
isolated view, is one that is widely shared. Readers who have had the
patience to reach this page will be aware that a great deal happened well
before 1908, even under the direct heading of 'social psychology'. Since so
much importance has been attached to the two books, they will be
discussed in some detail. Both authors had been subject to the influence
of evolutionary theory, though this applies far more to McDougall than
to Ross.

G. H. Mead, whose position has been outlined in the preceding chapter,
strongly criticised Ross, thereby highlighting the increasing gap between
'sociological' and 'psychological' social psychology. I shall argue that, far
from ushering in a new phase, the work of McDougall and Ross is more
properly seen as the end of an old one.

McDougall's psychological social psychology

William McDougall (1871–1938) was born in England, educated
first at what was then Owen's College in Manchester, where he read
Spencer, Darwin, and Huxley. In 1890 he won a scholarship to
Cambridge, and then went on to London to study for a degree in medicine. While in London he worked in the laboratory of the famous physiologist Charles Sherrington. After reading William James's *Principles* he
decided to turn to psychology. In 1897 he obtained a fellowship in
Cambridge, where he was advised by the psychologist and philosopher
James Ward. A year later he took part in the Cambridge Expedition to
Torres Strait, which was the beginning of what half a century later became
cross-cultural psychology. Under the direction of W. H. R. Rivers he
applied psychological tests to the Murray Islanders. In 1903 he was
appointed Wilde Reader in Mental Philosophy at Oxford, a title which

9   *William McDougall (1871–1938)*

has given rise to many jokes. The terms of the post explicitly prohibited any experimentation, so if he wanted to carry out experiments he was forced to ask for the hospitality of the physiology laboratory. Under these circumstances it is understandable that in 1920 he was pleased to accept an offer from Harvard, where he remained for seven years, finally moving to Duke University.

It will be evident that he was a noted figure, in touch with many of the major scientists and scholars of his time. His interests were wide and varied, including the classics as well as physiology and anthropology, but two of them were rather unusual. McDougall was a believer in Lamarckism, and spent many years trying to prove it by cutting off the tails of numerous generations of mice – all in vain. At Duke he also occupied himself with psychical research, creating a tradition there associated with J. B. Rhine, often regarded as 'the father of parapsychology'. This interest was connected with his strongly held view that mind is an 'emergent' and behaviour is purposive, which made him a leading opponent of Watsonian behaviourism.

McDougall's early work had been in physiological psychology, and he published a book which suggested a hydraulic model of nervous inhibition that was consistent with aspects of psychoanalytic theory. He combined such a physiological orientation with a strong belief in a teleological, purposive functioning of the human mind. It is not entirely clear what McDougall meant by 'purposive'. At times it seems to have referred to foresight of ends, in which case his speculations about animals would have been impossible to verify. At other times it seems to have meant sequences of behaviour continued until a goal is reached. In any case it later came to be known as 'hormic' theory. The first full statement of this viewpoint is contained in *An introduction to social psychology*, first published in 1908, which is said to have gone through more editions than any other book in psychology.

In the preface McDougall stressed the importance of Darwinian evolutionary theory for psychology, especially in relation to instinct as a spring of action, which he put rather dramatically:

> Take away these instinctive dispositions with their powerful impulses, and the organism would become incapable of activity of any kind; it would lie inert and motionless like a wonderful clockwork whose mainspring had been removed.   (McDougall 1908/1943, p. 38)

McDougall was only one of numerous psychologists influenced by Darwin, but hardly anyone else presented as coherent a theory of supposedly instinctive behaviour. Among McDougall's stated aims was that of providing a psychological basis for the social sciences; and although he did not mention Wundt in this connection, this is much the same as what Wundt had tried to do for the *Geisteswissenschaften* (humane disciplines). The psychology of his time, McDougall contended, was largely concerned with introspection, neglecting conation and affect, with the result that disciplines like anthropology, economics, or history had to resort to a do-it-yourself psychology. He promised to supply a motivational theory designed to remedy the lack, a theory founded on but enlarging and modifying Darwin's ideas.

McDougall's instinct theory

McDougall observed that Darwin had held that instincts can have two distinct origins: first, certain intelligent actions performed over several generations can become instinctive; secondly, and more frequently in the case of complex instincts, they can arise through natural selection acting upon variations in simpler instincts (Darwin 1871/1901, p. 102). The first alternative entails Lamarckism, which did not trouble McDougall. However, it should be said that his approach did not depend on the correctness of Lamarckism. Instincts in McDougall's sense are not rigid behaviour patterns, but become modified during development and influenced by external factors. The key question addressed is the following: what characteristics of the human mind fit her or him for social life? For McDougall this also involved the issue of moral behaviour, regarded by him as crucial:

> the fundamental problem of social psychology is the moralisation of the individual by the society into which he is born as a creature in which the non-moral and purely egoistic tendencies are so much stronger than any altruistic tendencies.   (McDougall 1908/1943, p. 16)

The substance of the work begins with a detailed discussion of the concept of instinct, the term having often been used loosely in several different senses. For McDougall, instincts were innately determined 'psycho-physical dispositions' characterised by three aspects:

1   perceptual – pay attention to objects of a certain class;
2   emotional – experience an emotional excitement of a particular quality on perceiving that object;
3   motor – react to such objects in a particular manner.

The most novel, yet at the same time most controversial aspect was the linking of emotion with instinct. For instance, it has been argued that emotion only arises when instinctive behaviour is thwarted, and McDougall tried to deal with such difficulties in a later work. At any rate he proposed that in the course of an individual's development instincts become modified in several different ways: the innate releaser of the instinctive behaviour is extended from objects to ideas; the movements triggered by the instinct become more diverse; several instincts may be triggered simultaneously and result in a blend; and the instinctive tendencies become more or less systematically organised around certain objects or ideas. As a further step in this direction, McDougall later adopted from Alexander Shand the notion of 'sentiment', which refers to an organised system of emotional tendencies centred on the idea of some object. It is a concept that has something in common with the later one of 'attitude', also referring to emotional dispositions. Instances of sentiments would be love or hate, which evoke particular emotions depending upon situational factors. For example, if a loved person wins the lottery, one is pleased, and if they suffer a misfortune one feels regret; but the converse will apply if the person is hated. Of central importance is the 'self-regarding sentiment', whose object is the ego and which is built up in the course of socialisation, incorporating the moral rules of the social environment. This happens as a result of the approval or disapproval of significant others, reminiscent once again of Adam Smith's 'impartial spectator'; he was familiar with the work of Smith, describing it as 'a first approximation'. The development of the moral sense of the child is discussed on the basis of Baldwin's theory, and four main stages are distinguished:

1   purely instinctive behaviour under the influence of pleasure and pain;
2   impulses come to be modified by rewards and punishment from the social environment;
3   conduct is controlled by anticipation of social praise and blame;
4   in the highest stage an ideal of conduct governs behaviour – doing what seems right irrespective of praise and blame from the social environment.

These stages, it may be noted, are basically rather similar to those later proposed by Kohlberg (1976) with regard to the development of moral cognition. In the course of these stages the child is transformed from a being whose behaviour is purely instinctive to a fully social one. The instincts themselves do not disappear, but their manifestations become modified. While such wide flexibility may be regarded as a strength of the theory, it is at the same time a weakness by making it harder to decide which instincts are innately given. The various conflicting classifications of instincts, ranging from a handful to hundreds, constituted a soft target for the behaviourist critics of the concept.

    The 'primary' instincts identified by McDougall, coupled with their respective emotional counterparts, are listed below:

flight – fear
repulsion – disgust
curiosity – wonder
pugnacity – anger
self-abasement – subjection
self-assertion – elation
parental – tender emotion

In the cases of the following instincts no corresponding emotions are mentioned; this does not imply that there are none, only that they may be highly variable:

reproduction
gregariousness
acquisition
construction

In addition to these instincts, a set of 'non-specific innate tendencies' are also postulated, namely sympathy, suggestion, imitation, play, and the 'emulative impulse'. In hindsight one cannot help feeling that such lists are bound to be very arbitrary. Another, perhaps more serious objection concerns the rather cavalier explanatory uses to which particular instincts are put.

The weaknesses of the theory become most apparent in the second part of the book, which seeks to show how instincts function in social life. The problematic nature of the claim that instincts *explain* behaviour may be illustrated in relation to 'gregariousness', described as being of far-reaching significance. In this connection McDougall referred to Giddings's phrase 'consciousness of kind'. In McDougall's view this concept is altogether redundant, and really boils down to the gregarious impulse:

> If we would state more accurately the facts vaguely implied by this phrase, we must say that the gregarious impulse of any animal receives satisfaction only through the presence of animals similar to itself ... Just so, in any human being the instinct operates most powerfully in relation to, and receives the highest degree of satisfaction from the presence of the human beings who most closely resemble that individual.   (McDougall 1908/ 1943, p. 258)

He further criticised Giddings's formulation on the grounds that 'consciousness of kind' as such lacks any motive force, and suggests that it constitutes merely the cognitive process through which the gregarious impulse is triggered. None the less, McDougall agreed that the instinct is most fully active in proportion as we are in the company of those who are most like ourselves. This is said to account for the fact that members of ethnic groups in American cities prefer to live together in the same districts. It also explains, according to McDougall, why occupational groups tend to be clustered in particular areas, e.g. London doctors in Harley Street or journalists in Fleet Street. He failed to consider that market forces are likely to be involved in such geographical concentrations.

Finally a broader evolutionary aspect is suggested: when populations were small, the gregarious instinct 'must have played an important part in social evolution by keeping men together and thereby occasioning the need for social laws and institutions'. Oddly enough, though, he regarded an excess of gregariousness as a bad thing, as when people congregate in large crowds to gape at some celebrity, or stay off work 'to spend the day in worse than useless idleness, confirming their already over-developed gregarious instincts'. It is even implied that it constituted a factor in the decline of the Roman empire! Here the alleged 'instinct of gregariousness' has been singled out because of its 'social' connotations, but similar observations could have been based on McDougall's discussions of other instincts. Putting it in a nutshell, they are made to explain too much, and in an *ad hoc* fashion, without considering possible alternative interpretations.

In sum, McDougall's approach began with a consideration of what he believed to be instinctive dispositions, originally part of our evolutionary heritage. He then went on to propose that these instincts made the creation of human social life possible. The instincts themselves underwent progressive changes when that life took on more complex forms, as 'barbarism' gave way to civilisation.

The brief critical account offered here fails to do justice to the power and verve of McDougall's exposition, which led to its having continued to be held in high esteem much longer than most psychological writings. The fact remains, however, that its main theme was motivation rather than social psychology, and as one critic cited by McDougall himself put it in a later edition: 'He seems to do a great deal of packing in preparation for a journey on which he never starts.' In his defence McDougall mentioned that he was about to publish another book which actually deals with part of social psychology proper. That was his highly controversial book on *The group mind* (1920), which took up and sought to update the ideas put forward by Espinas, Le Bon, Schäffle, and others, who postulated the existence of a collective mind over and above that of the constituent individuals. It was the last gasp of such a concept, and the work was widely criticised. In the preface to the second edition McDougall (1927) plaintively explained that his 'usage of the term "group mind" is not meant to denote some mental entity that exists over and above all the individuals comprised in the group and that might continue to exist though all the members ceased to be' (McDougall 1927, p. xiii). However, that is not an adequate justification, since even his predecessor had never gone so far as to believe in the possibility of a disembodied collective mind! Admittedly some of the questions he raised about groups of all kinds were pertinent; but his answers, often couched in simplistic appeals to 'race', bear the marks of his period.

Let us turn now to the second classical text, which presents an entirely different picture of the subject.

Ross's sociological social psychology

In his preface Ross wrote that he did not care about the success of his book, as long as social psychology flourished. He need not have worried about either – the book was very successful.

Edward Alsworth Ross (1866–1951) was an American sociologist who had been initially trained as an economist, a subject he taught at Stanford University from 1893 to 1900, when he was dismissed on an issue of academic freedom. He had objected to the use of migrant Chinese workers in the construction of the Union Pacific Railway, which offended the Stanford family, who had founded the university of that name and were involved in the project. He switched to sociology, which he saw as a discipline that would offer him a better opportunity to put his progressive ideas into practice. Subsequently he became professor of sociology at the University of Wisconsin and changed from a critic to a supporter of big business.

His mentor had been Lester Ward, a sociologist of the previous generation, whose *Dynamic sociology* was in the tradition of Comte and Spencer and who was also interested in more recent French sociology. He was a critic of Darwinism as applied to humans, on the ground that the environment transforms the animal, while man transforms the environment. In this he had probably been influenced by French writers sceptical of Darwinism, such as Le Bon, and particularly Tarde, who had also misunderstood the theory of evolution. But Ward (1883) did conceive mind as 'a social factor', albeit rather in the manner of Lindner and Schäffle.

Ward's influence is evident in Ross's *Social control* (1901) for which, together with his later *Principles of sociology* (1920), he was best known among sociologists. Here the critical work is his *Social psychology* (1908/1923), which incorporated much of his earlier *Social control*. Ross regarded social psychology as concerned with 'the psychic planes and currents that come into existence among men in consequence of their association'. The metaphor 'psychic planes and currents' presumably refers to beliefs, opinions, ideas, and so on resulting from associations. Such associations, according to Ross, take two main forms: one in which the individual is dominated by the group, and an opposite one in which a powerful person modifies the social environment. His major theme was the relationship between individuals and their group, entailing such issues as social influence and control. Ross did little more than pay lip-service to evolutionary aspects, though he agreed with McDougall that the 'original social forces are instinct'. Ross had been inspired by Tarde's theory and quoted him extensively, though he extended the concept of imitation from mere copying of the acts of others to a consideration of verbal and facial clues in interaction; and he placed relatively more emphasis on suggestion. In this connection he discussed crowds and mobs, proposing that the bodily movements, which he saw as maintaining individual self-consciousness, become suppressed in a crush, thereby leading to mental absorption by the mass. His description of crowds echoes the over-dramatised tone of Le Bon.

A striking aspect of the work is its applied orientation, seeking to relate theory to actual social issues, with a daring and perhaps somewhat rash readiness to lay down the 'laws' governing social phenomena. For example, he followed Tarde in differentiating 'crowd' and 'public', echoing Tarde's phrase that the era of 'publics' had dawned. Yet, Ross maintained, even a public is still liable to be crowd-like in following what he called 'crazes', citing instances that jumped in time from the children's crusades in the Middle Ages to modern financial 'crazes'. He felt able to propound a number of 'laws' in this connection, which range from the blindingly obvious (e.g. 'A craze takes time to develop to its height'), via the ambiguous (e.g. 'One craze is frequently followed by another' – at what interval?), to the possibly reasonable 'Ethnic or mental homogeneity is favourable to the craze.' It would be wrong to give the impression that the content is generally as vapid as that, but Ross like others among his contemporaries not merely sought to show that social life is lawful, but seemingly felt an obligation to enunciate such alleged 'laws'.

Since the work was intended as a text for students, each chapter is followed by a set of exercises, which are illuminating in at least two ways: first, they illustrate the range of content dealt with; second, they reveal then prevalent beliefs and attitudes – though of course the extent to which these were correctly identified by Ross remains an open question. At any rate a haphazard selection of these exercises, taken from different chapters, may be of some interest.

Why is it that a financial craze may bring in its train a religious craze, whereas the reverse is not true? (p. 82). Ross himself had provided no adequate evidence that this is the case.

Trace in detail the route by which a Parisian style reaches your neighbours (p. 109). Quite feasible, and might be fun to do, provided the student also has taken courses in economics.

Study closely some raw immigrant family and see if the process of their Americanization agrees with Tarde's law (p. 146). That would be a major project over a considerable period of time, but presumably students were only expected to describe how they would set about it.

Does any good thing spread by social gravity which might not be diffused by the school? (p. 165). By 'social gravity' he meant informal sources of influence such as peer groups. Note that an answer would require making moral judgements.

Show how the rise of romantic love helps to emancipate society from the past (p. 252). This assumes a causal direction that is rather doubtful.

Why is it a mistake to send the [American native] Indian girl back to her tribe when she finishes school? (p. 274). It was a widespread belief at the time (noted, for instance, by Galton) that any such person would revert to 'savagery'.

What is the rational way of ascertaining women's 'sphere'? (p. 259). At the time it was of course – rightly – taken for granted that there was such a clearly delimited sphere.

Why is little in the way of gift or stimulus to be expected from Oriental cultures? (p. 366). This reflects then current stereotypes about 'orientals'.

Finally, it will be evident from the above that Ross's *Social psychology* has almost nothing in common with McDougall's book of the same title. McDougall dealt with *individual* motives generated by evolution, and their

presumed social effects. Ross was mainly concerned with social phenomena as products of social interaction. Neither discussed groups as such,
but Ross explained that the topic is one that concerns 'psychological
sociology', and therefore is outside the scope of his book. It is not clear
whether or not 'psychological sociology' was seen by him as identical with
what he called 'sociology proper', whose subject was said to be 'groups
and structures'. In any case, the general orientation of the book is pre-
dominantly sociological.

Thus these two works, which are often supposed to have marked the
beginning of social psychology, took up positions that differed fundamentally. This prompted Mead, who took McDougall's side, to mount a
critical attack on Ross.

The debate between Mead and Ross

A year after the publication of McDougall's and Ross's books on
social psychology, G. H. Mead (1909) published an article in which he
commented on their positions, as well as on that of Baldwin. While
voicing some reservations about McDougall's instinct theory and
Baldwin's concept of 'imitation', he broadly agreed with their views. But
believing as he did in an evolutionary social science, he was very critical of
Ross on the ground that 'sociality is for Professor Ross no fundamental
feature of human consciousness, no determining form of its structure'. He
further offended Ross by declaring that sociologists, though not rejecting
psychology as Comte had done, did not seem to be clear as to what kind of
psychology they needed.

Ross was stung into a reply, published as part of the same article. He
began by stating that there were two kinds of social psychology in competition with each other: one, that of Baldwin and McDougall, concerned with
association and interactions among *individuals*; the other, in the tradition
of Tarde, focused on the macro scale – in other words a *psychology of
society*. Whoever wins will hold on to the label 'social psychology', while
the loser will have to find some other name. If the ideas of the former pair
were to prevail, then much of what is known as 'psychology' would have to
be turned over to social psychology, and that is unlikely to be accepted –
prophetic words! As for sociology, Ross proposed two divisions. One
should deal with mental uniformities produced by tradition, convention,
and rational imitation and would be called *social morphology*, the study of
social forms. The other should refer to 'the transient uniformity seen in
mobs, "booms", panics, stampedes . . . crazes, and fads', and for those Ross
reckoned that the term 'social psychology' would be very suitable.

This exchange epitomises some of the main issues widely debated from
the end of the nineteenth century into the 1920s. It was a period when the

previously ill-defined and overlapping spheres of the two disciplines of psychology and sociology were in the process of crystallisation. The crux of the debates, reviewed above, which are often confusing for the modern reader since they rest on assumptions no longer taken for granted, was about the relationship between psychology in general or social psychology in particular, and sociology. Another process was the gradual separation of psychological and sociological social psychology, that became more pronounced during the mid-1920s. The division was not equal, 'psychological' social psychology becoming relatively far more widespread, which is still the case today. However, during the early stages of this development there was no consensus about the nature of their subject even among the protagonists of 'psychological' social psychology.

Transition rather than a starting point

There are several reasons for regarding the claim that their texts mark the beginning of social psychology as unfounded. The roots of social psychology go much further back than 1908, and even if one ignores the prevalence of relevant ideas, or the effort of Herbart, it has to be recognised that the name itself was invented soon after the middle of the nineteenth century. Thereafter the possibility and scope of a social psychology were extensively debated, with books and papers having the term 'social psychology' as title or sub-title. If it were objected, as is sometimes done, that all of that old stuff was speculative and non-empirical, then the answer is that precisely the same applies to both McDougall and Ross.

Paradoxically, both McDougall and Ross, who are sometimes credited with ushering in a new era of social psychology, were in fact backward-looking. McDougall based his whole theoretical edifice on 'instinct', at a time when 'instinct' as an explanatory concept was on the way out. Ross largely reflected past views, especially those of Tarde.

However, given the very large circulation their books achieved, it has to be recognised that they managed to put the *name* 'social psychology' more generally on the map. This does not mean that their books helped to clarify the nature of the subject, so debates continued, as will now be illustrated in relation to the psychological version that gradually gained dominance.

What is social psychology? What should it become?

By the second decade of the twentieth century the centre of gravity of both types of social psychology had begun to shift decisively to America. Hence, although similar gropings took place in Germany for a while, examples of the – for us sometimes rather curious – ideas prevalent at the time will be confined to American sources. Robert Gault (1915), an associate professor of psychology at Northwestern University, defined social psychology as the study of social behaviour. This sounds just the same as a modern view, but here is a quote to show the difference: 'Social psychology implies a social consciousness distinct from a consciousness that is not social.' Furthermore, if one takes away social consciousness, what remains is a consciousness that has nothing to do with any relationship to other people. How one 'takes away' social consciousness is not explained, but in a later article Gault (1921) did indicate how, according to him, a stimulus becomes social. The noise of a truck outside a house is in itself not social. However, if I think of my new neighbour whom I have encouraged to move into what I told him is a quiet street, then 'the audible rumbling of the truck is the first step in the historical development of a series of definitely socio-psychic phenomena'. The behaviour of the artist, the reformer, or the manager of a large business are all said to be 'illustrations of socio-psychic phenomena'; the implication appears to be that the behaviour of the butcher, the baker, and the candlestick-maker has no such connection with 'socio-psychic phenomena', but it is not explained why not. More generally, Gault tried to show that members of a social group understand and mentally represent each other; but Adam Smith had done this kind of thing very much better.

Perhaps it is worth mentioning in passing William (1922), who, in a manner somewhat similar to McDougall though different from practically everyone else in America at that time, defined social psychology as 'the science of the motives of people living in social relations'. Although it was true that during the following two decades or so 'motivation' was treated as an integral part of social psychology, it was not regarded as the whole of it.

A more interesting contribution was that of Kantor (1923), who deplored the prevailing capriciousness in conceptions of what social psychology is about, and wanted to introduce some order and coherence. The major portion of his article deals with the *data* of social psychology. It begins with the assertion that 'it is concerned with the responses of individuals to stimuli', which indicates that like Floyd Allport (about whom more later) he was a behaviourist. Kantor distinguished individual from 'social or cultural' reactions and divided the latter into three types: (a) universal, (b) idiosyncratic, and (c) cultural. The first is really redundant, since according to him it simply consists of biologically determined reflexes. The second is rather odd, as shown by this description:

> in idiosyncratic reactions we find individualistic interpretations of the properties of objects. Thus red or some other particular color may or may not be reacted to as bookbinding material, and especially if combined with leather, silk, or some other material.   (Kantor 1923, p. 450)

The only really relevant ones are the cultural responses to *stimuli*, which may be things, natural situations, persons, or actions. Problems of social psychology as presented by Kantor may be summarised as follows. How does an individual become a member of a social group? What are the mutual influences of group members on each other? What are the patterns of adaptive traits produced by varied group memberships of individuals, which indicate their intelligence, social outlook, religious orthodoxy, etc.? What are 'the relations between the psychological phases of the development of institutions, groups, and other influences which play their part in the development of social behaviour'? Lastly, there is 'the problem of the psychological influences upon historical, anthropological, and sociological facts'. While some of this is rather quaint, the latter part anticipated to some extent what social psychology was to become in due course. As these examples show, the early 1920s in America was a period of uncertainty when the nature and objectives of 'psychological' social psychology were being extensively debated. In sum, neither Wundt's *Völkerpsychologie* nor our two texts made any significant impact on the subsequent development of the discipline. As far as the McDougall and Ross texts are concerned, these mark the *end* of a period rather than the beginning of a new one. After them the aim became that of making social psychology a real science, and that meant carrying out empirical research as well as – and sometimes instead of – propounding theories.

10 Social psychology becomes empirical: groups (social facilitation) and attitudes

The first two decades of the twentieth century saw the beginnings of research on two topics, groups and attitudes, which came to dominate the inter-war period. The story of how an interest in groups first arose is little known, and is therefore worth relating. Most of this early work dealt with the effects of the presence of other people on various performances, later dubbed 'social facilitation' by Floyd Allport. The label is somewhat misleading, since the presence of others could sometimes lead to a decrement of performance, depending on circumstances.

While social facilitation was the exclusive domain of psychologists, the study of social attitudes stemmed from the joint efforts of sociologists and psychologists, the former having been the initiators. However, as already noted, at that time the separation of the two disciplines was as yet incomplete. In due course methods for the systematic investigation of social attitudes came to be developed.

Although highly salient, these topics were certainly not the only ones featuring in the social psychology of the period, as will be shown in the two subsequent chapters.

The origins of experimental group studies

It has often been claimed that the tradition of social-psychological experimentation goes back to Norman Triplett, who published an article entitled 'The dynamogenic factors in pacemaking and competition' (Triplett 1898). It was well known then that cyclists who are paced or taking part in a competition are faster than when cycling alone. Several theories had been put forward to account for this, ranging from the sensible to the bizarre, all of them reviewed by Triplett, who also christened them. Here are three examples:

Suction theory: the vacuum created by the pacemaker pulls his follower along;

Shelter theory: the pacemaker shelters the follower from the wind;

Brain worry theory: the follower need not concentrate on where he is going, so does not exhaust his nervous system.

Triplett very sensibly did not believe in any of these and formulated his own hypothesis, that could be tested experimentally. It was related to the then prevalent notion of 'ideo-motor action', i.e. that a motor response is triggered or facilitated by an idea. He thought that the sight of other cyclists would have such a 'dynamogenic' effect, as well as stimulating the 'competitive instinct'. For the purpose of testing this he set up two fishing reels side by side, so that in the 'competition' condition subjects could see each other; there was also a control 'alone' condition. His child subjects were instructed to turn the reel as rapidly as possible, a trial consisting of four circuits over four metres, timed with a stopwatch. There is no need to go into the details of the study, which had some odd features. For instance, though the total number tested was 225, the results for only 40 children are reported; of these 20 had been stimulated positively, 10 negatively and another 10 were little affected – the numbers are suspiciously neat! At any rate the general conclusion was that 'the bodily presence of another contestant participating simultaneously in the race serves to liberate latent energy not ordinarily available'.

While it cannot be denied that the Triplett study was the first attempt to assess the influence of the presence of others on performance, there is no indication that he himself saw that as a social-psychological experiment, nor was there any connection between that study and social psychology as it then existed. Furthermore, no social or any other kind of psychologist directly followed up Triplett's work. Hence the claim that the Triplett study was the beginning of experimental social psychology has been described as little more than an 'origin myth' (Haines and Vaughan 1979).

The German roots

School work in individual and classroom settings

In reality the story is more complicated. The initial impetus for a coherent sequence of researches dealing with a topic similar to Triplett's dates back to imperial Germany at the turn of the nineteenth century. Curiously enough, the story is at least peripherally connected with the then emperor Wilhelm II of Germany. The period after German unification in 1871 saw extensive educational reforms, many of them concerned with the *Volksschule* (elementary school) and designed in part to meet the needs of rapid industrialisation. In several parts of Germany the amount of homework was strictly regulated by statute, but these regulations varied considerably across regional authorities. Hence the question of homework and its value relative to class work came to be extensively debated, and this debate reached the highest level: in a famous address at the opening of the Berlin School Conference the German emperor declared that when he was a student in the *Gymnasium* at Kassel, the pupils were obliged to report to the Director each morning the number of hours spent in preparing the task for the day.

In view of this preoccupation, efforts were made to investigate the matter, often in a merely impressionistic manner. However in Würzburg Oswald Külpe, well known as the founder of the Würzburg School on the psychology of the thought processes, encouraged an experimental approach. He was joined by Ernst Meumann, who had studied under Wundt and specialised in 'pedagogical psychology' or, as it came later to be known, 'experimental pedagogy'. They enlisted the help of two teachers, Friedrich Schmidt and August Mayer, who, together with Meumann, carried out the investigations. The amount of material collected was very extensive, and hence only some salient features will be singled out.

The basic design involved comparisons between children's performance together with others and on their own. Efforts were made to equate the difficulty of the tasks (e.g. arithmetic or composition) under the two conditions. In the case of Schmidt the comparison was between school and home work. He collected a vast amount of information on the characteristics of the home, which yielded little of substance. Mayer's comparison was between school work and the same pupils working in isolation at the Institute of Psychology, where Külpe acted as one of the observers. Meumann's (1904) strategy was in part more strictly experimental and was conducted in the laboratory, using a dynamometer and ergograph; he also introduced an element of competition. The results of all these numerous and varied studies converged on the conclusion that, with certain exceptions, group work is clearly superior to individual work. The effect of competition was noted, without any systematic attempts to separate it from group influence as such. The theoretical interpretation offered by Meumann was in terms of 'the will', supposedly optimised in the presence of other children.

These studies became known in the United States when William Burnham of Clark University published an account of the German researches. He summarised the outcome as follows: 'In general the result of the work of the pupils in groups was superior to their work as individuals' (Burnham 1905, p. 218). Burnham (1910) subsequently published an article in *Science* entitled 'The group as a stimulus to mental activity'. Intercalated in that text is one-quarter of a page describing the Triplett (1898) study. Clearly Burnham saw the German studies as more important, and did not regard their results as confined to school children: 'The investigations referred to have chiefly concerned the mere presence or absence of other individuals performing similar tasks. *In a true social group the relations are more vital*' (Burnham 1910, p. 766; my emphasis). Thereby Burnham raised an extremely important issue about the nature of a 'social group' that later came to be not just forgotten but categorically denied.

Experimental 'crowd'/group psychology and the transition to the USA

Subsequently another German psychologist, Walther Moede (1888–1958), carried out an extensive series of studies immediately prior to the First World War. He initially reported part of this in an educational journal (Moede 1914), and in his theoretical introduction linked his study to Wundt's *Völkerpsychologie*, which at first blush might seem odd. Yet Wundt had postulated an evolutionary process in the course of which the effects of social interactions had produced the mental and moral advance of humanity. He had written that 'the conditions of mutual mental effects will bring out new and special manifestations of the general psychic forces that could not be predicted from the mere knowledge of the properties of individual consciousness' (Wundt 1908, vol. 3, p. 227). Hence Moede saw his work as that of exploring such 'mutual mental effects'. The whole set of his empirical studies was eventually published in book form with the title *Experimental crowd psychology* and the sub-title *A contribution to experimental group psychology* (Moede 1920). This Janus-faced title on the one hand looked back towards Le Bon and, on the other hand, forward to a new approach radically opposed to his ideas. The book contains the first systematic and detailed consideration as to how the methods of general experimental psychology could be adapted to the study of groups. In the actual empirical studies the range of topics covered was wide, but all the experiments dealt with the effects of the presence of varying numbers of others on performance, mere presence being distinguished from competitive situations. The topics included collective influences on attention, memory, word association, and 'the will', which was then still a psychological category. In later life Moede did not continue with his experimental group studies, becoming instead a pioneer of applied psychology in Germany.

Another figure, who provided a crucial link between German and what was to become in due course the dominant American group psychology, was Hugo Münsterberg (1863–1916). He had studied medicine in Heidelberg and, like numerous others, came under the influence of Wundt and turned to psychology. He was in contact with many prominent German scholars of the period and in 1892 William James invited him to Harvard, where in due course he was appointed to the chair vacated by McDougall. Like Moede, he wrote and lectured on 'psychotechnology', as applied psychology was then known, but his interests were very wide and he wrote on themes including philosophy, education, criminology, and economics. Münsterberg sought to build cultural bridges between his adopted homeland and Germany. This did not endear him to his Harvard colleagues, especially after the outbreak of the First World War, and he was even suspected of being a German spy. Under considerable stress he died in harness, collapsing at the beginning of his 'Nine O'Clock Lecture'.

Floyd Allport and his 'science of the future'

In one of his numerous publications Münsterberg (1914) specifically advocated a scientific social psychology. In the same book he also described a group experiment somewhat reminiscent of Condorcet, since it was a simulated jury study that involved discussion followed by voting. The object, according to Münsterberg, was to find out how far such a procedure would help to arrive at the known 'objective truth'. His approach was therefore very different from that of Moede – though of course he was familiar with his work. When Münsterberg advised Floyd Allport (1890–1971) on his Harvard doctoral thesis, it was the Meumann and Moede type of approach he suggested; and with Floyd Allport began a new era in American social psychology, a move away from sociology towards experimental studies.

> In the recent rapid expansion and progress of general psychology one field ... has been sadly neglected and has been allowed to remain in a rationalistic and pre-experimental stage. This field is social psychology. Textbooks still cling to faculties of imitation, crowd consciousness, gregarious and other alleged social instincts ... True social psychology is a science of the future.   (Allport 1919, p. 297)

The above is the beginning of an early article in which Floyd Allport declared the need for a radical transformation of social psychology. As a Watsonian behaviourist he dismissed all explanations in terms of 'instincts', and was especially scathing about McDougall's 'social instincts'. He went so far as to state that the word 'social' has no significance except as 'denoting a certain type of environment and the part played by it in the post-natal behavior of the organism'. One must use observation and experiment with the aim of establishing the ways in which individuals react to social stimuli which constitute part of their environment.

In the last part of the article Allport claimed that studies of the kind he advocated could readily be undertaken by comparing subjects working alone and working together. He noted that 'practically all research on this problem had been done in Germany', but remarked that the aim of these studies had not been primarily social. Yet Floyd Allport did acknowledge his predecessors, which later writers almost invariably failed to do.

In a subsequent article Allport (1920) gave an account of his empirical studies, closely modelled on parts of Moede's work. He conducted five experiments on free association and one on 'Thought processes'. In the latter, subjects were presented with passages from Epictetus and Marcus Aurelius and instructed to think of as many counter-arguments as they could, in individual and group situations respectively. It anticipated so-called 'brain storming', i.e. tossing around ideas in a group, that in due course became fashionable in advertising and managerial circles.

The results of free association experiments indicated that co-workers in a majority of cases accelerated the rate of free association, though this varied with the nature of the task. Like Moede, Allport also found a greater effect for slow individuals. As regards 'thought processes', the *quality* of the contributions was found to be greater in the individual condition.

In his famous textbook of social psychology, often regarded as the foundation of the discipline, Allport (1924) laid down the principle, foreshadowed in the 1919 article, that

> There is no psychology of groups which is not essentially and entirely a psychology of individuals. Social psychology must not be placed in contradiction to the psychology of the individual; *it is a part of the psychology of the individual*, whose behavior it studies in relation to that sector of his environment comprised by his fellows.   (Allport 1924, p. 4; emphasis in the original)

All behaviour, he maintained, is fundamentally a biologically driven mode of adjustment to one's environment, be that social or non-social; but in a footnote rather than the text he did concede that other people do not just serve as stimuli – they also react. The empirical work reported is essentially that already described, and much of the other content is what one finds in books of general psychology, so only some brief additional comments are needed. There is a chapter on social attitudes, on which his brother Gordon had more to say. From a chapter entitled 'Personality – the social man' it emerges that Floyd Allport regarded personality as largely a social product:

> many of the characteristic reactions to be judged are evoked only through the social environment. A man's self-assertion, submission, quickness of temper [etc.] are all dependent upon the existence of other human beings toward whom these attitudes [*sic*] may be displayed.   (Allport 1924, p. 101)

A section on 'race' indicates that Allport's views on the matter were somewhat ambivalent, and he had not escaped the climate of opinion of his time. On the one hand he criticised Le Bon for writing about superior and inferior races, suggesting that 'differences in cultural adaptation' are to a considerable extent due to environmental rather than innate factors. However, he went on to say that the intelligence of whites is more versatile and complex than that of blacks, as shown by 'a greater variability in blood pressure in the negro than in the white man'!

In evaluating Floyd Allport's contribution, he must be credited with putting experimental social psychology on the map in America. On the other hand his insistence that the focus of social psychology should be purely on the individual, and that 'the group' is little more than a fiction, was misguided. He was certainly justified in dismissing the old notion of a 'group' or 'collective' *mind*. Unfortunately he also rejected the possibility that some processes can be identified that result from shared membership of a social group, thereby throwing out the baby with the bathwater. In practice he could not stick to his rejection consistently, and in his book he was unable to avoid numerous references to the concept of 'the group'. He had a whole chapter dealing with various group situations, and in the final one on 'Social behavior in relation to society' one finds him adopting several concepts like Cooley's 'primary group' or Giddings's 'consciousness of kind'. Yet in the introduction to that chapter he still maintained that 'all behavior phenomena of groups are reducible to mechanisms of individual behavior in the social environment' (Allport 1924, p. 382).

Many American social psychologists of that period did not agree with Allport's stark and narrow position, casting their net wider. But the consequences of Allport's radical stance proved far-reaching in the long run, its effects still being manifest in what Greenwood (2004) called *The disappearance of the social in American social psychology*. For instance, two of Floyd Allport's former students, Katz and Schanck, published a widely used textbook on social psychology in 1938, that was reprinted several times over the following decade. In it they discussed what Floyd Allport had called the 'group fallacy', by which he had meant using the notion of 'the group as an entity external to the individual, which makes demands upon the loyalty of the individual apart from his own welfare' (Katz and Schanck 1938, p. 550). They went so far as to compare a belief in the existence of groups, or of institutions like a college fraternity, to belief in ghosts!

This was of course an absurd position that could not be sustained. In fact Katz and Schanck themselves, when introducing the so-called 'J-curve hypothesis', had written 'More and more we live our lives within the confines of institutions and organized groups. We are a nation of joiners. The business man has his Rotary Club ... The working man has his labour union, his sick and death-benefit society.' So in practice they, like Floyd Allport himself, were unable to remain consistent.

Katz and Schanck devoted a good deal of space to the 'J-curve hypothesis of conforming behavior', put forward by Floyd Allport (1934) and at one time much in vogue.

The 'J-curve hypothesis'

The 'J-curve hypothesis' postulated that much of collective behaviour can be shown to result in a distribution that takes the form of a reversed letter J: The reversed ʟ symbolises a line on a graph sharply descending from top left and then gradually to bottom right. Allport sent out his students to collect data, which they did assiduously. There was for instance the study of car parking in a location where it was confined to 30 minutes. The investigators noted the actual parking times in nearly 30,000 cases, displaying heroic endurance! In about 20,000 of the these the rule was observed; some 5000 exceeded it by no more than half an hour; thereafter half-hour intervals contained progressively fewer cases. Another rather remarkable study was that of the 'Holy Water Ceremony' in a Catholic church. For this the scale set out below was devised:

1   Complete compliance: dipping the fingers and making the sign of the cross;
2   touching the font without dipping, but making the sign of the cross;
3   making the sign without dipping or touching the font;
4   dipping the fingers but not making the sign;
5   doing none of these.

Once again, out of a total of 1557 cases some 63 per cent conformed fully, with subsequent decline.

It was not claimed that all collective behaviour follows such a pattern, but the regularity is sufficiently widespread that it gave rise to the hope that, like physical regularities, social ones would be amenable to quantitative analysis. Alas, that hope in its original form was not fulfilled and the 'J-curve hypothesis', hardly different from common-sense expectations, has slid into well-deserved oblivion. None the less, Floyd Allport was responsible for putting experimental social psychology on the map and for giving it a direction that was, and remains, controversial.

How studies of 'social attitudes' became a core topic

While Floyd Allport did not altogether ignore the issue of attitudes and opinions, it was relatively peripheral to his main concerns. Other social psychologists such as Bogardus (1923) or Folsom (1931) regarded the study of attitudes as central to social psychology, and the same was true of Floyd Allport's brother, Gordon W. Allport (1935), whose contribution will be discussed in chapter 11.

The origins of the term 'attitude' as a social psychological concept are to be found among a group of scholars at the Department of Sociology at the University of Chicago. They included Ernest Burgess, John Dewey, George Herbert Mead, Robert Park, William Thomas, and Florian Znaniecki. It was the last two who carried out a massive empirical study based on a decade of research. It had a powerful impact on later developments in both sociological and psychological social psychology. Thomas, with Znaniecki as his collaborator, published *The Polish peasant in Europe and America* (1918–20).

On 'the Polish peasant'

William I. Thomas (1863–1947) began teaching in the Chicago Department in 1894, and in his work the influence of G. H. Mead and Dewey is apparent. Another influence was his wife, trained as a statistician. Early on he published a short paper on 'The province of social psychology' (1904), where he characterised it as an extension of individual psychology to collective life. In the same year appeared a paper which described prejudice as an 'instinct' produced by evolution, a view he later abandoned. In fact he was exceptional in arguing against the then orthodox notion of the inferiority of women and non-Europeans.

Florian Znaniecki (1882–1958) was by origin a Pole who taught at the University of Poznań and subsequently went to the United States, where he began at Chicago and then held posts at several other American universities. He was highly critical of behaviourism, which he regarded as a kind of scientific superstition. In his *Laws of social psychology* (1925) Znaniecki discussed the extent to which such laws could be said to have been established. He concluded that although significant regularity had been demonstrated, 'the expressions of this regularity are still hovering between philosophical doctrines and more or less vague, empirical approximations' (1925, p. 47). This is somewhat reminiscent of what J. S. Mill had said about 'empirical laws'.

Thomas and Znaniecki's *magnum opus* of more than 2000 pages was essentially concerned with the adjustment of immigrant Polish peasants to the radically different social environment of the United States. They saw the fundamental issue in terms of the acquisition of new values, and the focus was on attitudes. They defined an attitude as a state of mind of the individual towards a value, which governs real or potential actions in the social world. Unlike most later studies of attitudes, they used a wide range of materials: personal documents such as biographies, autobiographies, diaries, letters, newspaper articles, and official records of various kinds. Here is just one example among thousands, based on a letter to the correspondence column of a Polish newspaper:

> Josef Pawlowski, blacksmith from the village of Parchocin, after bidding good-bye to his wife and two young children, had to go, as soldier of the reserve, to a distant war in Manchuria. The woman was pretty and, what is worse, fickle. Temptations came; she could not resist and went the wrong way. Having colluded with her lover, a young boy, she sold whatever she could – cows, pigs, grain from the barn – obtained a passport for [a journey abroad] and, taking the money and the bed-furnishings, ran away at night from her children sleeping in a cradle. She covered then with straw and left them so without pity. It seems that she went to America.   (Thomas and Znaniecki 1918–20, vol. 2, p. 1162, cited in Blumer 1949, p. 49)

A huge variety of materials of this kind about people emigrating to America was minutely analysed, and from it they drew inferences about the motives and underlying attitudes for such a move. The theoretical principle they adopted may be contrasted with that employed by Durkheim, who had stated that 'The determining cause of a social fact must be searched for among antecedent social facts, and not among the states of individual consciousness.' They held, on the contrary, that 'The cause of a social or individual phenomenon is never another social or individual phenomenon alone, but always a combination of a social and an individual phenomenon' (Thomas and Znaniecki 1918–20, vol. 1, p. 44). They sought to tease out such combinations, but there are of course difficult problems of interpretation in dealing with such complex material, and they were criticised for often basing their inferences purely on declared individual attitudes. In reply to the critiques, Thomas maintained that how a person sees things is the key to his or her behaviour. In a phrase that has become famous he stated that 'If men define situations as real, they are real in their consequences.'

The methodological debate prompted by that work continued over the years in the context of the relation between attitudes and behaviour, which still features in social psychology texts. What concerns us here is that *The Polish peasant* was the starting point of a preoccupation with 'attitudes' that dominated the inter-war years. Thomas and Znaniecki themselves actually defined social psychology as 'the scientific study of attitudes'. Theoretical approaches to the concept of 'attitude' will be further surveyed in the next chapter.

Techniques of measuring attitudes and opinions

The rise into prominence of the study of attitudes, opinions, and beliefs – which were often not clearly distinguished – has to be seen in its social and political context that has been lucidly analysed by Danziger (1997). As mentioned previously, Robert Park had taken up and developed Tarde's notion of 'publics'. Walter Lippmann, an able journalist, published an influential book on *Public opinion* (1922) in which he suggested that people's ideas and opinions are to a considerable extent determined not by 'objective' facts or events, but by their personal representations of the external world. These, he argued, are based on pre-existing 'pictures in the mind' which he likened to 'stereotypes', literally printing-plates; and thus began the metaphorical use of the term. Lippmann also stressed the need for scientific studies of public opinion that could serve as guides for framing policies.

The era following the First World War was one of rapid social changes in the United States as elsewhere, and President Hoover in 1929 commissioned studies of 'social trends'. The methods used for this purpose consisted almost wholly of content analyses of newspapers, prominent magazines, popular fiction, and such-like. From this material dominant themes were laboriously teased out, leading to a number of broad conclusions. Some of these were that the authority of religion had declined, sexual mores had become more lax, and opposition to prohibition had increased. Prohibition was the law enacted in the USA in 1920 forbidding all alcoholic drinks. It was a law honoured more in the breach than the observance, which created a huge bootlegging industry. It was in fact ended in 1933, the year the report appeared.

The kind of approach adopted by the President's Research Committee, like that of Thomas and Znaniecki, naturally did not lend itself to any routine ascertainment of social attitudes, and so more readily applicable methods were being sought. One of these was already at hand, namely the questionnaire, whose use dates back centuries. For instance, a French economist in the eighteenth century devised a questionnaire dealing with trade between countries. Well in advance of his time, he formulated it in such a way that respondents would not be unduly burdened. Thus answers could be given either in terms of a simple 'yes' and 'no', or by giving sums and quantities. This he sent to French consuls and ambassadors in various countries. Unfortunately, in spite of his precautions, not a single one responded!

One of the earliest and most durable attitude measures was the 'Social Distance Scale' devised by Emory Bogardus, whose PhD was from Chicago. Bogardus was not the originator of the concept of 'social distance', since it was already extant. Robert Park defined it as follows:

> The concept of 'distance' as applied to humans ... has come into use among sociologists, in an attempt to reduce to something like measurable terms the grades and degrees of understanding and intimacy which characterize personal and social relations generally ... The point is that we are clearly conscious, in all our personal relationships, of degrees of intimacy.   (Park 1924, pp. 339–40)

Bogardus (1925) published his method, and its initial version, as shown below (slightly abbreviated), is self-explanatory:

> <u>Directions</u>: According to my first feeling reactions, I would willingly admit members of each race (as a class, not the best I have known, nor the worst members) to one or more of the classifications I have circled.

	Close kinship by marriage	My club as chum	Job in my occupation	In my street	Citizen- ship	Visitor only	Would exclude
Canadians	1	2	3	4	5	6	7
Chinese	1	2	3	4	5	6	7
English	1	2	3	4	5	6	7
French	1	2	3	4	5	6	7
Germans	1	2	3	4	5	6	7
Hindus	1	2	3	4	5	6	7

The scale has the virtue of being easy to understand and simple to administer, hence it has been extremely popular and used internationally. This is not to say that it is perfect. It entails the assumption of unidimensionality, i.e. if someone indicates acceptance of a French person as a fellow-worker, this should mean that the person is acceptable for admission to citizenship; but that is not always the case. Moreover, when an imaginary country like Ruritania is included, people are often quite willing to oblige. None the less, by and large the scale has undoubtedly proved very useful.

Bogardus devoted much of the rest of his life to studies using the renamed 'Ethnic Distance Scale', and with the help of colleagues in other US universities surveyed more than 8000 people. A biographical note issued by the University of South Carolina, which he joined in 1915, states his optimistic conclusion that 'brotherhood and sympathetic understanding had increased progressively during that 40-year period'.

The work of Bogardus came to the notice of Thurstone, arousing his interest. Louis Thurstone (1887–1955) had begun to study engineering, but later turned to psychology. He obtained a chair at Chicago, where he taught psychophysics and also some statistics to psychology students, then a new departure. His main research at the time was concerned with testing intelligence, and other forms of educational testing. When he came across the Bogardus scale he became interested in attitudes. After corresponding with Floyd Allport, who was concerned with political opinions (as professor of social and *political* psychology at Syracuse University), Thurstone decided to move into that field. Given his background, it is not surprising that he sought to apply the methods of psychophysics to the study of attitudes. In 1928 he published a paper with the title 'Attitudes can be measured'. In order to understand the phrasing of the title and reactions to the paper, it should be explained that the gurus of the period took the view that such measurement was impossible. Undaunted by the critical onslaught directed at him, Thurstone developed his method. A few years later he abandoned social psychology, gaining fame as an exponent of multiple factor analysis.

As one might guess Thurstone's method, unlike that of Bogardus, is very complicated and involves a large undertaking. I shall make no attempt to expound it in detail, only sketching the bare bones. At the beginning a set of statements relevant for the attitude to be measured is assembled. Then several hundred (!) people acting as judges are asked to sort these into sets of eleven categories ranging from extremely favourable to the attitude object to extremely unfavourable, via a neutral position. It must be understood that the judges themselves are not asked for their opinion, but merely where the statement should go along the dimension. Each statement is then assigned a score based on the median value assigned to it by the judges. The resulting attitude scale consists of some twenty statements with which those tested have to agree or disagree. For scoring, only those items with which the person agrees are counted, and the total attitude score consists of the sum of the score values of each item agreed.

The object of the exercise is to arrive at equal-appearing intervals from one step on the scale to the next, something that the Bogardus scale could not claim. However, such neatness and elegance is achieved at a heavy price, and the scale is now mainly of historical rather than practical interest.

A more straightforward and widely used technique was designed by Rensis Likert (1903–81), while working with Gardner Murphy at Columbia on a project concerned with the influences producing liberal and conservative attitudes. It is known as the method of summated ratings, or simply the Likert scale (Likert 1932). An attitude statement is accompanied by a series of grades of agreement or disagreement. The scoring consists of assigning values from 1 to 5 to the alternatives. There are several forms of this, and examples are shown below.

Slapping children when they misbehave: *Score*
(a) is entirely reasonable and right   *(5)*
(b) has some questionable aspects, but on the whole is right   *(4)*
(c) has about as many justifiable aspects as unjustifiable ones   *(3)*
(d) has some justification, but is on the whole wrong   *(2)*
(e) is entirely unreasonable and wrong   *(1)*

An alternative version involves a series of statements relating to a particular dimension of attitudes. An example of a hypothetical item might be the following:

'Intelligent design' should be taught in schools.
   Strongly agree Agree No opinion Disagree Strongly disagree
      (1)   *(2)*   *(3)*   *(4)*   *(5)*

Since the values of the response categories in a consistent direction are simply added up, it is also known as one type of the 'method of summated ratings'. Owing to their ease of construction and proven value, Likert scales are still being widely used.

The popularity of attitude studies and the relation of attitudes to behaviour

Using this tool kit, two main types of investigations were undertaken, one purely descriptive, the other experimental or quasi-experimental. As regards the former, attitudes towards a huge variety of 'attitude objects' were assessed, which included kinds of people, practices, or institutions; many reflected the political or social concerns of the period, such as race relations or political radicalism; others ranged far and wide (cf. Danziger 1997). In this connection it should again be noted that the term 'attitudes' lacked an agreed precise meaning, including beliefs and opinions.

All this began during the 1930s and continued to grow into a major preoccupation of social psychology until about the 1960s. In 1934 the American Institute of Public Opinion was founded, polling samples of the general population. Here, chosen more or less randomly, are some of the 'objects' of attitudes during the period preceding the Second World War (from Shaw and Wright 1967):

Children telling lies	God
Chinese	Law
Church	Negroes
Evolution	Punishment of criminals
Feminism	United States Constitution
Germans	War

One of the reasons why studies of attitudes were so popular is that they were widely assumed to be indicators of corresponding behaviours. Thus if some people rated Chinese favourably, it was expected that they would behave positively towards them; and the converse if they expressed a negative attitude. Then a classic piece of research threw serious doubt on the assumption.

Richard LaPiere (1934) travelled with two Chinese friends, booking into hotels and inns all over the United States. Out of fifty-five cases, only a single hotel categorically refused to accommodate Chinese guests. Six months later LaPiere wrote to these same establishments, asking if they would be willing to accept Chinese guests. Among forty-seven who replied, exactly the reverse was found: only one of them declared an unconditional willingness, and that was a woman proprietor who had previously been host to a Chinese couple and had found them very pleasant.

Another such demonstration was by Corey (1937), who tested students on their attitudes to cheating. The results failed to predict which of the students would actually be found cheating in their examinations. This kind of study opened up the issue of the relationship between attitudes and behaviour, an issue that has been debated ever since. In spite of the evidence to the contrary, there has been a reluctance to abandon the view of a close link between them. Moreover, individual attitudes, beliefs, and opinions have sometimes even been seen as simple and direct *causes* of behaviour. A striking example is a report on the causes of war by UNESCO, which stated: 'The manipulation of beliefs ... [is] one of the most important factors causing both hot and cold wars' (UNESCO 1972, p. 269).

Experiments on attitude change and effects of propaganda

The above does of course not imply that there is *no* connection between attitudes and behaviour, only that it is much more complex than was at one time envisaged. The assumption of some causal link between attitudes and behaviour underlies the numerous experimental attempts during the 1930s to produce attitude *changes*. The objects or targets of such attitudes reflect areas of concern at that time, such as 'race', nationality, internationalism, war, and liberalism/conservatism. The large majority of such studies were carried out in school or college settings, where teachers or college staff introduced material designed to influence students in a particular direction (the 'treatment'). The typical design is shown below:

Experimental group: Attitude test > treatment > repeat attitude test
Control group: Attitude test > interval > repeat attitude test.

A more sophisticated design was used by Thurstone (1931) to assess the impact of war films on children's attitudes to war. With that design it was possible to gauge the effects of particular factors, e.g. the sequence of presentation of the films.

Sequence of administrations		Types of effects	
A,B,C,D,E	took attitude scale	A	scales only – control
B, C	saw war film X	B	effect of film X
B	took attitude scale	D	effect of film Y
C,D,E	saw war film Y	C	effect of X + Y
C,D,A	took attitude scale	E	effect of Y + X
E	saw war film X		
E	took attitude scale		

In hindsight it may be noted that one condition is missing here, namely a group F which is given the attitude scale only once, right at the end. The reason is that between the start and the end of the experiment, external events may have taken place (in this case the outbreak of a war) that affected attitudes and thereby confounded the results. These kinds of issues have been discussed by Cook and Campbell (1979).

While most influence attempts were fairly straightforward others were more adventurous, such as Cherrington's (1934) ambitious project that dealt with attitudes to war and international relations. Nine groups of adult students were exposed, respectively, to conferences, a summer school in Geneva, lecture discussions, and other influence attempts. Alas, that massive battery seems to have had little effect. By contrast, a study undertaken for a Columbia PhD thesis by F. T. Smith (1933) succeeded in producing substantial changes. It was concerned with the effects of personal contact on attitudes to 'Negroes'. Mature graduate students in education were invited to visit Harlem and be entertained by prominent black professionals of various kinds, an experience not shared by a matched control group. However, a possible 'volunteer bias', such that those accepting the invitation had been more ready to change, does not seem to have been adequately controlled.

The 1930s saw the first systematic efforts to assess the impact of various forms of *propaganda*. The main questions usually asked were 'Is propaganda effective?' and 'Which form of propaganda is most effective?' An example of the former is an investigation by Chen (1933) related to the Manchurian conflict between China and Japan. Groups of students were orally given either neutral information or, respectively, pro-Chinese or pro-Japanese propaganda by instructors who switched roles in order to avoid any bias due to personality. Large changes were obtained.

Among comparisons, an extensive one with a complex design was that by Wilke (1934), using psychology students as subjects. It involved four different issues: the existence of God, the necessity for war, the justification of birth control, and inequalities of wealth. There were also three methods of delivery of the propaganda: public address with or without loudspeaker, and print. Direct public address without a loudspeaker produced the largest shifts. There were a number of variations on this theme, e.g. hearing a passionate advocate of pacifism, versus reading a pamphlet; not surprisingly, the live advocate prevailed. This was confirmed in a series of studies that took advantage of the intense public debates regarding Prohibition. For instance Knower (1935, 1936) investigated the relative effectiveness of message delivery intended to change attitudes towards Prohibition in the years just before it was abolished in 1933. Some 1300 students took part, divided into the initially 'dry' (pro-Prohibition) and the 'wet'. The variables investigated were:

1   exposed to identical messages, either spoken or printed, *against* the initial attitude;
2   exposed alone or in a group;
3   message either 'logical' or 'persuasive' in tone.

In addition some other variables such as sex of speaker and strength of initial attitude were also considered. Once again the spoken version resulted in more change, but there was no difference between the 'logical' or 'persuasive' versions.

What is important here is not really the detail of the findings, many of which are open to question, but the fact that this kind of work was the start of a movement in social psychology known as 'persuasive communication research'. It was greatly accelerated by the demands of the US War Department during the Second World War, when social psychologists were commissioned to study ways of influencing the attitudes of American soldiers. Such work continued during the post-war period (e.g. Hovland et al. 1953), and in due course became increasingly oriented towards politics and advertising.

11 The wider panorama of social psychology in the mid-1930s

It has already been shown that a great deal of uncertainty reigned during the 1920s about the aims and methods of social psychology. During the 1930s, by which time the centre of gravity had moved firmly to the United States, two handbooks were published. The editor of one, Murchison, had strongly held beliefs about the social sciences in general and social psychology in particular, and was perturbed by what he saw as their shortcomings. The book is therefore to a considerable extent a blueprint for a future social psychology, though it does also deal with then current topics. The other volume is very different in its orientation, seeking to provide a comprehensive overview of the state of social psychology at that time, and it does so very successfully.

Taken together, these volumes provide a kind of map of the landscape of social psychology in the mid-1930s. Many of its features will be familiar, while others have now disappeared. Interestingly the concept of 'culture' was then quite salient, only largely to vanish during the postwar period, re-emerging only fairly recently. This and other important topics covered rather briefly in the handbooks will be more fully presented in the final chapter.

The *Handbook of social psychology*: a grand vision

Carl Murchison (1887–1961), editor of the *Handbook of social psychology* (Murchison 1935), had taken his PhD under Knight Dunlap, one of the first to have questioned the 'instinct' approach (Dunlap 1919). Murchison was appointed at Clark University in 1923 and became head of undergraduate teaching. This was odd, since he had acquired a reputation as a poor teacher – nor was he a great researcher. However, he made his mark as a brilliant editor of numerous journals and books. He also added to the renown of Clark by establishing the Powell Lectures, named after his father-in-law, which attracted a galaxy of famous names, including Koffka, Köhler, McDougall, and Watson. Like Hamon before him and some 'critical' psychologists since, Murchison was a radical in outlook. He had published a book with the title *Social psychology: the psychology of political domination* (1929), with chapter titles such as 'Control over the labor of others', 'International relations', and 'Human rights'. Hence it is not surprising that in preparing the *Handbook* he had a moral and political agenda in addition to a scientific one. In his preface he lamented the immaturity of the social sciences in a rapidly changing world, a world, it must be remembered, which suffered from the Great Depression and witnessed the rise of Nazism:

> The social sciences at the present moment stand naked and feeble in the midst of the political uncertainty of the world. The physical sciences seem so brilliant, so clothed with power by contrast. Either something has gone all wrong in the evolution of the social sciences, or their great day in court has not yet arrived. It is with something akin to despair that one contemplates the piffling, trivial, superficial, damnably unimportant topics that some social scientists investigate with agony and sweat. And at the end of all these centuries, no one knows what is wrong with the world or what is likely to happen in the world.   (Murchison 1935, p. ix)

There is nothing left here of the optimism of the Enlightenment and its high hopes for permanent progress. Yet Murchison could not have been altogether despairing, for he brought together a notable set of contributors from an astonishingly wide range of fields, as shown by the first six chapter headings listed below:

1   Population behavior of bacteria
2   Social origins and processes among plants
3   Human populations
4   Insect societies
5   Bird societies
6   The behavior of mammalian herds and packs.

For us today that makes strange reading, and one wonders what it has to do with social psychology. The first sentence of his very brief preface (less than a page) provides a clue: 'This is the initial attempt to organize a representative cross-section of serious methods of investigating *social mechanisms*' (my emphasis). He evidently took the view that such 'mechanisms' operate throughout the organic world. It was probably prompted by evolutionary ideas, though he did not say so. Here I shall merely touch upon some topics and discuss others that are directly relevant for the present theme.

   In the idiom current at the time, four chapters are concerned with the social histories, respectively, of the 'Negro', 'Red', 'White', and 'Yellow Man'. They are authored by anthropologists rather than historians, and deal largely with cultural features. A chapter on 'Language' is kept at a rather general level and does little to foreshadow what later became psycho- and sociolinguistics. Another one on 'Magic and cognate phenomena' tackles a problem that has long fascinated anthropologists and later also psychologists. Although somewhat peripheral to social psychology, it has also been discussed in that context (e.g. Jahoda 1969). The title 'Material culture', by an anthropologist, is self-explanatory. The same applies to 'Age in human society' and 'Sex in social psychology'. A comment in the latter, by one of the only two women authors in the book, is worth quoting: 'It is interesting in this connection to note that the new day for women and the manifold investigation of sex as a scientific subject in social psychology have appeared simultaneously.' The term 'feminism' had yet to see the light of day.

Gordon Allport on the concept of 'attitudes'

The salience of the topic of 'attitudes' during the inter-war years has already been demonstrated. The *Handbook* chapter with that title will help to throw some light on the reasons why the topic was so important at the period. At the outset some account will be provided about the background of its distinguished author, Gordon Willard Allport (1897–1967), one of the outstanding personality and social psychologists of the twentieth century. Born in Montezuma, Indiana, he was the youngest of four brothers, one of them Floyd (see above); their father was a doctor of Scottish origin. When Floyd graduated from Harvard, he suggested to Gordon that he apply there, which he did. After graduating, he obtained a position teaching English and sociology in Turkey for two years. He then went to see another brother then working in Vienna, and took the opportunity of obtaining an interview with Freud. In the course of this encounter, much discussed subsequently, Freud suggested that Allport had a 'dirt phobia'. Allport was not too pleased, and it led to his mixed feelings about psychoanalysis.

On returning to America he studied for a PhD with McDougall, and two other supervisors (he was not favourably impressed by McDougall). Allport then obtained a fellowship for further studies in Europe and went to Berlin, where he met Eduard Spranger, a follower of Dilthey. After a period in Hamburg with Heinz Werner, he came to England and spent some time with Frederick Bartlett in Cambridge. These experiences shaped his outlook, which was far less parochial than that of many of his contemporaries.

When he came back he began to teach what was a new course on 'personality' at Harvard, where he remained till the end of his life. The problem of 'personality' continued to be one of his major interests, which he approached in a variety of ways, including individual case histories involving what he called 'the intuitive method' (Allport 1929). He presented his students with the autobiography of a professor of English who had an acute phobia of railways, so much so that he was unable to cross a track. Students thereby were able to gain an insight into the personality of a particular individual that could hardly have been gained in another way. The idea stemmed from his contact with Spranger, who in turn had

10 *Gordon W. Allport (1897–1967)*

adopted Dilthey's concept of *Verstehen*, rendered in this case as 'intuition'. His famous book on 'personality' appeared in 1937, and his more social psychological studies were published after the war.

Among the most innovative of these was *The psychology of rumor* (Allport and Postman 1947). Although it appeared in the early post-war period, beyond the time boundary of the present book, it will be briefly sketched. A series of richly detailed drawings depicting somewhat ambiguous social situations were used. For each part of the experiment one of the scenes was projected on to a screen, and the first participant had to describe it. Those who followed had to repeat the description without, of course, seeing the picture themselves. The distortions that occurred were often revealing of prevalent stereotypes. For instance, one picture shows a white man wielding a razor and facing a black man, but in the reports the razor was sometimes transferred to the black man. It is likely that this study was inspired by Bartlett's work on 'serial reproduction' (about which more later) which Allport would have encountered at Cambridge (England). Lastly, mention should be made of his book on *The nature of prejudice* (Allport 1954b), that has become a classic and was celebrated half a century after its first publication (Dovidio et al. 2005).

Allport's chapter in the *Handbook* begins with the sentence 'The concept of attitude is probably the most distinctive and indispensable concept in contemporary American social psychology.' After an initial historical outline, the bulk of the chapter offers a conceptual analysis rather than details of empirical work. Any community, it is argued, shares a set of common attitudes which are a combined product of culture and innate dispositions. The notion of a 'group mind' resulted from a mistaken impression that a group has a mental life of its own, gained from the existence of common attitudes.

If all attitudes were common, it would be possible to arrive at social laws based on a constant human nature. But they are not, and so social psychology has to take account of 'individual perturbations' which are more numerous than common attitudes. Yet the stability of society rests on common attitudes. These two kinds together constitute states of readiness to act, forming a total system, and it is that system, rather than any single attitude, that leads to action. Given that the effects of attitudes are indirect, how do we know that there really are such things as attitudes? The answer is that we infer their existence from the regularity of human behaviour:

> Attitudes are not faculties, but neither are they fictions. Without assuming them as actual neurophysical facts no psychologist can give an intelligible account of human behavior ... If they did not exist as fairly *organized* and *coherent* dispositions in the mental life of each individual it would be impossible to account for the patent stability and consistency in human conduct.   (Allport 1935, p. 836, emphasis in original)

Apart from the common attitudes which alone concern the social psychologist, there is a vast range of individual attitudes and traits that make up the individual human personality. This leads on to a discussion of the relationship between attitudes and personality.

There are those, like Bogardus, who hold that there is no difference – personality is simply the sum total of a person's attitudes. Others, agreeing with that, go further and believe that since attitudes are determined by culture, personality is a cultural phenomenon. Allport rejected that view, on the ground that *traits* form an integral part of personality, and traits, unlike attitudes, are not directed at particular objects but constitute particular response styles. It follows, according to Allport, that personality has a unique integration which is the business of general and not social psychology. However, and here he returns to social psychology, it is possible to abstract common attitudes and study cultural differences. At this point he cites an example: between two-thirds and three-quarters of northern college students regarded lynching as *never* justified, as compared with only a third of southern students. In conclusion, he states again that while one cannot directly observe attitudes, they are an indispensable concept for explaining the consistency of individual behaviour and the stability of society.

The above is of course a highly condensed version of a lengthy and complex argument, but the upshot is clear: attitudes are not merely the royal road for explaining social behaviour, they are the *only* road. Hence it becomes understandable why attitudes were so central, and why so much effort was devoted to their study. It should be added that in later years Allport's ideas changed, and he no longer treated attitudes as the sole key to the social.

Dashiell, a follower of Floyd Allport, on experiments

In contrast to Gordon Allport's theoretical discussion, a chapter by J. F. Dashiell reports on 'Experimental studies of the influence of social situations on the behavior of individual human adults'. Already the title shows that the focus is on the *individual*, and the framing of the issues reveals the influence of Floyd Allport. Dashiell states explicitly that the stress is on stimulus-response, and that the principles entailed in the studies of social situations are exactly the same as those applying to stimuli concerning non-social objects. In this field, Dashiell notes, one compares '*measured achievements of the individual person when under influences from other persons physically present with the measured achievements ... of the same individual when working alone*' (Dashiell 1935, p. 1099, emphasis in original). The other persons present may (1) be merely a passive audience; (2) work alongside; (3) compete against her or him; (4) make remarks about the individual or her or his work; (5) cooperate by exchanging ideas; (6) act as sole source of information; (7) exert influence through sheer majority or as a function of personal prestige.

It is of course not possible to go into the details of the numerous and often quite elaborate experiments, some of which are also described in the other handbook to be examined shortly. Many of the studies were concerned with 'social facilitation' of the kind already described, and so only a couple of examples illustrating other approaches will be offered. One was a study of jury deliberations where the focus was on the personal backgrounds of the jurors, namely the extent to which they had been trained in sifting evidence. Use was made of a method widely employed in Germany around the turn of the century for studying the validity of testimony. For instance, the famous German psychologist William Stern carried out such an experiment. He arranged for a graduate student to create a small incident in the course of a seminar, and students were later asked to describe what had taken place. In the present study the witness reports were submitted to a judge, to juries consisting of individuals trained in fact-finding such as historians and journalists, and to groups of college students. It was found that a single trained person was able to come closer to a true account of what had actually happened than a group of students. It was also noted that 'The female jury exercised much greater care in considering the details of the testimony.'

Another study juxtaposing groups and individuals compared group discussion with individual performance in arriving at the correct solution of problems. The experimenter divided half the class into groups of four who discussed the problems, while the other half worked individually.

Group discussion proved far more effective than individual efforts to find the correct solution (40 per cent versus 7 per cent). Subsequent research over many years has shown that group superiority is only found under certain conditions. Altogether this chapter provides a comprehensive inventory of the work done in this sphere until the mid-thirties.

Apart from its more esoteric content the Murchison volume also has two chapters by Lois and Gardner Murphy, dealing with topics they developed much more fully in the other handbook they edited; and this will now be surveyed.

Experimental social psychology: a faithful mirror

There is a sharp contrast between Murchison's somewhat esoteric *Handbook* and Murphy et al.'s *Experimental social psychology* (1937), in which the reader in the early third millennium will recognise many familiar themes. The volume has the sub-title *An interpretation of research upon the socialization of the individual*, and this formulation is important to note, since it signalled a radical shift away from the earlier sociological focus on society and social groups towards social aspects of the individual. In mainstream social psychology this focus has persisted, and has given rise to some critiques (cf. Greenwood 2004). Given this orientation, the work presents an extensive, coherent, and research-based account of the social psychology of the period. A massive volume of more than 1100 pages and a similar number of references, it provides an account of what the authors saw as comprising social psychology.

On the scope and methods of social psychology

This begins with a brief historical sketch in which McDougall features prominently, though the authors made it clear that 'instinct' theory was dead. There is a shrewd discussion of the place of experiments in social psychology. While clearly in favour, they are not uncritical and some of their observations are still pertinent:

> It has become very evident . . . that the social psychologist has thrust many of his problems into the laboratory without adequate consideration of the matrix in which his most certain and valuable data lie. He has simplified his phenomena in such a way as to exclude essential facts necessary in the understanding of social life, and has succeeded in experimental and quantitative control by leaving out most of the variables about which we really need to know.   (Murphy et al. 1937, p. 10)

This is why, they further explain, much of the material they present has to be non-experimental. In this connection they refer also to anthropology, which at that time was having a considerable impact on social psychology, an issue more fully discussed in chapter 12. One consequence was that the concept of 'culture' played an important role in their account. They regarded it as the business of social psychology to study the relations of individual human beings to one another in American culture. In order to understand the beginnings of such relationships, it is according to them necessary to undertake a detailed scrutiny of the ways in which children become socialised. This explains why about one-third of the work is devoted to infancy, childhood, and to a lesser extent adolescence, topics that largely dropped out of social psychology and became for a period the exclusive domain of developmental psychology. However, more recently a field bridging the two disciplines has once more emerged (e.g. Durkin 1995).

The specific mention of 'our own culture' and 'our society', with its implied restriction of range, is worth pointing out as something one does not often encounter in current social psychology. The same idea is expounded in connection with experimentation:

> It must be recognized that nearly all the experimental work in social psychology ... has value and is definitely meaningful only in relation to the particular culture in which the investigation was carried on. Such psychological laws as we can discover are for the most part statements of relations discoverable between stimuli and responses in civilized man, and perhaps many of them hold good only in specific groups or under specific social conditions.   (Murphy et al. 1937, p. 7)

This is similar to the broad distinction drawn by J. S. Mill, in his discussion of what he called 'the laws of mind', between 'universal' and 'empirical' laws, with the latter having a restricted range of application (see p. 89). It has become one of the aims of *cross-cultural psychology* to investigate the extent to which psychological generalisations hold beyond these limits (cf. Berry et al. 2002).

At this point a few general comments will be offered. The huge amount of material already available during the mid-1930s is astonishing. Throughout the volume there are, apart from numerous studies discussed at greater length, over 300 research summaries. These provide basic information sufficient to convey a useful picture of the type of research undertaken. Three abbreviated examples are given below.

General area:	aggression in children
Specific topic:	ascendancy
Author:	Jack, L. M. (1934)
Subjects:	18 four-year-old Iowa nursery school children
Method:	Time-sampling observation of paired children behind a one-way screen, 5-min. periods.
Findings:	Social responsiveness correlates with ascendancy [A].65. Resistance to adult authority correlates with A.56. Lack

of self-confidence associated with non-A. By specific training designed to increase self-confidence, children became more ascendant.

General area:	effects of praise and reproof
Specific topic:	encouragement and discouragement
Author:	Gilchrist, E. P. (1916)
Subjects:	50 educational psychology students
Method:	Given Courtis English Test. Random division into group A reproved, group B praised, and test repeated
Findings:	Group A gained 79%, group B no improvement (group B 23% better on first test).

General area:	influence of birth order upon social behavior
Specific topic:	atheism
Author:	Vetter, E. G. (1932)
Subjects:	members of the American Association for the Advancement of Atheism
Findings:	36% of the atheists were oldest children; only 15% were youngest children, and about 9% only children. These people came from families averaging 5 children.

While the above examples are certainly not representative, they do serve to illustrate some common features. For reasons already stated, a large proportion of studies dealt with children; and, as remains even more true today, many of the older participants were college students. The members of the American Association for the Advancement of Atheism (one wonders if it still exists!) constitute a rare instance of an adult population sample belonging to a group whose members shared certain views. All results shown above are quantitative, which is also true of the majority of the summaries. Measures are mostly expressed in percentages or, less frequently, correlations. Today's readers will be struck by the absence of significance levels – a considerably later development in psychology – though the 'probable error' was sometimes reported to indicate the significance of differences. The summaries of course form only a small fraction of the content of the *Handbook*, which consists of theoretical discussions and rich descriptive materials. What follows is an inevitably highly selective survey of some of the contents.

On the process of socialisation

The content of this part is not what one might have expected. It includes a chapter on learning in social situations, that really only amounts to an account of then current theories of learning. The chapter on 'The biology of motives' is equally general, though part of its eminently sensible conclusion is worth citing:

> It is important not to conclude that all emotional patterns are simply 'cultural products'; the smile, the startle patterns, the collapse of facial tone in grief, are examples of physiological responses which appear to occur in all sorts and conditions of men ... there is no heredity-environment problem as usually conceived; the physiology of emotion, though basically the same in all human beings, undergoes selective socialization, and group differences are superimposed upon the existing individual differences.   (Murphy et al. 1937, p. 154)

A chapter on 'nature and nurture' treats a perennial theme, and it is nice to find that here again the authors are on the side of the angels. In their preliminary remarks they refuse to take part in what they call a 'meaningless debate' between supporters respectively of biology or culture, a debate we have not yet left behind. The chapter is mainly concerned with 'social differences', and I single out those of sex and 'race'. As regards the former, they are quite clear in stating that sex differences in intelligence have not been found either in America or, with minor exceptions, elsewhere.

In their summary of intellectual differences between 'Negroes' and whites, the authors state that the former have much lower scores. However, they note that schooling and urban residence have a considerable effect on scores, so that one cannot be sure how they would perform if environmental differences were eliminated. This may be compared with Francis Galton's comments nearly a century earlier:

> If the Negro race in America had been affected by no social disabilities, a comparison of their achievements with those of the whites in their several branches of intellectual effort, having regard to the total number of their respective populations, would give the necessary information. As matters stand, we must be content with much rougher data.   (Galton 1869/1892, pp. 326–7)

One of the classic studies in the sphere of 'race' differences in intelligence is briefly mentioned, and will be more fully described in the next chapter. The issue of differences between ethnic groups is again a matter that is still being discussed, though there is now wide agreement that differences, if any, are relatively minor. Moreover, as already pointed out by Waitz in the mid-nineteenth century, and reiterated by the authors of *Experimental social psychology*, within-group variations are much greater than between-group differences.

A genetic study of social behaviour

All except the last chapter deal with various aspects of social development. Since most of this is no longer an integral part of social psychology and has largely been taken over by developmental psychology, only a few aspects will be considered. The issue of 'stages' of development is discussed, curiously without mention of Piaget, though he appears elsewhere. Emphasis is placed on 'the social situations' in which children become socialised under the guidance of adults and acquire the values of American culture, and throughout one finds extensive descriptive accounts of children's social behaviour in relation to adults and peers. It is worth noting again that such behaviour is said to be characteristic of children 'in our culture'. In this connection the authors draw for comparisons on Margaret Mead's ethnographic studies of the Arapesh, Mundugumor, and Tchambuli of New Guinea (Mead 1935).

Given the important functions attributed in the eighteenth and nineteenth centuries to 'sympathy' and 'imitation', one observes that these had been relegated to a minor role by the 1930s, being only briefly discussed in connection with friendships and cooperation among children. In fact these concepts were on the way out, and during most of the second half of the twentieth century they largely disappeared from social psychological texts; it is only fairly recently that they have come to the fore again as a result of neuropsychological advances.

Somewhat oddly, a chapter on 'Some adult behavior patterns in our own society' is tacked on right at the end of over 400 pages devoted to child development. The content of this chapter overlaps both with the history of group experiments in the present work (cf. chapter 10), and with the piece by Dashiell in the Murchison handbook. However, most of the studies by Floyd Allport already described were confined to social facilitation in connection with cognitive tasks, and in this section one finds some different approaches which will be illustrated. One investigation included an attempt to assess motivational factors in a group situation, namely a poker game. This was set up in the laboratory with students as players. In the course of the games the participants were asked at intervals to respond to questions about their feelings, such as 'How anxious are you to beat each player?' on a scale of $+100$ to -100. A set of correlations were then computed between the players' own cards, the bet they placed, and their desire to win. From the analysis it was concluded 'that the bet acts as a stimulus to desire rather than desire as a stimulus to bet'. The experiment of course referred to a quite specific social situation hardly amenable to wider generalisation.

As already stated, a majority of social facilitation experiments dealt with problems to which there is a single correct solution. This is atypical of real life, where issues in areas like politics involve choices between incompatible alternatives. It is probably no coincidence that a study of 'group thinking' of this kind was conducted in a sociology rather than a psychology class, and that it was not an experiment in the strict sense. Students were asked to discuss an open-ended topic related to everyday life, such as how they would spend their free time, with a view to arriving at an agreed plan. Detailed notes were taken of the unfolding of the discussion so that the stages in the emergence of a plan could be isolated. For this purpose a recording scheme was devised, with categories like 'positive suggestion', 'opposition to given solution', 'extraneous material', and so on. On the basis of this a flow diagram was prepared, plotting the course of the interactions. Essentially the same method, though greatly elaborated, was later developed by Bales (1950), who called the procedure 'interaction process analysis'.

Observational studies

So far all the studies cited have been carried out in laboratory settings, but there are also some that took place in natural conditions, using observations. There is, for instance, a section on 'suggestion and imitation in groups' in the chapter on 'Adult behavior patterns', where a project on 'crowd laughter' is described. The investigator, armed with a stop watch, attended four performances of an amusing piece by Gilbert and Sullivan and timed the duration of laughter episodes. Unsurprisingly, the responses of the four audiences were very similar in terms of what they found funny and how long they laughed. This initial exploration was followed by an elaborate experiment involving nine high school audiences numbering 100 students each, intended to isolate the factors that make people laugh. A comedienne sang a song with or without gestures, a burlesque dance, and an amusing costume, in a kind of quasi-analysis of variance design. The findings need not detain us, but what *is* interesting is that the research is described as 'a study analysing the contagion of feeling and attitude in a crowd'. So the term 'crowd' is here employed in the manner of Le Bon.

Elsewhere another set of studies dealt with the 'phenomenon' of conversation. In one of these the investigator wandered through Broadway in New York recording conversations – no doubt by pen and pencil, since tape recorders had not yet been invented. The main topics were classified and the episodes divided into men only, women only, and mixed. Women talked mainly about clothes and social affairs, men about money and business. In mixed pairs women more often adjusted their talk to the interests of men. The exercise was replicated by another researcher in London's Oxford Street and Regent Street with essentially the same results, excepting that 'the Englishman tends to adapt his conversation to the interests of the woman'. With the rise of feminism half a century later, the issue became topical again under the banner of 'conversational politics'. A study by Zimmerman and West (1975) found that irrespective of the relationship between the partners in the conversation, or the kind of situation, women are more often interrupted by men than vice versa. The interruptions are said to be assertions of superior power.

In the section entitled 'Competition and cooperation in the light of ethnological material' there is some reference to a famous sociological study of a small mid-western American town given the name *Middletown* (Lynd 1930). But the bulk of the data is drawn from Mead's (1937) survey of cooperation and competition in various 'primitive' cultures. The sample ranges widely over thirteen cultures, from native Americans, to Africans, to peoples of New Guinea, and the emphasis in Murphy et al.'s discussion is mainly on competition. Mead proposed that one of the most crucial areas of competition is power over other persons; other areas relate to valued objects, property rights, and the gratification of vanity. The portrayals of the different peoples' dominant values are, perhaps inevitably, so grossly simplified as to constitute caricatures. For example it is said about the Dakota that their 'glory hunger is so great that apparently nothing else matters much'. The fault is only partly that of the authors – Margaret Mead herself was apt to generalise rather too readily.

The main point to be made here is that the authors of *both* handbooks displayed considerable awareness of the importance of culture, regarding anthropological approaches as highly relevant for social psychology. The way in which this came about will be discussed in the next chapter. Meantime there remain two topics to be considered in the Murphy et al. volume, namely 'Measurement of adult personality' and 'Social attitudes and their measurement'. The latter has already been adequately covered here, but is mentioned since it would have been inconceivable for a book on social psychology at that time to have omitted it.

Measurement of the adult personality

In defining the scope of the chapter it is stated that 'The data in the present chapter consider the adult as a *formed* individual in our own society.' Here again one finds the implication that there are cultural differences, and a few comparative studies are included. The basic idea underlying this chapter is that personality as such is social. This idea still remains a significant strand in modern social psychology, as indicated by the fact that the largest organisation of social psychology in North America is still called The Society for Personality and Social Psychology. However, the study of personality *per se* has now split off from social psychology, and the various tests and measurements described are no longer part of it. Yet much of the material remains relevant, since personality is viewed in its social context. For instance, the ascendance–submssion test devised by Floyd and Gordon Allport is a rating scale that requires people to say how they usually behave in particular social situations. The same is true of a study of 'dominance' in which people were judged on that dimension on the basis of how they behaved in an interview setting, and of another one used to assess 'suggestibility'.

Among the various tests devised, one concerned with 'values' and devised by Gordon Allport and Phillip Vernon (1931) is of particular interest here. This is because it is based on a theory by Spranger, who had himself been strongly influenced by Dilthey. As has been mentioned already, Allport met Spranger when he was staying in Germany. Spranger elaborated what he called a 'structural' psychology in which 'meaning' was central; like Dilthey, he saw it as being in direct opposition to 'atomistic' or 'explanatory' psychology. For him 'personality' as a unique whole has to be viewed in the context of a historically evolved socio-cultural environment. This is characterised by a set of *values*, and Spranger postulated a set of the following value-types: 1 theoretical; 2 economic; 3 aesthetic; 4 social; 5 political; 6 religious. Naturally he did not believe that these existed in pure form, but proposed that any individual person embodies some or all of these to varying degrees. In their test Allport and Vernon designed a set of statements incorporating these values, and by making choices between alternatives those tested displayed the relative appeal each of these values had for them.

In this chapter there are also reports of all kinds of other proposed personality traits that were investigated, one dealing with the sense of humour. In this a sample consisting of Jewish and gentile respondents were presented with sixteen jokes, half of them disparaging Jews, and the duration of laughter measured. There was no difference in the case of the neutral jokes, but the Jewish ones were less appreciated by the Jewish subjects. Curiously enough, the same patterns of responses were obtained when Scottish jokes were presented to the same people, leading to the conclusion that Jews tend to 'affiliate themselves mentally with Scots'!

Among the methods of personality study discussed is one where pairs of individuals were brought together in the laboratory and given tasks such as making models, thereby given the impression that their manual skills were being tested. In fact, the aim was to get at personality characteristics such as helpfulness, competitiveness, honesty, and so on. Among the topics was that of the qualities of leadership, which remained popular for decades thereafter. One such study involved getting 'leaders' from such institutions as the army, penitentiaries, or universities, and administering personality tests to them as well as to samples of 'followers'. The outcome was inconclusive, as was true of many subsequent studies, until it came to be recognised that leadership is not something absolute but is relative to particular groups and situations.

The survey of the handbooks will have served to convey a general impression of what social psychology was like from about 1920 to the mid-thirties. However, the handbooks suffer from the drawback that their content was rather kaleidoscopic, touching on numerous topics and failing to distinguish clearly between the ephemeral and the enduring. An attempt will be made to remedy this in the final chapter, by elaborating on some of the themes adumbrated and discussing other significant ones that found no place in the handbooks.

12 Highlights of the inter-war years

The contents of the two handbooks discussed in chapter 11 by no means provide the full picture of social psychology in the era. Certain topics were covered only partially or not at all, and of course there were further developments after they had been published. Hence the present chapter is intended to supplement them so as to offer a more comprehensive account.

It might well be asked how I decided what should be regarded as particularly important and therefore be included as a 'highlight'. One way that suggests itself is that one should choose those still to be found in textbooks. Unfortunately that would not be a satisfactory criterion, since most texts are apt to be biased in favour of what is most recent; and while some texts contain references to some of the work that will be described, on the whole it receives little mention. So it comes down to my personal and subjective judgement, which means that other writers might have come up with a rather different – but probably not totally different – selection.

How American social psychology discovered culture

Curiously enough, the story goes right back to the tradition of Herbart and Humboldt, Lazarus and Steinthal, Wundt and Dilthey. It was that inheritance which formed the outlook of Franz Boas (1858–1942). Although by no means the first American anthropologist, he was the founder of 'cultural anthropology' that became the dominant school.

Boas was born at Minden in Westphalia to a prominent Jewish family, his father a textile merchant and his mother a member of a liberal circle influenced by the ideas of the 1848 revolution. Boas recalled that while still at school his interest in far-off lands was aroused by Daniel Defoe's *Robinson Crusoe*, and later he read accounts of Alexander von Humboldt's voyages of exploration. Alexander's brother Wilhelm (see p. 49) as well as Gottfried Herder stimulated his interest in language, culture, and the history of peoples. He did not initially follow these lines, but for a short time studied chemistry and mathematics at the University of Heidelberg, then went to Bonn where he switched to physics, biology, and geography. There he met the geographer Theobald Fischer, who introduced him to polar research and became a friend. Boas then went on to Kiel, where

11 *Franz Boas (1858–1942)*

at the age of twenty-three he completed a doctoral thesis on the seemingly
odd question of the colour of water! He rapidly lost interest in the topic of
his thesis, and under the influence of Benno Erdmann, who had been a
student of Helmholtz and Steinthal, was led towards psychophysics and the
problems of the relationships between humans and their environment. At
that point he decided to follow his youthful dreams and went to Berlin to
prepare for an expedition to Baffinland. In Berlin he was introduced to the
Society of Anthropology, Ethnology and Pre-history. There he also met
and worked with Adolf Bastian (1826–1905), who had attended lectures by
Lazarus as a student. Bastian was an intrepid ethnographic traveller who,
unlike the usual run of explorers, was most interested in the psychological
characteristics of peoples.

   In 1883 Boas left for Baffinland, where under the harsh conditions of the
Arctic he conducted researches in geography, meteorology, and demogra-
phy as well as studying the Eskimo (now Inuit), for whom he developed a
high regard. On his return he passed the *Habilitation*, an examination
necessary for university teaching (among the members of the examination

committee were Helmholtz and Dilthey). He became a *Privatdozent*, a status which obliged him to teach, but without either pay or tenure.

This background has been rehearsed in some detail to show the extent to which he was steeped in the German intellectual traditions. Yet owing to the then prevalent anti-Semitism, something he had already experienced in the course of his studies, he found it impossible to obtain a permanent position in Germany. Accordingly Boas moved to America, where in 1889 he obtained a post at Clark University and began to study the ethnography and languages of native Americans. In 1899 he became the first professor of anthropology at Columbia University.

Back in Germany at that time the connotations of the term *Kultur* may be gauged from the then current opposition of *Kulturmensch* (civilised human) and *Naturmensch* ('primitive' or 'savage'). This usage is also to be found in the writings of Wundt. Although Boas initially adhered to it, he gradually transformed the meaning of 'culture' into the modern anthropological concept, referring broadly to a cluster consisting of norms, roles, customs, and modes of thought and behaviour transmitted through the generations within a particular society. Curiously, in the last great work of Wundt, the meaning he attached to *Kultur* had undergone a radical shift, as shown by this passage: '*Kultur* is national. It is confined to the particular national community which constitutes a coherent unity in terms of language, custom, and intellectual cultivation' (Wundt 1920b, p. 20). One wonders whether perhaps this change came about by echoes of Boas that had reached him.

Another great contribution by Boas was his analysis of the causes of differences between cultures. Since the Enlightenment there had been theories of social evolution (not to be confused with the Darwinian kind) whereby it was held that societies pass through a series of lawful stages from 'savagery' to civilisation, and that 'savages' are basically the same as the civilised but have moved more slowly. With the efflorescence of biological racism in the nineteenth century this came to be modified by the view that certain peoples are innately incapable of advancing. Boas deployed a radical critique of that position, using the results of his field-work to argue that cultural differences are the outcome of environmental circumstances and historical contingencies.

Boas was always very much concerned with psychology, which he saw as closely linked with anthropology, and he envisaged a two-way traffic between these disciplines. For instance, at the twentieth anniversary celebrations of Clark University in 1909, attended by Freud, Jung, Ernest Jones (biographer of Freud), and other luminaries, Boas gave a talk on 'Psychological problems in anthropology', suggesting that anthropological data would be useful for psychologists. At Columbia he lectured his students on Wundt, and on mental functioning in traditional societies; the lectures were subsequently published (Boas 1911). He also encouraged them to take courses in psychology, which most of those who subsequently became prominent did. One of them even wrote a paper on 'The possibility of a social psychology' (Kroeber 1917/18) intended, as he explained many years later, to call for a science that would account causally for cultural processes.

Among Boas's most distinguished students at Columbia were two close friends, Ruth Benedict and Margaret Mead. Like their mentor, both made use of psychology in developing their theories, which began a trend that after the Second World War led to the emergence of a 'psychological anthropology'. Both wrote books that became best-sellers and put the notion of 'culture' more widely on the map. Benedict's best-known book, entitled *Patterns of culture* (1934/1946), was influenced by the writings of Wilhelm Dilthey and Gestalt psychology. Cultural diversity, she pointed out, is not to be taken as random assemblies of traits and behaviours but consists of different patterns, each of which constitutes a coherent whole. She saw cultures as analogous to the personalities of the individuals who collectively constitute them: 'A culture, like an individual, is a more or less consistent pattern of thought and action.' Benedict sought to categorise broad *types* of cultures, the most notable one being the dichotomy of 'Apollonian' versus 'Dionysian' (both terms adopted from Nietzsche). The former, exemplified by Pueblo Indians, are described as avoiding extremes of any kind, conforming to their traditions, being even-tempered and disinclined to assert themselves. The latter, by contrast, are said to be the direct opposite. The name is derived from Greek mythology, in which Dionysus was the god of wild and unbridled ecstasy. Accordingly, the Plains Indians displaying this pattern are competitive, violent, and subject to extremes of emotion. It has since been shown that such rigid categorisations, based on doubtful evidence, are untenable. None the less, Benedict's dramatic presentation compelled attention to the nature of cultural differences.

While Benedict worked among what are now known as 'native Americans', Margaret Mead did all her fieldwork in various parts of the South Pacific. Perhaps to an even greater extent than Benedict, she sought to draw lessons for modern western societies from her research findings. Two major and related themes of her studies were gender differences and the outcomes of child rearing in various cultures; she was also a forerunner of the women's liberation movement. Boas suggested to her that she should investigate the effects of culture on personality, and she focused on issues of sexuality, especially in the context of adolescence. This was the topic of her first book, *Coming of age in Samoa* (1928), which had the significant sub-title *A psychological study of primitive youth for modern civilization*. This implied that the study of adolescent development in traditional cultures is relevant for the understanding of that transition stage in modern societies. She tried to show that in cultures like that of

Samoa adolescence is merely a smooth transition to adulthood, without the conflicts and stresses it entails in the western world. Margaret Mead's thesis was later shown by Derek Freeman (1983) to be seriously flawed, but at the time it made a great impression and the book became very popular. In subsequent publications she further developed her theme that culture is vastly more important than biology in determining gender roles, and the sexual division of labour, as well as personality and temperament. Thus in her *Sex and temperament in three primitive societies* (1935) she claimed that in Tchambuli the temperaments characterising the sexes in the United States are reversed, so that males have a female temperament and vice versa. Many of her claims have not stood up to critical scrutiny, yet even so her numerous publications stimulated a great deal of research and her reputation as an outstanding figure is well deserved. Margaret Mead remained for several decades *the* anthropologist – often the only one – whose name was familiar to psychologists. References to her could be found in social psychology texts of the second half of the twentieth century, and she appeared already in the *Experimental social psychology* discussed above.

In 1937 Ralph Linton came to replace Boas as chairman of the Columbia Department, a position to which Benedict had aspired. Unlike her, he was more interested in psychoanalysis than in psychology. Linton invited Abram Kardiner, a psychoanalyst, to take part in a seminar in which anthropologists presented their field data and Kardiner interpreted them in neo-Freudian terms. The group came up with the concept of 'Basic Personality Structure' (BPS), supposed to describe the dynamic interactions between personality and culture. The integration of culture, they maintained, arises from a system that has three main aspects:

1   *primary institutions*, mainly subsistence economy, family type and child training; this produces
2   *a specific BPS*, meaning psychodynamic trends including anxieties and neuroses; in turn, the BPS shapes the
3   *secondary institutions*, e.g. religion and folklore.

The first book on this by Kardiner and Linton (1939) was followed by several others, and an alternative but rather similar formulation of 'modal personality' was popular for a while. The whole enterprise began to fizzle out during the post-war period, since it was flawed by the fatal circularity of the scheme and the weakness of its methods. In retrospect Jerome Bruner called it 'a magnificent failure'. The reason for noting it here is that it usually featured in social psychology texts of the period.

Going back for a moment to Boas, it should be said that he and W. I. Thomas (see p. 177) were among the foremost anti-racists of the period. Boas and his students influenced Otto Klineberg (1899–1992), whose brilliant study will now be described.

Migration and intelligence

During the First World War the American army applied what were then novel group intelligence tests to recruits, and their now notorious results included race differences. It was claimed that recruits of northern European origins were more intelligent than southern ones, and whites in general were found to be superior to 'Negroes'. But as shown in the table below, the most dramatic difference was between the scores of northern and southern blacks.

Median scores on the Army Alpha Test

Whites	57.9
Northern blacks	40.5
Southern blacks	14.4

Since that difference could not be attributed to 'race', the most common interpretation was that of 'selective migration'. In other words it was believed that the most intelligent blacks had moved north, while their duller fellows stayed behind.

This interpretation was challenged by Klineberg (1935), a social psychologist, in an investigation that consisted of two parts. First he compared the school records of black children aged between ten and twelve years in three southern areas for the period from 1915 to 1930. Then he divided them into those who subsequently moved north and those who remained. When comparing the school performance of the two groups, he found no significant difference.

For the second part of the study he administered intelligence tests to black children of the same age range in New York, and ascertained the length of their residence in the city. He found that such residence tended to raise IQ scores and school performance roughly in proportion to its duration. Thereby he conclusively disproved selective migration hypothesis in favour of environmental influences. In his later social psychology text Klineberg was led to comment:

> It must be borne in mind, however, that even in New York city the environment of the Negroes cannot be regarded as completely equal to that of the Whites ... It seems to the writer highly probable, if not certain, that with complete environmental equality, the present differences between Negroes and Whites would entirely disappear. (Klineberg 1940, p. 301)

This again is a matter that is still being discussed, and there are some who maintain that there are large genetically determined race differences in intelligence. Prominent among them is Rushton (1994), though he has demoted whites to a position between Asians and blacks.

The next piece is concerned with some developments in Britain, justifiable, I submit, since they were widely diffused and influential in the United States.

An excursion to anthropology and social psychology in Britain

In 1898 members of the Cambridge Anthropological Expedition to Torres Strait set sail for a cluster of islands situated between Australia and Papua New Guinea. The expedition was organised and led by Alfred Haddon, an outstanding natural scientist and ethnologist, who took the decision to make the expedition a multi-disciplinary one. Hence it included linguists, medical men, and psychologists in addition to anthropological specialists. The group of psychologists was headed by W. H. R. Rivers, an experimental psychologist at Cambridge, and had William McDougall (see chapter 9) as another of its members. The investigations conducted by the team were mainly psychophysical: perception (visual acuity, colour, susceptibility to visual illusions), auditory perception, reaction time, sense of smell, and muscular sense. It was the first time that experimental procedures in the tradition of Fechner and Wundt, and their followers in the United States, came to be applied in non-literate cultures. The psychological researches of the Expedition were a harbinger of the cross-cultural psychology that was to emerge more than half a century later. Incidentally, several of the pioneers in that field started as social psychologists.

After the expedition Rivers turned to anthropology, without abandoning his psychological interests. His experiences led him towards a consideration of social psychology: 'To me ... the final aim of the study of society is the explanation of social behaviour in terms of psychology' (Rivers 1926, p. 5). He advocated the study of psychology for intending field anthropologists. One of his students at Cambridge was Frederic Bartlett (1886–1969), who had been undecided whether he should pursue a career in anthropology or psychology, opting eventually for the latter. In 1913 he served as a subject for a study on perception conducted by Charles Myers – another of the members of the Cambridge Expedition. This inspired him to embark on a long series of studies which eventually saw the light some two decades later. The book was called *Remembering*, and had the sub-title *A study in experimental and social psychology* (Bartlett 1932). It demonstrated the effects of social factors on higher mental processes, and gained him international fame.

One of the chief methods he employed was that of 'serial reproduction'. In one version of this an individual is given a story to read, and asked to relate the story to another person after an interval, and so on through several reproductions. In one of the best known of these experiments Bartlett investigated the influence of culture on recall, selecting a story Boas had obtained from native Americans. The story in its original form is set out below.

The War of the Ghosts

One night two young men from Egulac went down to the river to hunt seals, and while they were there it became foggy and calm. Then they heard war-cries, and they thought: 'Maybe this is a war-party.' They escaped to the shore and hid behind a log. Now canoes came up, and they heard the noise of paddles, and saw one canoe coming up to them. There were five men in the canoe, and they said:

'What do you think? We wish to take you along. We are going up the river to make war on the people.'

One of the young men said: 'I have no arrows.'

'Arrows are in the canoe', they said.

'I will not go along. I might be killed. My relatives do not know where I have gone. But you', he said, turning to the other, 'may go with them.'

So one of the young men went, but the other returned home. And the warriors went on up the river to a town on the other side of Kalama. The people came down to the water, and they began to fight, and many were killed. But presently the young man heard one of the warriors say: 'Quick, let us go home: that Indian has been hit'. Now he thought: 'Oh, they are ghosts'. He did not feel sick, but they said he had been shot.

So the canoes went back to Egulac, and the young man went ashore to his house, and made a fire. And he told everybody and said: 'Behold I accompanied the ghosts, and we went to fight. Many of our fellows were killed, and many of those who attacked us were killed. They said I was hit, and I did not feel sick.'

He told it all, and then he became quiet. When the sun rose he fell down. Something black came out of his mouth. His face became contorted. The people jumped up and cried.

He was dead.

It will be noted that the story contains a considerable number of (for Europeans) strange cultural elements, which Bartlett rightly expected to become transformed or altogether omitted. The ninth reproduction given below will serve to illustrate this.

The War of the Ghosts

Two Indians of Mombapan were fishing for seals when a boat came along bearing five warriors.

'Come with us' said the warriors, 'and help us in the fight we are going to wage'.

The first Indian said: 'I have an old mother at home who would grieve terribly if I did not return.'

The second Indian said: 'I have no weapons.'

'We have plenty on the boat' said the warriors. The Indian stepped in and was taken with them.

In the fight farther on he was mortally wounded, so that his spirit fled.

'I am going to die,' he said, 'take me back to Mombapan'.

'You are not going to die', said the warrior. But in spite of this he did die, and his spirit left the world. (p. 124)

Bartlett analysed the striking transformations, omissions, and condensations that had taken place, showing how they followed cultural lines. Thus the 'canoe' became a boat, names were forgotten or changed, and odd elements such as something black coming out of the mouth disappeared entirely. The somewhat disconnected character of the original tale became smoothed into a continuous narrative. Perhaps most remarkable was the fact that, in spite of the title, there was no mention of any ghosts.

In the years before *Remembering* appeared Bartlett had published a book on *Psychology and primitive culture* (1923) in which he sought to undermine many of the stereotypes about 'primitives'. He also went on a field trip to Africa, and on the basis of systematic observations Bartlett described aspects of social influence on memory. At the time it was believed that Africans have a memory that is vastly superior to that of Europeans, whereas they are deficient in intelligence. Bartlett found that Africans were no better than Europeans in recalling socially neutral stimuli. However, in Swaziland, where cattle were central to the culture, people displayed an extremely detailed and accurate recall of each of their animals. In his general conclusions Bartlett discussed the significance of his various studies of memory for social psychology. Perhaps it is also worth mentioning that a later book on social aspects of thinking (Bartlett 1958) was, together with Durkheim's writings, a major source for Moscovici's 'theory of social representations'.

Bartlett was one of the very few European psychologists who featured in Murphy et al., *Experimental social psychology* (see pp. 192–9). Another was Piaget, and one of his groundbreaking experiments (hardly ever found in modern social psychology texts) will now be discussed.

Piaget on the rules of the game

There is hardly any need to say that Jean Piaget (1896–1980) ushered in a new era in child psychology. What is rather less well known is that he held chairs in sociology as well as in psychology, and that some of his work is highly pertinent for social psychology. This was recognised by Murphy et al. (1937), who included an account of Piaget's (1932) book on *The moral judgement of the child*. In that work Piaget wrote about his investigation of the processes whereby children acquire moral rules and norms. He also discussed Durkheim's theory of morality as having its source in society, agreeing with some of Durkheim's views. However, he found himself in fundamental opposition to the doctrine set out in Durkheim's book on *Moral education* (1925) regarding the way moral rules are inculcated. He described Durkheim's position in the following passage:

> In the family altruistic leanings and feelings of solidarity are stronger than duty. At school, on the contrary, there must be rules. These rules must be cultivated for their own sake. They constitute 'an instrument of moral education which it would be hard to replace.' It is therefore the master's business to impose them. 'Since it is by the master that rules are revealed to the child, everything rests with him. Rules can have no other authority than that which he confers upon them: that is to say, than that of which he suggests the idea to the children.'   (Piaget 1932, p. 360)

Hence Durkheim attributed the acquisition of moral rules entirely to the authoritarian pressures exerted by teachers in the school situation. It was a doctrine that went against the grain of Piaget's more democratic sentiments – he always placed great emphasis on the importance of cooperation as compared with coercion. He set out to demonstrate the validity of an alternative account of the origins of moral rules, and diagnosed the basic flaw in Durkheim's attempted explanation:

> Durkheim thinks of children as knowing no other society than adult society or the societies created by adults (schools), so that he entirely ignores the existence of spontaneously formed children's societies, and of the facts relating to mutual respect. Consequently ... Durkheim's pedagogy ... for lack of being sufficiently informed on the subject of child sociology ... simply leads to a defence of the methods of authority.   (Piaget 1932, pp. 358–9)

Something might be added which Piaget himself did not mention, namely that schooling is not universal. Hence Durkheim's position would imply that there could be no moral rules in pre-literate societies, which is evidently nonsense.

Naturally it would not be feasible to summarise here the rich material obtained by Piaget in a whole series of investigations. Instead, a necessarily condensed account of one key study will be provided. This dealt with the manner in which children come to understand the nature of rules.

The game of marbles

Piaget's method was as straightforward as it was ingenious. He simply asked children between the ages of four and thirteen to show him how to play with some marbles he presented, saying he had forgotten how to play since his childhood and wanted to play again. In the course of the games, during which he made sure to let the child feel in command, it was natural to ask questions about the rules, their fairness, their origin, and so on.

In order to explore the level of understanding they had reached, Piaget asked children questions like 'Can rules be changed? Have rules always been the same as they are today? How did rules begin?' A couple of protocols are cited below, the first one being of a child who had great respect for the rules and attributed them to his father:

> FAL, age 5. 'Long ago when people were beginning to build the town of Neuchâtel, did little children play at marbles the way you showed me?' – *Yes* – 'Always that way?' – *Yes* – 'How did you get to know the rules?' – *When I was quite little my brother showed me. My Daddy showed my brother.* – 'And how did your Daddy know?' – *My Daddy just knew. No one told him.* – 'How did he know?' – *No one showed him.* (p. 46)

At a later age the relativity of rules of games comes to be recognised:

> ROSS, age 11. 'Why are there rules in the game of marbles?' – *So as not to be always quarrelling you must have rules, and then play properly.* – 'How did these rules begin?' – *Some boys came to an agreement among themselves and made them.* – 'Could you invent a new rule?' – *Perhaps ...* [thinks and suggests one] – 'Could one play that way?' – *Oh, yes.* – 'Is that a fair rule like the others?' – *The chaps might say it wasn't very fair because it's luck. To be a good rule, it has to be skill.* – 'But if everyone played that way, would it be a fair rule or not?' – *Oh, yes, you could play just as well with that rule as with any others.* (p. 58)

Generally, the youngest children have as yet little or no conception that there are any rules. Then they become aware of the existence of rules, but regard these as absolute – there could be no other ways of playing the game. From about ten onwards the relativity of rules of games starts to be understood, the fact that they are a function of group consensus and cooperation, and could be modified. During the same period the concept of 'fairness' emerges. Thus authority gives way to reciprocity.

These are of course only the bare bones of the story which, as Piaget showed, also holds lessons for understanding adult social behaviour. I have singled this theme out since this part of Piagetian theory constituted an important contribution to social psychology and has inspired a great deal of subsequent research. For instance Turiel (1983) took the issues further by tracing the emergence in children's minds of a distinction between morality and convention.

It is a little-known fact that, as shown by Hsueh (2002), Piaget came to be known to social scientists in the United States in the context not of child study but, oddly, of industrial psychology.

The surprising results of the Hawthorn Experiments

In the early years of the twentieth century Frederick Taylor, an American engineer, put forward a theory of 'scientific management' designed to make industry more efficient. He introduced time-and-motion study in order to standardise working procedures with a view to maximising output. Among other factors considered, the physical setting of the workplace was prominent. The prevailing assumption was that a workforce is motivated only by monetary rewards. It was no coincidence that

Münsterberg (see p. 173), one of the pioneers of industrial psychology, called it 'economic psychology'. In the system of 'scientific management', workers were more or less treated as cogs in the machine, to be homogenised as far as possible.

It was this ethos that came to be undermined by a series of studies conducted under the aegis of the Harvard Graduate School of Business Administration at the Hawthorn Works of the Western Electric Company of Chicago (Roethlisberger and Dixon 1939). The series began in the mid-1920s and lasted for twelve years. The initial aim was to answer the simple question of the effect of different levels of illumination on performance. Accordingly, the performance of women workers was measured at first under existing conditions, to provide a standard against which the outcome of changes could be assessed. Illumination was then systematically varied, but this appeared to have no consistent effect. Consequently the design was refined, with an experimental and a control group matched for initial base rates, and the illumination was changed only for the experimental group. The result astonished the researchers: experimental and control groups *both* increased production to the same degree.

With the object of clarifying the matter, various other manipulations were tried out. It was thought that fatigue might be a confounding factor, and so rest pauses of varying lengths were introduced, the working day shortened, followed by a return to the initial conditions. Once again expectations were not fulfilled: taking the original base line as 100 per cent, output gradually increased irrespective of the nature of the manipulations; and instead of being reduced by the return to conditions at the outset, it reached a level of 131 per cent.

It then became obvious that the researchers had been on the wrong track, by failing to consider the feelings and attitudes of the women who had participated. The experimenters' presence, coupled with the fact that the women had been singled out for special attention and observation, meant that a particular *social situation* had been created, and it was this that explained the findings.

This now classical series of experiments was one of the first large-scale field studies. Its major significance, however, was that it brought about a fundamental revision of ideas not merely in industrial/organisational psychology but also in social psychology (cf. Miller 1972). It came to be generally accepted that what used to be known as 'subjects' are themselves *reactive*, and this fact has gone down in the literature as 'the Hawthorn effect'.

One of the main figures from the Harvard Business School who participated in the Hawthorn studies was Elton Mayo, a friend of the great French psychologist Pierre Janet (1859–1947), whose intellectual descendant had been Piaget. Thereby Mayo became interested in Piaget's ideas, later even publishing a paper on his work (Mayo 1930). When planning for his part in the Hawthorn studies, Mayo decided on an extensive programme for interviewing 20,000 workers over the years 1929–32, adapting for this purpose Piaget's method of clinical-type interviews which Piaget had used with children. Compared with the then popular attitude studies, it was open, flexible, and exploratory. Mayo (1933) expounded the lessons learnt from his project for an understanding of the modern industrial scene. Given the impact of the Hawthorn project, it is understandable that Mayo's investigations contributed to the diffusion of Piaget's ideas among the wider social science community in America. For instance, when Margaret Mead went into the field, one of her objectives was to test Piagetian theory in a non-European population.

Before leaving the Hawthorn studies, a brief note on a less dramatic though by no means negligible finding seems worth adding. At a later stage, when the investigators had become fully aware of the social implications, they undertook a study of fourteen male workers in the 'Bank Wiring Observation Room'. These men were paid by piecework, and the traditional assumption had been that they would make every effort to maximise their earnings by producing as much as possible and putting pressure on their slower colleagues to speed up, since their rewards were interdependent. In fact the investigators discovered that the group had evolved a set of norms that governed their output, which may be summarised as follows: you should not work too hard, or you are a 'rate buster'; you should not slacken unduly, or you are a 'chiseler'; you should not give away your mates to the supervisor, or you are a 'squealer'. The norms had a rational basis, for if a member was too slow, the group earnings would diminish; and if some worked too hard, management might adjust the piece rate so that all would have to work more without corresponding benefit. In this way, in spite of considerable individual differences in ability and skills, the group produced at a uniform rate.

However, perhaps more often than not such group norms are not deliberately devised but emerge in the course of interaction between group members. How this can happen was elegantly demonstrated by Sherif.

Sherif on the formation of norms

A classic study dealing with the emergence of social norms was carried out by Muzafer Sherif (1935), a social psychologist of Turkish origin who went to live in the United States. Unlike most of the inter-war contributions described in the present chapter, Sherif's experiment still features in most social psychology texts. For that reason it will be dealt with rather briefly.

The problem of how social norms develop was then also debated by sociologists, and Sherif decided to tackle it experimentally in an ingenious manner by making use of the 'autokinetic effect'. This effect was first discovered by astronomers who were looking at one particular star, and found that it appeared to move. The phenomenon can be produced by having a single point of light in a completely darkened room. Although the light is stationary, the illusion of movement is extremely powerful, and subjects were asked to estimate the distance the light had moved during the few seconds it had been exposed. During individual trials there was a tendency for each person to converge on a rather narrow range, but individuals differed widely in their mean estimates. When subsequently tested in small groups the estimates converged on a common magnitude. In a condition where subjects were tested first in a group and then individually, the group norm tended to persist. It was later shown by Jacobs and Campbell (1961) that if group members are progressively replaced by others, so that the new groups contained none of the original participants, their members still adhered to the same norm transmitted through the 'generations'.

Later Sherif and colleagues (e.g. Sherif et al. 1961) conducted an equally famous series of extended experimental field studies of inter-group relations with boys at summer camps. This kind of field experiment with artificially created, and yet in an important sense 'natural', groups had previously been done by Lewin.

Lewin, and a new generation of American 'stars'

Experimental studies during the 1920s and 1930s were carried out in laboratory settings, but towards the end of that period a new approach was pioneered by Kurt Lewin (1890–1947). After having studied psychology and philosophy at the University of Berlin he fought and was wounded in the First World War. On his return he joined the staff of the Psychological Institute in Berlin, where the prominent Gestaltists Wolfgang Köhler and Kurt Koffka were his colleagues, and Fritz Heider (see p. 35) was a close friend. Already at that time Lewin had written about the logical foundations of physics and biology, which he later used in his attempts to elaborate a theoretical basis for a 'topological' psychology that would be truly scientific. By the time the Nazis had come to power in Germany he had already acquired an international reputation, and being Jewish he decided to leave for the United States where Cornell University had offered him a temporary post. On his way there he stopped over at Cambridge to visit Frederick Bartlett, with whom he discussed his ideas.

After two years Lewin moved to what was then called the Iowa Child Welfare Research Station, where he remained until 1944. There he developed his 'field theory' intended as a tool for the analysis of individual and social behaviour. It was a theory that used terms from physics and mathematics, yet remained firmly psychological. Two of his fundamental concepts were those of the *life space* consisting of a combination of persons and their environments, and the concrete *situations* in which they find themselves. During the early period Lewin experienced some difficulties, since his inadequate command of English combined with his unfamiliar ideas meant that his listeners were unable to understand him. However, his intellectual brilliance was evident, and unlike traditional German professors he did not remain remote from his students. He became a highly successful teacher, and the brightest students flocked to him for their dissertations.

Lewin's enduring contribution to social psychology was not so much his theoretical formulations, which have somewhat receded into the background, but his espousal of a group psychology. Nowadays one would not see anything remarkable about that; but at the time many psychologists, following the lead of Floyd Allport, denied the psychological reality of 'groups'. Older theories of 'group mind' such as those of Espinas or McDougall had discredited the concept of a group viewed as more than an assembly of individuals; and referring to a 'group atmosphere' or 'group goals' tended often to be regarded as unscientific or even mystical. It was due in no small measure to Lewin that the notion of a 'group' became scientifically respectable. Moreover, he devised appropriate methods for the study of what he named 'group dynamics'. In order to illustrate this, an early version of one of his best-known experiments (Lewin et al. 1939) will be outlined.

It all began with Ronald Lippitt's interest in problems of leadership, which he discussed with Lewin, and they jointly drew up plans for the first of what became several field studies. They organised activity clubs for small numbers of eleven-year-old children, dedicated to making masks and other objects. They were formed into two groups of five children each, and came together for eleven sessions. The same adult leader (Lippitt) took both groups, but with one he functioned in a 'democratic' and with the other an 'autocratic' style. As an autocratic leader he determined objectives, allocated tasks to individuals, decided who should work with whom, and praised or criticised each participant individually. As a democratic leader he encouraged group discussion, did not tell the group what to do, and if asked proposed alternatives among which the group members had to choose; praise or criticism was addressed to the group as a whole. Five observers took continuous notes on the behaviour of the children and of the leader.

Analyses of the data indicated that democratic groups were more relaxed, displayed more cooperative behaviour, showed more initiative, and produced more and better work. With hindsight it is clear that this outcome was to some extent predetermined, and one also has to view this particular study in the context of a tense international situation that pitted democracy against fascism. What matters, though, is not that particular result, but the demonstration that group processes are amenable to empirical study.

Lewin was also involved in dealing with applied problems. Thus when America entered the war, a committee concerned with nutrition was established, to which Lewin and also Margaret Mead were invited. At the meetings the problem of changing customary behaviour was discussed, and in the course of this the concept of 'group decisions' was developed. Consequently Lewin and his students embarked upon what became known as the 'food habits study', which yielded some useful insights about ways to bring about changes. He later called such approaches, which relate a theoretical framework to real-life issues, *action research.*

Generally, the impact of Lewin's work was very great, so much so that he was one of those who have been described as 'the father of social psychology'. Not least among his achievements was the enthusiasm he generated among his students. Out of his stable came prominent contributors, including Morton Deutsch, Leon Festinger, Harold Kelley, Albert Pepitone, Stanley Schachter, and John Thibaut. It was they who largely shaped the mainstream social psychology of the second half of the twentieth century.

Concluding reflections

Time present and time past
Are both perhaps present in time future,
And time future contained in time past.

(T. S. Eliot, *Four Quartets*)

As the preceding pages have shown, the path towards a scientific social psychology has been a slow and tortuous one, with many halts and even backward moves. Such slow progress is not unusual, since it also took centuries for astrology to become astronomy or alchemy chemistry. Moreover, while all such developments were influenced by the prevailing *Zeitgeist*, this is particularly true of efforts to understand the social nature of humans. Owing to what is known as 'reflexivity', the existing social power and epistemological assumptions of a period were, and always are, apt to constrain the available perspectives. It was largely for this reason that many of the insights gained during the eighteenth century came to be lost, only to be rediscovered later. None the less, there has been a certain continuity, with ideas being passed on, sometimes misinterpreted, often modified. It may have come as a surprise that many concepts usually regarded as modern had been anticipated long ago.

The present work has been confined to a broad mapping of the historical landscape up to the Second World War. Hence the kinds of transformations undergone by old ideas in the more recent past are beyond its scope. However, the issue is sufficiently important to warrant some brief comments, illustrated by an example. What has tended to happen is that interesting and wide-ranging if perhaps somewhat diffuse ideas are narrowed into a form where they become amenable to an empirical and preferably quantitative approach. A case in point is that of 'attribution theory', whose origin is credited to Fritz Heider, a member of the Gestalt school. Its roots in Germany and Austria have been traced back to Goethe and Kant via Franz Brentano, Ernst Mach, Alexius von Meinong and Carl von Ehrenfels, to Kurt Koffka, Wolfgang Köhler, Kurt Lewin, and Max Wertheimer. This dropping of names is partly to point to another history not touched upon here, but mainly to note that Heider drew extensively on the ideas of the last four mentioned in formulating his approach. As far as 'attribution' is concerned, something like it in the sense of making judgements of the actions of others is already implicit in the writings of Adam

Smith; and Heider was thoroughly familiar with them (see p. 35). Furthermore, in discussing whether an attribution is a function of the perceiver or of external factors, he refers to J. S. Mill's *method of difference* as providing a decision tool (Heider 1958, p. 68).

Now it is necessary to stress that, contrary to what is often assumed, neither his initial journal publication (Heider 1944) nor the 1958 book was primarily concerned with 'attribution'. Although the term recurs frequently in the book, it was only one of the concepts he employed, and there is no chapter with that heading. The focus of both publications was far wider, dealing with social perception in general. Then Harold Kelley (1967) introduced his famous cube, representing three causal dimensions of attributions, namely persons/actors, time/situations, and entities/ targets. Thereby Kelley on the one hand produced an elegant scheme designed to render 'attribution' amenable at least in principle to empirical analysis; on the other hand, much of the richness of Heider's original approach was thereby lost. In this way 'attribution theory' became, at least for a time, the dominant topic in social-psychological research.

Such periodic shifts in major research interests are, of course, also to be found in other fields. They can be quite healthy, as long as there is a central body of knowledge that is cumulative. The extent to which this is the case in social psychology is debatable, and it can be argued that the solid foundations which exist in other sciences are still awaited. This may soon change, as there have been promising developments. The background of three of these will now be sketched. They are, respectively, evolutionary social psychology, social neuropsychology, and 'critical social psychology' (CSP). I shall call the last one CSP for the sake of brevity, though it is also known as 'discursive psychology' or 'social constructionism'. It might be best to begin with some comments on this area, since its historical depth is rather shallow.

On 'critical social psychology'

The epistemological stance of most CSP roughly matches that of Vico, who had maintained, contrary to most Enlightenment figures, that Newtonian science is *not* applicable to human affairs. A view in some respects similar was put forward by Dilthey (see p. 133), though he did not deny the legitimacy of 'scientific' psychology, as most CSP is apt to do. There is probably no direct relationship between the position of Dilthey and that of CSP, which constitutes 'postmodernism' in its psychological garb (it has many others), and began to flourish around the 1970s (see Burr 2003 and Tuffin 2005).

It is not easy to pin down 'postmodernism' beyond saying that it emphatically rejects what its adherents usually call 'the Enlightenment project'. All CSP is critical of any experimental approaches, which are regarded as misplaced or even 'oppressive', and in any case pointless. This is because of the view that all knowledge is a product of 'social construction', and so experiments have no special claim to truth. Far from trying to be entirely objective and value-free, rightly seen as unattainable, CSP adherents openly advocate what are often radically reformist values. At the same time they are not anti-empirical, since they view 'discourse' and 'text' as crucial for understanding social life. Their main method is 'discourse analysis', and they have made interesting contributions using it. It should be added that the above characterisation is somewhat artificial, since adherents of CSP do not constitute a homogeneous group; some even accept conventional social psychology, seeing their role as that of complementing it. In my opinion this last point of view will gain ground, since CSP is unlikely ever to achieve its aim of completely supplanting more tough-minded social psychology.

On evolutionary social psychology

Unlike CSP, evolutionary social psychology (see Simpson and Kenrick 1997; Ellis and Bjorklund 2005) has a long line of precursors, at least in the sense that people have long been asking 'how did we become as we are?' Prior to the Renaissance there was a widespread belief in a past Golden Age, followed by degeneration. In 1566 Jean Bodin postulated a succession of periods dominated first by Orientals, then by Mediterraneans, and lastly by northern Europeans. Their respective dominant features were in turn religion, practical skills, and warfare and invention. He tried to explain this sequence causally in terms of climate and geography.

Let me jump now to the Enlightenment when, as already mentioned, the past was viewed as a succession of ascending stages from primitive hunters to commercial civilisations. It was envisaged that the ascent of humanity would continue unabated, and Condorcet was one of those who had faith in continuous progress, an optimism that continued to prevail for more than a century. It can be seen in the writings of Comte, and also Spencer who referred to the *necessity* of progress; and both linked this to features of the human mind. The term 'evolution' in the sense of development of animals and plants dates back to the seventeenth century, but it was Spencer who applied it systematically to the social sphere. At that time philologists also studied the evolution of languages, and so evolutionary ideas were then common. However, it was of course Darwin who showed *how* past evolutionary processes had shaped human nature. Psychologists of the period eagerly adopted the new insights, and Wundt for instance focused on the long-term effects of social interaction. Most others chose to concentrate on 'instinct' as an evolutionary product in the expectation that it would explain behaviour, an attempt that eventually had to be abandoned.

During the following three-quarters of a century Darwinian theory came to be extended and refined into 'neo-Darwinism', and in the 1960s and 1970s biologists became interested in biological analyses of social behaviour. In 1975 E. O. Wilson published his *Sociobiology*, initially much criticised by social scientists who resented what they felt to be an intrusion into their field. Gradually this kind of approach gained adherents among psychologists, culminating in the recent emergence of evolutionary social psychology. Its aim is to answer the old question of how we have become what we are, by framing and testing hypotheses about the way the challenges faced by early humans had resulted in a neural architecture that still influences our social behaviour. In other words, it constitutes a search for human social universals, a search that is tricky since the genetic inheritance is confounded by cultural variations.

All this has been rather abstract and general, and so a concrete example will perhaps be useful, and for that I return once again to Adam Smith. One of the principles he enunciated was that of *reciprocity*:

> It is thus that man, who can subsist only in society, was fitted by nature to that situation for which he was made. All the members of human society stand in need of each others' assistance, and are likewise exposed to mutual injuries. Where the necessary assistance is reciprocally afforded ... the society flourishes and is happy.   (Smith 1790/1984, part I, p. 1)

Smith was far from having been the first to enunciate that principle. It is reported that when Confucius was asked for a single word that would encompass all morality, he responded by 'reciprocity'. Hobbes suggested that it was necessary to end 'a condition of war of every one against every one'. Yet in spite of it long having been regarded as a fundamental prerequisite of sociality, reciprocity has not figured prominently in social psychology.

During the 1970s biologists noted that under certain conditions what they called 'reciprocal altruism' could be observed in animals. It is therefore a product of evolution, and when Smith attributed it to 'nature', it was a more accurate statement than he could have known. In recent years there have been an increasing number of studies of this topic across a wide range of cultures by psychologists, anthropologists, and economists. Why economists, it may be asked? The answer is that they were testing the assumption of classical economics that people act in terms of rational self-interest, and found it wanting. People everywhere consider reciprocity and 'fairness', though the extent to which they do so varies according to culture and circumstances. It would appear, therefore, that reciprocity constitutes a universal principle of human sociality, of prime concern to social psychology.

On social neuropsychology

This is a complex and varied field (see Frith and Wolpert 2004; Cacioppo and Berntson 2005), and here I shall confine myself mainly to the twin categories of 'sympathy' and 'imitation' already discussed in the context of the Enlightenment, though social neuropsychology as such is much wider. Before going further, a brief digression is necessary. I am referring throughout to 'sympathy', but readers will be well aware that the term 'empathy' has come into increasing use and is now more frequent than 'sympathy' in the psychological literature. Since this is liable to create confusion, it should be explained that when Titchener coined the term in 1909 it was as the result of a misunderstanding; and in spite of claims to the contrary, there is no discernible difference in meaning between 'sympathy' and 'empathy' (see Jahoda 2005).

Returning to sympathy and imitation, the physiologist Cabanis coupled them under the heading of 'moral' [read 'social'] processes and proposed that they, 'like those one calls "physical", result from the actions of either certain particular organs or from the whole of the living system' (Cabanis 1802/1985, p. 337). Although few followed him in his physiological speculations, sympathy and imitation continued to be discussed by many prominent figures during the nineteenth century, as will now be shown.

Alexander Bain wrote that 'Sympathy and imitation both mean the tendency of one individual to fall in with the emotional or active state of others' (1859, p. 210). When discussing the 'moral sense', Darwin referred to 'The all-important emotion of sympathy' (1871/1901, p. 162), and argued that it will have been strengthened by natural selection, since communities where it is most prevalent would increase relative to others. Like his grandfather, though in a rather different manner, he also gave considerable weight to imitation: 'It deserves notice that, as soon as the progenitors of man became social ... the principle of imitation, and reason, and experience would have increased, and much modified the intellectual powers' (Darwin 1871/1901, p. 198). Applying his principle of selection, Darwin suggested that if a clever man in a group invents something important and others imitate him, then the group will flourish and become larger, thereby increasing the chances of other inventive people being born. One of the earliest followers of Darwin to apply evolutionary theory to human society was Walter Bagehot, who stated that 'the propensity of man to imitate is one of the strongest parts of his nature' (Bagehot 1872/1905, p. 92), and in his *Principles of psychology* (1870–2) Herbert Spencer had a chapter entitled 'Sociality and sympathy'.

The salience of sympathy and imitation was by no means confined to Britain. In France, Tarde's whole theoretical edifice rested on imitation. The eminent French psychologist Théodule Ribot described sympathy as a 'highly plastic psychophysiological property' and, rather like Adam

Smith, saw it as 'one of the foundations of social and moral life' (Ribot 1896, p. 227). In America, Baldwin and William James, among others, held similar views. Like Baldwin, James traced imitation back to its onset in early childhood and his comments on its far-reaching implications are reminiscent of the views of Erasmus Darwin: 'And from this time [i.e. childhood] onward man is essentially *the* imitative animal. His whole educability and in fact the whole history of civilization depend on this trait' (James 1891, vol. 2, p. 408). It would be easy, but futile, further to multiply examples.

In early twentieth-century social psychology sympathy and imitation still figured prominently, e.g. in McDougall's 1908 text, but later this declined progressively over the remainder of the century. It is probably no coincidence that this decline occurred *pari passu* with an increasing emphasis on empirical, and especially experimental, approaches. Sympathy/empathy does not lend itself to any direct measurement, and although imitation involves behaviour, its study was chiefly confined to children. Imitation came to the fore in the evolutionary conjectures of Dawkins (see p. 145), yet at that time the modes of functioning of imitation and sympathy still remained shrouded in mystery.

The breakthrough took place during the 1980s, with developments in neuroscience. A crucial advance was made possible by the advent of Magnetic Resonance Imaging (MRI), providing insights into the living brain. This led to the discovery of so-called 'mirror neurons', which are activated in the presence of other people and throw fresh light on the mechanisms underlying both sympathy and imitation. This discovery has been likened to that of DNA, and, while that is going rather too far, there is little doubt about its considerable importance. Another advance was related to 'attachment theory', and in this connection it has been shown that certain types of interpersonal behaviour affect key neurochemical systems in the brain. These discoveries contribute to a deeper understanding of what happens during social interactions, confirming the speculative ideas put forward by Cabanis two centuries ago and justifying the importance attached to sympathy and imitation by so many past writers.

Towards the future

Beginning with the Enlightenment, scholars in many different fields have been concerned with themes germane to what in due course became social psychology. About a century ago social psychology achieved the status of a distinct discipline, marking it off from neighbouring specialisms. During the 1970s it experienced a 'crisis' of confidence, in the course of which 'critical' social psychology began to split off; but this had little effect on the mainstream.

Since then a number of new developments have arisen which to some extent challenge what might be called the orthodoxy. In addition to those noted above, there is Moscovici's theory of social representations. Another is 'dialogical' social psychology (see Markova 2003). This takes its original inspiration from the Russian writer Mikhail Bakhtin (1895–1975), who put forward an epistemology of human cognition and communication based on dialogical relationships. Today, however, 'dialogism' refers to a number of approaches that emphasise the value of dialogue like those of George Herbert Mead, Buber, and Habermas among others. These different forms of dialogism provide new theoretical tools for the analysis of the social world, and as such have also been adopted by some sociologists (see Camic and Joas 2004). Significantly, their sub-title refers to 'the postdisciplinary age', suggesting that the boundaries between academic disciplines are becoming increasingly permeable.

There is no doubt that this trend will affect social psychology in relation not merely to other social but also to the biological sciences. At the time of writing, such cross-fertilisation is already in its initial stages (see van Lange 2006), and holds out the prospect of a greatly enriched and truly scientific social psychology.

Select bibliography

Allport, F. H. (1919). Behavior and experiment in social psychology. *Journal of Abnormal Psychology* 14: 297–306.

   (1920). The influence of the group upon association and thought. *Journal of Experimental Psychology* 3: 159–82.

   (1924). *Social psychology*. Boston: Houghton Mifflin.

   (1934). The J-curve hypothesis of conforming behavior. *Journal of Social Psychology* 5: 141–83.

Allport, G. W. (1929). The study of personality by the intuitive method: an experiment in teaching from *The Locomotive God*. *Journal of Abnormal and Social Psychology* 24: 14–27.

   (1935). Attitudes. In C. Murchison, ed., *A handbook of social psychology*. Worcester, MA: Clark University Press.

   (1937). *Personality: a psychological interpretation*. New York: Holt, Rinehart and Winston.

   (1947). *The use of personal documents in psychological science*. New York: Social Science Research Council.

   (1954a). The historical background of modern social psychology. In G. Lindzey, ed., *Handbook of social psychology*, 2 vols. Reading, MA: Addison-Wesley.

   (1954b). *The nature of prejudice*. Reading, MA: Addison-Wesley.

Allport, G. W. and Postman, L. (1947). *The psychology of rumor*. New York: Holt.

Allport, G. W. and Vernon, P. (1931). A test for personal values. *Journal of Abnormal and Social Psychology* 26: 231–48.

Ashton, R. (1991). *G. H. Lewes: a life*. Oxford: Clarendon Press.

Bagehot, W. (1872/1905). *Physics and politics*. London: Kegan Paul, Trench, Trübner.

Bain, A. (1859/1899). *The emotions and the will*. London: Longmans, Green.

Baker, K. M. (1975). *Condorcet: from natural philosophy to social mathematics*. Chicago: University of Chicago Press.

Baldwin, James Mark (1895). *Mental development in the child and the race*. New York: Macmillan.

   (1897). *Social and ethical interpretations in mental development: a study in social psychology*. New York: Macmillan.

   (1899/1911). *The individual and society*. London: Rebman.

   (1906–11). *Thought and things: a study of the development and meaning of thought: or genetic logic*, 3 vols. London: Swan Sonnenschein.

   (1915). *Genetic theory of reality: being the outcome of genetic logic as issuing in the aesthetic theory of reality called pancalis, with an extended glossary of terms*. New York: Putnam.

Bales, R. F. (1950). *Interaction process analysis: a method for the study of small groups*. Reading, MA: Addison-Wesley.

Bandura, A. (1965). Influence of models' reinforcement contingencies on the acquisition of imitative responses. *Journal of Personality and Social Psychology* 1: 589–95.

Bartlett, F. C. (1923). *Psychology and primitive culture*. Cambridge: Cambridge University Press.

(1932). *Remembering: a study in social and experimental psychology*. Cambridge: Cambridge University Press.

(1958). *Thinking: an experimental and social study*. London: Allen and Unwin.

Benedict, R. (1934/1946). *Patterns of culture*. New York: Mentor.

Berry, J. W., Poortinga, Y. H., Segall, M. H. and Dasen, P. R. (2002). *Cross-cultural psychology: research and applications*. 2nd edn, Cambridge: Cambridge University Press.

Blumer, H. (1949). *Critiques of research in the social sciences: I. An appraisal of Thomas and Znaniecki's 'The Polish peasant in Europe and America'*. New York: Social Science Research Council.

Boas, F. (1911). *The mind of primitive man*. New York: Macmillan.

Bogardus, E. S. (1923). *Essentials of social psychology*. Los Angeles: Miller.

(1925). Measuring social distance. *Journal of Applied Sociology* 9: 299–308.

Burnham, W. H. (1905). The hygiene of home study. *Pedagogical Seminary* 12: 213–30.

(1910). The group as a stimulus to mental activity. *Science* 31: 761–7.

Burr, V. (2003). *Social constructionism*. London: Routledge.

Cabanis, P. J. G. (1802/1985). *Rapports du physique et du moral de l'homme*. Paris: Ressources.

Cacioppo, J. T. and Berntson, G. G., eds. (2005). *Social neuroscience: key readings*. New York: Psychology Press.

Camic, C. and Joas, H. (2004). *The dialogical turn: new roles for sociology in the postdisciplinary age*. Lanham, MD: Rowman and Littlefield.

Cattaneo, Carlo (1864). Dell'antitesi come metodo di psicologia sociale [On antithesis as a method of social psychology]. *Il Politecnico* 20: 262–70.

Chen, W. K. C. (1933). The influence of oral propaganda material upon students' attitudes. *Archives of Psychology* 150.

Cherrington, B. M. (1934). Methods of education in international attitudes. *Teachers' College Contributions to Education* 595.

Comte, Auguste (1853/1876). *System of positive polity*, 4 vols. London: Longman.

(1855/1974). *The positive philosophy*. Tr. Harriet Martineau. New York: AMS Press.

Condillac, E. B. de (1746/1971). *An essay on the origins of human knowledge*. Gainesville, FL: Scholars, Facsimiles and Reprints.

Condorcet, M. J. de (1794/1966). *Esquisse d'un tableau historique des progrès de l'esprit humain*. Paris: Editions Sociales.

Cook, T. D. and Campbell, D. T. (1979). *Quasi-experimentation: design and analysis issues for field settings*. Chicago: Rand McNally.

Cooley, C. H. (1902/1912). *Human nature and the social order*. New York: Scribner.

(1909/1912). *Social organization: a study of the larger mind.* New York: Scribner.

(1918). *Social process.* New York: Scribner.

Copans, J. and Jamin, J. (1978). *Aux origines de l'anthropologie française.* Paris: Le Sycomore.

Corey, S. M. (1937). Professed attitude and actual behavior. *Journal of Educational Psychology* 28: 271–80.

Cournot, A. A. (1861). *Traité de l'enchainement des idées fondamentales dans les sciences et dans l'histoire.* 2 vols. Paris.

Danziger, K. (1990). *Constructing the subject.* Cambridge: Cambridge University Press.

(1992). The project of an experimental social psychology: historical perspectives. *Science in Context* 5: 309–28.

(1997). *Naming the mind.* London: Sage.

(2000). Making social psychology experimental: a conceptual history, 1920–1970. *Journal of the History of the Behavioral Sciences* 36: 329–47.

Darwin, C. (1871/1901). *The descent of man.* 2nd edn, London: John Murray.

(1872). *The expression of the emotions in man and animals.* London: John Murray.

Darwin, E. (1803/1824). *The temper of nature; or, the origin of society: a poem with philosophical notes.* London: Jones.

Dasen, P. R. (1975). Concrete operational development in three cultures. *Journal of Cross-Cultural Psychology* 6: 156–72.

Dashiell, J. F. (1935). Experimental studies of the influence of social situations on the behavior of individual human adults. In C. Murchison, ed., *A handbook of social psychology.* Worcester, MA: Clark University Press.

Dawkins, R. (1976). *The selfish gene.* Oxford: Oxford University Press.

Degérando, J.-M. (1800/1969). *The observation of savage peoples.* Tr. F. T. C. Moore. London: Routledge and Kegan Paul.

Dilthey, Wilhelm (1894/1964). Ideen über eine beschreibende und zergliedernde Psychologie. In *Gesammelte Schriften*, 18 vols. 4th edn, Stuttgart: Teubner; Göttingen: Vandenhoeck and Ruprecht.

Dovidio, J. F., Glick, P. and Rudman, L. A. (2005). *On the nature of prejudice: fifty years after Allport.* Oxford: Blackwell.

Du Bois, C. (1944). *The people of Alor.* Minneapolis: University of Minnesota Press.

Dunlap, K. (1919). Are there any instincts? *Journal of Abnormal Psychology* 14: 307–11.

Durkheim, E. (1897/1952). *Suicide: a study in sociology.* London: Routledge and Kegan Paul.

(1901/1947). *Les règles de la méthode sociologique.* 2nd edn, Paris: Presses Universitaires de France.

(1915). *The elementary forms of religious life.* London: Allen and Unwin.

Durkin, K. (1995). *Developmental social psychology.* Oxford: Blackwell.

Ellis, B. J. and Bjorklund, D. F., eds. (2005). *Origins of the social mind: evolutionary psychology and child development.* New York: Guilford.

Ellwood, C. A. (1901). *Some prolegomena to social psychology.* Chicago: University of Chicago Press.

(1917). *An introduction to social psychology.* New York: Appleton.

Espinas, Alfred (1878). *Des sociétés animales.* 2nd edn, Paris: Baillière.

Eulenburg, Franz (1900). Ueber die Möglichkeit und die Aufgaben einer Sozialpsychologie. *Jahrbuch für Gesetzgebung, Verwaltung und Volkswirtschaft im Deutschen Reich* 24: 202–37.

Festinger, L. (1954). A theory of social comparison processes. *Human Relations* 7: 117–40.

Flugel, J. C. (1933). *A hundred years of psychology.* London: Duckworth.

Folsom, J. K. (1931). *Social psychology.* New York: Harper.

Freeman, D. (1983). *Margaret Mead in Samoa: the making and unmaking of an anthropological myth.* Cambridge, MA: Harvard University Press.

Fresenius, F. C. (1866). Die Natur der Masse. *Deutsche Vierteljahrschrift* 29: 112–78.

Frith, C. and Wolpert, D., eds. (2004). *The neuroscience of social interaction: decoding, influencing and imitating the actions of others.* Oxford: Oxford University Press.

Gaddis, J. L. (2002). *The landscape of history.* Oxford: Oxford University Press.

Galton, F. (1869/1892). *Hereditary genius.* London: Macmillan.

Gault, R. H. (1915). On the meaning of social psychology. *The Monist* 25: 255–60.

(1921). The standpoint of social psychology. *Journal of Abnormal and Social Psychology* 16: 41–6.

Gergen, K. J. (1973). Social psychology as history. *Journal of Personality and Social Psychology* 26: 309–20.

(2001). *Social construction in context.* London: Sage.

Gergen, K. J. and Gergen, M. M. (1984). *Historical social psychology.* Hillsdale, NJ: Erlbaum.

Giddings, Franklin Henry (1896). *The principles of sociology.* New York: Macmillan.

Greenwood, J. D. (2004). *The disappearance of the social in American social psychology.* Cambridge: Cambridge University Press.

Habermas, J. (1972). *Knowledge and human interests.* London: Heinemann.

Haines, H. and Vaughan, G. H. M. (1979). Was 1898 a 'great date' in the history of experimental social psychology? *Journal of the History of the Behavioral Sciences* 15: 323–32.

Hamon, A. F. (1894). *Psychologie du militaire professionnel (Etudes de psychologie sociale).* Brussels: Rosez.

Haney, C., Banks, C. and Zimbardo, P. (1973). A study of prisoners and guards in a simulated prison. *Naval Research Reviews* September: 1–17.

Heider, F. (1944). Social perception and phenomenal causality. *Psychological Review* 51: 358–74.

(1958). *The psychology of interpersonal relations.* New York: Wiley.

Helvétius, C. A. (1758/1973). *De l'ésprit.* Verviers: Gérard.

Herbart, J. F. (1821/1890). Ueber einige Beziehungen zwischen Psychologie und Staatswissenschaft [On some relationships between psychology and political science]. In K. Kerbach, ed., *Joh. Fr. Herbart's sämtliche Werke*, vol. 5. Langensalza: Hermann Beyer.

(1825/1892). Psychologie als Wissenschaft [Psychology as science]. In K. Kerbach, ed., *Joh. Fr. Herbart's sämtliche Werke*, vol. 6. Langensalza: Beyer.

(1834/1891). *Lehrbuch zur Psychologie*, 2nd edn. In K. Kerbach, ed., *Joh. Fr. Herbart's sämtliche Werke*, vol. 4. Langensalza: Beyer.

Herman, A. (2003). *The Scottish Enlightenment: the Scots' invention of the modern world*. London: Fourth Estate.

Hovland, C. I., Janis, L. L. and Kelley, H. (1953). *Communication and persuasion*. New Haven: Yale University Press.

Hsueh, Y. (2002). The Hawthorn experiments and the introduction of Jean Piaget in American industrial psychology, 1929–1932. *History of Psychology* 5: 163–89.

Hume, David (1739/1911). *A treatise on human nature*, 2 vols. London: Dent.

(1741/1894). Of national characters. In *Essays literary, moral and political*. London: Routledge.

(1748/1975). *Enquiries concerning human understanding*. Oxford: Clarendon Press.

Ibanez, T. and Iniguez, L., eds. (1997). *Critical social psychology*. London: Sage.

Jacobs, R. C. and Campbell, D. T. (1961). The perpetuation of an arbitrary tradition through several generations of a laboratory microculture. *Journal of Abnormal and Social Psychology* 76: 675–89.

Jahoda, G. (1962). Social class. In G. Humphrey and M. Argyle, eds., *Social psychology through experiment*. London: Methuen.

(1969). *The psychology of superstition*. London: Allen Lane.

(1988). J'accuse. In M. H. Bond, ed., *The cross-cultural challenge to social psychology*. Newbury Park, CA: Sage.

(1991). Dessins primitives, dessins d'enfants et la question d'évolution. *Gradhiva. Revue d'Histoire et d'Archives de l'Anthropologie* 10: 60–70.

(1993). *Crossroads between culture and mind*. Cambridge, MA: Harvard University Press.

(1999). *Images of savages*. London: Routledge.

(2000). Piaget and Lévy-Bruhl. *History of Psychology* 3: 218–38.

(2002). The ghosts in the meme machine. *History of the Human Sciences* 15: 55–68.

(2005). Theodor Lipps and the shift from 'sympathy' to 'empathy'. *Journal of the History of the Behavioral Sciences* 41: 151–63.

James, W. (1891). *The principles of psychology*, 2 vols. London: Macmillan.

Kant, I. (1797/1974). *Anthropology from a pragmatic point of view*. Tr. M. J. Gregor. The Hague: Martinus Nijhoff.

Kantor, J. R. (1923). What are the data and problems of social psychology? *Journal of Philosophy* 20: 449–57.

Kardiner, A. and Linton, R. (1939). *The individual and his society*. New York: Columbia University Press.

Katz, D. and Schanck, R. L. (1938). *Social psychology*. New York: Wiley.

Kelley, H. H. (1967). Attribution theory in social psychology. In D. Levine, ed., *Nebraska Symposium of Motivation*, vol. 15. Lincoln: University of Nebraska Press.

Kim, U., Triandis, H. C., Kagitcibasi, C., Choi, S.-C. and Yoon, G. (1994). *Individualism and collectivism*. Thousand Oaks, CA: Sage.

King, E. G. (1990). Reconciling democracy and the crowd in turn-of-the-century American social-psychological thought. *Journal of the History of the Behavioral Sciences* 26: 334–44.

Klineberg, O. (1935). *Negro intelligence and selective migration.* New York: Columbia University Press.

    (1940). *Social psychology.* New York: Holt.

Knower, F. H. (1935). Experimental studies in changes in attitudes: I. A study of the effect of oral argument on changes of attitudes. *Journal of Social Psychology* 6: 315–47.

    (1936). Experimental studies in changes in attitudes: II. A study of the effects of printed argument on changes in attitude. *Journal of Abnormal and Social Psychology* 30: 522–32.

Kohlberg, L. (1976). Moral stages and moralization: the cognitive-developmental approach. In T. E. Lickona, ed., *Moral development and behavior.* New York: Holt, Rinehart and Winston.

Kroeber, A. L. (1917/18). The possibility of social psychology. *American Journal of Sociology* 23: 633–50.

Lamprecht, K. (1896/7). Was ist Kulturgeschichte? Beitrag zu einer empirischer Historik. *Deutsche Zeitschrift für Geschichtswissenschaft, N. F.* 1: 75–150.

    (1900). *Die kulturhistorische Methode.* Berlin: Gaertner.

    (1905). *Moderne Geschichtswissenschaft.* Freiburg: Heyfelder.

    (1912). *Einführung in das historische Denken.* Leipzig: Voigtländer.

LaPiere, R. T. (1934). Attitudes versus actions. *Social Forces* 13: 230–7.

Lauken, U. (1998). *Sozialpsychologie.* Oldenburg: BIS.

Lazarus, M. (1851). Ueber den Begriff und die Möglichkeit einer Völkerpsychologie. *Zeitschrift für Literatur, Kunst und Oeffentliches Leben* 1: 112–26.

Lazarus, M. and Steinthal, H. (1860). Einleitende Gedanken über Völkerpsychologie. *Zeitschrift für Völkerpsychologie und Sprachwissenschaft* 1: 1–73.

Le Bon, G. (1881). *L'homme et les sociétés,* 2 vols. Paris: Rothschild.

    (1895/1966). *The crowd.* London: Fisher Unwin.

Lewes, G. H. (1860). *The physiology of common life.* Leipzig: Tauchnitz.

    (1874). *Problems of life and mind.* First Series. *The foundation of a creed,* vol. 1. London: Trübner.

    (1879). *Problems of life and mind.* Third Series. Problem the first. *The study of psychology: its object, scope, and method.* London: Trübner.

Lewin, K. (1952). *Field theory in social science.* London: Tavistock.

Lewin, K., Lippitt, R. and White, R. K. (1939). Patterns of aggressive behavior in experimentally created 'social climates'. *Journal of Social Psychology* 10: 271–99.

Likert, R. (1932). A technique for the measurement of attitudes. *Archives of Psychology* 140: 1–55.

Lindner, G. A. (1868). *Das Problem des Glücks.* Vienna: Gerold.

    (1871). *Ideen zur Psychologie der Gesellschaft.* Vienna: Gerold.

Lubek, I. and Apfelbaum, E. (1989). Les études de psychologie sociale de Augustin Hamon. *Hermès: Cognition, Communication, Politique* 5/6: 67–94.

Lukes, S. (1973). *Emile Durkheim, his life and work.* London: Penguin.

Lynd, R. S. (1930). *Middletown.* New York: Harcourt, Brace.

Markova, I. (2003). *Dialogicality and social representations.* Cambridge: Cambridge University Press.

Marston, W. M. (1924). Studies in testimony. *Journal of Criminal Law and Criminology* 15: 5–31.

Mayo, E. (1930). The work of Jean Piaget. *Ohio State University Bulletin* 35: 140–6.

(1933). *The human problems of an industrial civilization*. New York: Viking.

McDougall, W. (1908/1943). *An introduction to social psychology*. 25th edn, London: Methuen.

(1927). *The group mind*. Cambridge: Cambridge University Press.

McGuire, W. (1999). *Constructing social psychology*. Cambridge: Cambridge University Press.

Mead, G. H. (1909). Social psychology as counterpart to physiological psychology. *Psychological Bulletin* 6: 401–8.

(1917/18). The psychology of punitive justice. *American Journal of Sociology* 23: 577–602.

(1934). *Mind, self and society*, ed. Charles Morris. Chicago: University of Chicago Press. Selected parts reprinted in Strauss (1956).

(1982). *The individual and the social self: unpublished work of George Herbert Mead*, ed. D. L. Miller. Chicago: University of Chicago Press.

Mead, M. (1928). *Coming of age in Samoa*. New York: Morrow.

(1935). *Sex and temperament in three primitive societies*. London: Routledge.

(1937). *Cooperation and competition among primitive peoples*. New York: McGraw-Hill.

Meumann, E. (1904). Haus- und Schularbeit: Experimente an Kindern der Volksschule. *Die Deutsche Schule* 8: 278–303; 337–59; 416–31.

Mill, John Stuart (1843/1879). *A system of logic*. 10th edn, 2 vols. London: Longmans Green.

(1865). *Auguste Comte and positivism*. London: Reprinted from Westminster Review.

Millar, John (1771/1806). *The origin of the distinction of ranks*. Edinburgh: Blackwood.

Miller, A. G. (1972). *The social psychology of psychological research*. New York: The Free Press.

Moede, W. (1914). Der Wetteifer, seine Struktur und sein Ausmass [Competition, its structure and its extent]. *Zeitschrift für Pädagogische Psychologie* 15: 353–68.

(1920). *Experimentelle Massenpsychologie: Beiträge zur Experimentalpsychologie der Gruppe*. Leipzig: Hirzel.

Montesquieu, C. (1748/1964). *Œuvres complètes*. Paris: Editions du Seuil.

Moscovici, S. (1984). The phenomenon of social representation. In R. Farr and S. Moscovici, eds., *Social representations*. Cambridge: Cambridge University Press.

(1985). Innovation and minority influence. In S. Moscovici, G. Mugny and E. van Avermaet, eds., *Perspectives on minority influence*. Cambridge: Cambridge University Press.

Münsterberg, H. (1914). *Psychology and social sanity*. Garden City, NY: Doubleday, Page.

Murchison, C. (1929). *Social psychology: the psychology of political domination*. Worcester, MA: Clark University Press.

Murchison, C., ed. (1935). *Handbook of social psychology*. Worcester, MA: Clark University Press.

Murphy, G., Murphy, L. B. and Newcomb, T. M., eds. (1937). *Experimental social psychology*. Rev. edn, New York: Harper.

Park, Robert E. (1904/1972). *The crowd and the public*, ed. H. Elsner. Chicago: University of Chicago Press.

    (1924). The concept of social distance. *Journal of Applied Sociology* 8: 339–44.

Piaget, J. (1932). *The moral judgement of the child*. London: Routledge and Kegan Paul.

    (1950). *The psychology of intelligence*. London: Routledge and Kegan Paul.

    (1962). *Play, dreams and imitation in childhood*. London: Routledge and Kegan Paul.

    (1965). *Sociological studies*. London: Routledge and Kegan Paul.

Quetelet, A. (1835). *Sur l'homme et le développement de ses facultés, ou, Essai de physique sociale*, 2 vols. Paris: Bachelier.

    (1848). *Du système social et des lois qui le régissent*. Paris: Guillaumin.

    (1869). *Physique sociale ou essai sur le développement des facultés de l'homme*. 2nd edn, 2 vols. Brussels: Muquardt.

Reid, Thomas (1785). *Essays on the intellectual powers of man*. Edinburgh: Bell.

Ribot, T. (1896). *La psychologie des sentiments*. Paris: Felix Alcan.

Richards, R. J. (1987). *Darwin and the emergence of evolutionary theories of mind and behavior*. Chicago: University of Chicago Press.

Rivers, W. H. R. (1901). *Reports of the Cambridge Anthropological Expedition to Torres Straits*, vol. 2, *Physiology and psychology*. Cambridge: Cambridge University Press.

    (1926). *Psychology and ethnology*. London: Kegan Paul, Trench, Trübner.

Roethlisberger, F. J. and Dixon, W. J. (1939). *Management and the worker*. Cambridge, MA: Harvard University Press.

Ross, E. A. (1901). *Social control*. New York: Macmillan.

    (1908/1923). *Social psychology*. New York: Macmillan.

    (1920). *The principles of sociology*. New York: The Century.

Rushton, N. P. (1994). *Race, evolution and behavior*. New Brunswick, NJ: Transaction.

Saint-Simon, C.-H. de (1813/1965). Mémoire sur la science de l'homme. In G. Gurvitch, *La physiologie sociale*. Paris: Presses Universitaires de France.

Samelson, F. (1974). History, origin myth and ideology: 'discovery of social psychology'. *Journal for the Theory of Social Behaviour* 4: 217–31.

Schäffle, A. E. F. (1875–8). *Bau und Leben des socialen Körpers: encyclopädischer Entwurf einer realen Anatomie, Physiologie und Psychologie der menschlichen Gesellschaft mit besonderer Rücksicht auf die Volkswirtschaft als socialen Stoffwechsel*, 4 vols. Tübingen: Laupp.

Shaw, M. E. (1932). A comparison of individuals and small groups in the rational solution of complex problems. *American Journal of Psychology* 44: 491–504.

Shaw, M. E. and Wright, J. M. (1967). *Scales for the measurement of attitudes*. New York: McGraw-Hill.

Sherif, M. (1935). A study of some social factors in perception. *Archives of Psychology* 17: 17–22.

Sherif, M., Harvey, O. J., White, B. J., Hood, W. R. and Sherif, C. W. (1961). *Intergroup conflict and co-operation: the robber's cave experiment.* Norman, OK: University of Oklahoma Press.

Sighele, S. (1901). *La foule criminelle: essai de psychologie collective.* Paris: Alcan.

Simmel, G. (1897–9). The persistence of the social group. *American Journal of Sociology* 3: 662–98, 829–36; 4: 35–50. Tr. A. Small.

(1898). Die Rolle des Geldes in den Beziehungen der Geschlechter. *Die Zeit* (Vienna) 172: 38–40; 173: 53–4; 174: 69–71.

(1900/1978). *The philosophy of money,* tr. T. Bottomore and D. Frisby. London: Routledge.

(1908). Ueber das Wesen der Sozialpsychology. *Archiv für Sozialwissenschaft und Sozialpolitik* 26: 285–91.

Simpson, J. A. and Kenrick, D. T., eds. (1997). *Evolutionary social psychology.* Mahwah, NJ: Erlbaum.

Slotkin, J. S. (1965). *Readings in early anthropology.* Chicago: Aldine.

Small, A. W. and Vincent, G. E. (1894). *An introduction to the study of society.* London: Appleton.

Smith, Adam (1790/1984). *The theory of moral sentiments.* 6th edn, ed. D. D. Raphael and A. L. Macfie. Indianapolis: Liberty Fund.

Smith, F. T. (1933). An experiment in modifying attitudes towards the Negro. PhD thesis in the Library of Teachers' College, Columbia University.

Spencer, Herbert (1851). *Social statics: or, the conditions essential to human happiness specified, and the first of them developed.* London.

(1855/1870–2). *The principles of psychology.* 2nd edn, 2 vols. London: Williams and Norgate.

(1864). *The classification of the sciences to which are added reasons for dissenting from the philosophy of M. Comte.* London: Williams and Norgate.

(1873/1894). *The study of sociology.* 17th edn, London: Kegan Paul, Trench, Trübner.

(1885). *The principles of sociology.* 3rd edn, vol. 1. London: Williams and Norgate.

(1904). *An autobiography.* London: Williams and Norgate.

Steinthal, H. and Misteli, F. (1871). *Abriss der Spachwissenschaft.* Berlin: Dümmlers.

Strauss, A., ed. (1956). *The social psychology of George Herbert Mead.* Chicago: University of Chicago Press.

Sumner, W. G. (1907). *Folkways.* Boston: Ginn.

Taine, H. A. (1870). *De l'intelligence.* 2nd edn, Paris: Hachette.

(1878). *The Revolution,* 2 vols. London: Daldy, Isbister.

Tarde, G. (1890/1895). *Les lois de l'imitation.* 2nd edn, Paris: Alcan.

(1898). *Etudes de psychologie sociale.* Paris: Giard and Brière.

(1898/1999). *Œuvres de Gabriel Tarde,* 5 vols.; vol. 4, *Les lois sociales.* Paris: Synthélabo.

(1901/1989). *L'opinion et la foule.* Paris: Presses Universitaires de France.

Taylor, S. E. (1998). The social being in social psychology. In D. T. Gilbert, S. T. Fiske and G. Lindzey, eds., *The handbook of social psychology.* 4th edn, 2 vols. Boston: McGraw Hill.

Thomas, W. I. (1904a). The province of social psychology. *Psychological Bulletin* 1: 392–3.

(1904b). The psychology of race prejudice. *American Journal of Sociology* 11: 593–611.

Thomas, W. I. and Znaniecki, F. (1918–20). *The Polish peasant in Europe and America*, 5 vols. Boston, MA: Gorham.

Thurstone, L. L. (1928). Attitudes can be measured. *American Journal of Sociology* 33: 529–54.

(1931). Influence of motion pictures on children's attitudes. *Journal of Social Psychology* 2: 291–305.

Tomasello, M., Kruger, A. C. and Ratner, H. H. (1993). Cultural learning. *Behavioral and Brain Sciences* 16: 495–552.

Triplett, N. (1898). The dynamogenic factors in pacemaking and competition. *American Journal of Psychology* 9: 507–33.

Tuffin, K. (2005). *Understanding critical social psychology*. London: Sage.

Turgot, A. R. (1750/1973). A philosophical review of the successive advances of the human mind. In R. L. Meek, ed., *Turgot*. Cambridge: Cambridge University Press.

Turiel, E. (1983). *The development of social knowledge: morality and convention*. Cambridge: Cambridge University Press.

UNESCO (1972). *In the minds of men*. Paris: UNESCO.

van Lange, P. A. M., ed. (2006). *Bridging social psychology*. Mahwah, NJ: Lawrence Erlbaum.

Vico, G. (1744/1948). *The new science*, tr. T. G. Bergin and M. H. Fish. Ithaca, NY: Cornell University Press.

Vyse, S. A. (1997). *Believing in magic*. Oxford: Oxford University Press.

Wagner, A. (1864). *Die Gesetzmässigkeit in den scheinbar willkürlichen menschlichen Handlungen vom Standpunkt der Statistik* [The lawfulness of seemingly arbitrary human actions from the standpoint of statistics]. Hamburg: Geisler.

Waitz, T. (1849). *Lehrbuch der Psychologie als Naturwissenschaft*. Braunschweig: Vieweg.

(1859–72). *Anthropologie der Naturvölker: ueber die Einheit des Menschengeschlechts und den Naturzustand des Menschen*, 6 vols. Leipzig.

(1863). *Introduction to anthropology*. London: Anthropological Society of London.

Ward, L. (1883). *Dynamic sociology*. New York: Appleton.

Wassmann, J. (1995). The final requiem for the omniscient informant? *Culture and Psychology* 1: 167–201.

Wheeler, M., Ziman, J. and Boden, M. A. (2002). *The evolution of cultural entities*. Oxford: Oxford University Press.

Wilke, W. H. (1934). An experimental comparison of the speech, the radio, and the printed page as propaganda devices. *Archives of Psychology* 169.

William, J. M. (1922). *Principles of social psychology*. New York: Knopf.

Wundt, W. (1863). *Vorlesungen über die Menschen- und Thierseele*, 2 vols. Leipzig: Voss.

(1908). *Logik*, 3 vols.; vol. 3: *Logik der Geisteswissenschaften*. 3rd edn, Stuttgart: Enke.

(1910). *Völkerpsychologie*, vol. 4, *Mythus und Religion*, part 1. Leipzig: Engelmann.

(1920a). *Erlebtes und Erkanntes*. Stuttgart: Kröner.

(1920b). *Völkerpsychologie*, vol. 10, *Kultur und Geschichte*. Leipzig: Kröner.

Zimmerman, D. H. and West, C. (1975). Sex roles, interruptions and silences in conversation. In B. Thorne and N. M. Henley, eds., *Language and sex: difference and dominance*. Rowley, MA: Newbury House.

Znaniecki, F. (1925). *The laws of social psychology*. Chicago: University of Chicago Press.

Index